The Golfer Mindset

Addressing Confidence and Mind State Issues

Warren St. Peter

Copyright © 2016 Warren St. Peter.

All rights reserved. No part of this book may be reproduced, stored, or transmitted by any means—whether auditory, graphic, mechanical, or electronic—without written permission of both publisher and author, except in the case of brief excerpts used in critical articles and reviews. Unauthorized reproduction of any part of this work is illegal and is punishable by law.

ISBN: 978-0-9949-3941-8 (sc)
ISBN: 978-0-9949-3940-1 (e)

Because of the dynamic nature of the Internet, any web addresses or links contained in this book may have changed since publication and may no longer be valid. The views expressed in this work are solely those of the author and do not necessarily reflect the views of the publisher, and the publisher hereby disclaims any responsibility for them.

Any people depicted in stock imagery provided by Thinkstock are models,
and such images are being used for illustrative purposes only.
Certain stock imagery © Thinkstock.

Lulu Publishing Services rev. date: 4/15/2016

Dedication

From the day my Father gave me my first set of clubs, consisting of 5 irons and a putter, I have always played the game to improve and learn more about it. My Father was most certainly responsible for kindling my interest in the game, and as a respectable player himself, is still adding to hundreds of rounds played competitively over the past six decades. As a youngster, I was exposed to an organized caddy program within a short bike ride of my home, providing opportunities to carry the clubs for a number of tour players; a dream come true. There was a chance to learn from better players, by getting to know them, and mustering enough courage to ask questions.

My entire life being touched by golf certainly had an impact on my desire to write this book, but it was primarily through the encouragement of my grandmother, Norah O'Donnell, that sparked the desire to complete it. I immediately reflect on her "good-nature", always having a positive outlook on life, and her ability to "roll with the punches" when things were turning for the worst. She certainly had an approach toward life reflective of a sound basis for being a good player herself. Over the course of the compilation of this book, I also lost my Mother, whose endless support for the project gave me the tenacity to persevere. She has always been there when I needed her.

In the couple weeks prior to my final edit of this book, my life changed forever with the passing of my only Son, Riley Warren St. Peter. One of the most cherished memories of my life was caddying for him during his attempt to attain his golf professional playability qualification. It was a proud moment to experience my son's excitement qualifying for his card as the youngest competitor in the field. I certainly was the proud father on that memorable day. During the compilation of The Golfer Mindset, my son regularly provided valued comments on different portions of the book. It became his insistent " this is really good Dad, you have to get the booked finished", validating what I hoped the book would achieve. The memory of my discussion with my son on the eighteenth tee of his final qualification round was the reaffirmation I needed to complete what I started almost 20 years ago. I am indebted to many, and appreciate the influence my family has had on my life and their steady encouragement to pursue my dreams. I also thank my daughter Kaeley for being a pillar of strength for family and friends during the difficult time since the loss of her brother. I am extremely proud of dedicating this book to my inspiring Grandmother, loving Mother, and a dearly missed Son.

Reflecting on the journey of making this book a reality immediately wells up my love for my wife Lori. Her consistent encouragement, understanding and support gave me the thrust I needed to complete my goal. As "My Partner in Crime" our love is reflected in everything we do, and is still growing in the things we share together.

Contents

Preface ix

Chapter 1: A Game In Flux 1
Section 1 - Golf's Lure and the Popularity Paradox 3
Section 2 - The Golfer's Frustration 5
Section 3 - Golfers and Mind State Issues 7

Chapter 2: Golf's Changing Paradigm 9
Section 1 - The Nebulous Nature of Mindset. 11
Section 2 - The Progressive Benefit of Instilling Mindset Competencies 15

Chapter 3: Setting The Demeanour. 17
Section 1 - Golfers Have The Greatest Intentions 19
Section 2 - Essential Commitments. 21
Section 3 - Focusing Efforts 27

Chapter 4: The Positive Competitive Mindset 31
Section 1 - Foundational Elements 33

Chapter 5: PCM Implementation 43
Section 1 - Strategy Integration 45

Chapter 6: Benchmarking 53
Section 1 - Prerequisite of a Goal Setting Plan. 55

Chapter 7: Goal Setting And Planning 61
Section 1 - The Essential Element 63
Section 2 - Process Overview 66
Section 3 - Reaping The Benefits Gained 67
Section 4 - Considerations and Pitfalls. 70
Section 5 - Basic Principles and Concepts 75
Section 6 - Supports and Linkages. 83

Chapter 8: Practice. 89
Section 1 - The Building Blocks of Practice 91
Section 2 - The Cost of Inaction. 93
Section 3 - The Outcomes of Practice. 95
Section 4 - Make Time For Quality Practice. 98
Section 5 - Creating Progressive Practices. 100

Chapter 9: Stress And Anxiety ... 103
Section 1 - Preliminary Considerations ... 105
Section 2 - Optimizing Overall Tension Levels ... 107
Section 3 - Effects of Stress and Anxiety ... 109
Section 4 - Stress ... 111

Chapter 10: Proximity Acceptance ... 115
Section 1 - Overview ... 117

Chapter 11: Distraction Management ... 121
Section 1 - Correcting Mind State Instability ... 123
Section 2 - Distraction Management - Tools and Tactics ... 131

Chapter 12: Routine ... 141
Section 1 - Preliminary Considerations ... 143
Section 2 - What's Trying To Be Achieved ... 145
Section 3 - Principles and Primary Activities ... 148
Section 4 - The Shot Assessment Routine ... 152
Section 5 - The Putt Assessment Routine ... 163
Section 6 - The Shot Execution Routine ... 167
Section 7 - The Putt Execution Routine ... 172

Chapter 13: Game And Course Management ... 175
Section 1 - Game and Course Management Defined ... 177
Section 2 - Course Management Considerations ... 179
Section 3 - Game Management Tactics ... 181
Section 4 - Game Management, Preparing For Play ... 189

Chapter 14: On-Course Assessment ... 191
Section 1 - Overview ... 193
Section 2 - Implementation Benefits ... 195
Section 3 - The Shot Assessment Tool ... 197

Preface

The creation of this book is the culmination of cherished experiences and memories playing what I consider to be the ultimate game. Golf is a unique sport for a wide range of reasons, but foremost is the sport's unique trait of offering consistent opportunities for learning wise lessons about self. Golf truly takes our egotistical attitudes and exposes just how fragile and helpless we can truly be. The game is a reflection of life itself, where simple compelling hopes and wishes are not usually the result, and what transpires is often unexpected, and sometimes puzzling. The game brings with it the full spectrum of raw human emotions, with weaknesses being exposed regularly, leaving the golfer the sole source of resolve for whatever is encountered. There is no source of support in a teammate able to cover for mistakes and weaknesses. Maintenance of accountability for what transpires during play is relentless and must be maintained for top performance to be sustained. Golf is a solitary game, ranging from the serenity of a perfect sunny day with everything seemingly normal, stable, and comfortable, to the turmoil of missed opportunities and feelings of helplessness and despair, when things go array.

Golf can be enjoyed and competitively played between a senior and a youngster, beginner and expert, or an uncle and his niece. Whether you're ten years of age or ninety-five, the game can be played spanning a lifetime or played competitively between players of any age. As a result, golf is a sport ideally fitting family values related to a healthy lifestyle and the sharing of time together.

At the same time, golf is a game demanding integrity, honesty, and respect, as reflected in its rules, history, and traditions. Exhibiting these qualities almost seems a prerequisite to excel at the sport due to the emerging importance of the deeply personal nature of a golfer's own impression of themselves and how this influences performance. The respect and honesty the golfer has for themselves and others, coupled with the integrity displayed through their actions establish their playing environment. A golfer's impression of himself or herself as a player, coupled with a belief in their capabilities is a key factor for how well they perform. This defines the confidence a player possesses or feels while playing, and is essential to successful play. How the golfer feels about their ability to successfully address difficult and unfamiliar situations is reflective of the confidence they have in themselves to address most shot making circumstances. The stature or health of a golfer's self-impression of himself or herself is the impetus for superior performance and is a primary focus of <u>The Golfer Mindset.</u>

The game is an extremely simple in concept, but extremely diverse and changing, both physically and mentally, creating a uniquely challenging sport to master. It is my hope you find value in the ideas and information presented in this book and that it provides the mechanism for golfers to manage the mental aspects of the game to become more complete and well-rounded players.

CHAPTER 1

A Game In Flux

"We have to learn to be our best friends because we fall to easily in the trap of being our worst enemies."
Roderick Thorpe

Section 1 - Golf's Lure and the Popularity Paradox

Why is golf such an addictive sport? Even newcomers display a passion for the game, despite the frustration felt for any self-perceived weaknesses, or gross inconsistencies in performance. With popularity of the game growing, its mastery still remains elusive to golfers, despite many playing the sport for numerous years. The game continues to draw thousands of new participants, but most golfers experience disappointing performance levels, stagnated improvement, and the frustration of only occasionally making true solid contact with the ball in an intended manner. The nature of the game provides a great deal of satisfaction to those attracted to the sport because of its social aspects. Golf is unquestionably a game offering ample opportunity to socially interact with others. The sport provides ample time for social activities and occasions to build new relationships. Some are attracted to the sport because of the exercise and positive health effects associated with playing golf. The health benefits of the walking associated with the sport has surely contributed to the appeal of the game. Still others appreciate the ability to play the game into the elderly years, and the advantages this brings to involving friends and family. Other golfers are attracted to the challenge and strategy of the sport. There are still others that see golf as an outdoor game having close ties to nature, and are drawn to the natural beauty of its venues. There are many things that attract newcomers to the game, holding their interest and participation for a lifetime. There may be numerous reasons contributing to attract people to the game, but the desire of the majority of golfers is to see satisfying levels of improvement and acceptable levels of performance.

Golfers have forever been searching for methods, strategies, systems or the technology that will provide solutions to problems or issues inhibiting their ability to perform consistently, at a personally satisfying level of play. It is interesting and ironic that the popularity of the game is at an all-time high, while golfers perceive their playing skills, personal development, and frequency of intended ball contact as below their personal expectations. Popularity of the sport certainly cannot be attributed to the satisfaction of hitting a high percentage of quality shots, consistency of play, or pleasing rates of improvement. If golfers were surveyed determining the ratio satisfied with their on-course performance, the percentage would be surprisingly low. This percentage will be even lower for golfers actively working and making a dedicated effort to improve. Satisfaction levels of golfers are low regarding their expected skill improvement and their actual progress. Many golfers hope for improvements to come, admit making some progress, but at levels well below expectations.

Collectively, most golfers have not had satisfying levels of success remedying their personal issues and problems. Even seasoned players often become frustrated with their play, experiencing a majority of shots falling well short of expectations. Golfers have spent billions of dollars on activities, aids, and equipment directed specifically at game improvement. Despite this diligence and the money spent to improve, frustration and deflated levels of confidence persist, leaving many bewildered with their limited improvement, and helplessness to deal with their shortcomings. Many years of questionable practice methods, reluctance to commit to the effort required to improve, and not having a practical means of controlling mental aspects of the game are a few of the major factors contributing to dissatisfaction with performance and improvement rates.

What is it that draws or attracts so many to play the game, when anticipated ball contact is only an occasional event for newcomers, and a minority event for seasoned players? Is the draw or lure to golf kindled by the desire to more frequently experience the pleasure and satisfaction gained when solid ball contact is achieved? Is it possible the exhilaration and excitement of occasionally sizzling a drive down the middle of the fairway, or dropping a laser-like long iron shot close to the pin, sufficient to keep golfers motivated and actively coming back to the game? Perhaps the golfer's attraction to the game originates with the realization of their shortcomings kindling a desire to improve and increase the frequency of the satisfying ball strikes. Whatever a golfer's skill level, there is a lure back to the game to better a previous performance, remedy a problem or issue, implement strategies for improvement, or personally experiment with personal ideas for better execution of various types of shots.

Ultimately, every individual golfer's definition of what they will accept as representing personal success is the primary determining factor for how well they play the game and the satisfaction they gain from it. Golfers are seeking continuous and steady improvement to elevate their caliber of play to a level at least equaling a previous superior performance. Generally, most golfers closely approaching, equaling or bettering a previous best score are satisfied with their play, because they have had the opportunity of re-experiencing a time of above average performance. The golfer's unending search to experience the repeated instances of superior play could be a primary source of the motivation that brings them back to the game. No matter what the draw may be, the desire to play at a better performance levels on a consistent basis is a common hope of most golfers because of the satisfaction gained playing at this level.

Even the professional shooting a rare score of 59 will look at the missed opportunities during the round, despite this sort of brilliant play happening rarely. The golfer scoring 59, sets 58 as the new target score to surpass their previous level of performance. Golfers are the true epitome of the search for perfection.

Section 2 - The Golfer's Frustration

Ultimately, the probability of playing the perfect round of golf is a near impossibility. Despite this, the golfer never stops trying to achieve a personally satisfying score for every round played. What is more important, golfer realize that the condition of mind state is one of the most important determining factors in attempting to achieve this goal. Golfers soon find their level of performance is dependent on the condition of their mindset, which is the product of their own thoughts and actions. Whatever your state of mind on any given day, you as an individual are the sole determining factor for how well you play. As a result, there is the constant struggle of maintaining mental stability to establish conditions increasing the likelihood more "better performances" are experienced with greater frequency.

As golfers' overall skills are elevated over time, they soon learn the mental aspects of the game have an increasingly more dominant impact on successful competitive play. It is also realized how quickly playing situations can change causing the emergence of self-created issues, concerns, and problems, often leading to unfavorably elevated scores on holes. Golfers also experience the percentage of satisfying rounds played to be much lower than expected, but despite this, don't lose sight of the fact you were the architect of those cherished rounds, and have already demonstrated the capability to equal these excellent performances. Golfers are frustrated with very erratic levels of play, plagued by better performances being a minority event occurring a limited number of times over a season. This last point will be revisited later as a key factor related to building self-confidence and performing at better performance levels.

During a season, a limited number of rounds are experienced where everything seems to go just right. The result is a better performance. There have been times when you displayed ball striking skills that may have even surprised yourself, but find maintaining this quality of play is elusive. One day your shot making is satisfying, and the next day feels like you just started playing the game. A primary source of golfer frustration is their difficulty with keeping performances more consistent, without huge fluctuations in scores and performance levels. Why is it that we consistently witness golfers having a number of holes with ballooned scores during a round, resulting in scores they wish had never occurred? Whatever the reasons for these disasters, there are those rounds you were more confident scoring a better performance. An important fact to always remember is that outcomes of rounds will vary, and that you have already displayed the capability of playing well above the quality of play demonstrated in the majority of rounds over a season. So, what is the problem?

I contend these elusive glimmers of genius in shot making are based on a mind state free of distractions, which normally sabotages efforts to reach superior levels of play. For a minority number of rounds during the season, you experience a greater number of shots in the upper echelons of your repertoire. You played well because your confidence was higher than normal, and you were able to ward off or expel any negative factors that could possibly blemish your performance. There is also the possibility that circumstances were such that negative influences didn't't arise during these better rounds of play, and you never had to deal with them, but despite this, the fact still remains that the omission or absence of negative influences and distractions during play can only have a positive influence on performance. Whether the negative influences or distractions are controlled or nonexistent, the result is effectively the same; enhanced likelihood of superior performance.

Your memorable scores may have been the result of one or two aspects of your game going well. Your putting may have been superb, your driving may have been strong, or your short game happened to be clicking on a particular day. Whatever aspect of your game was working, I contend you were playing with a higher level of self-confidence, and able to thwart off damaging negative distractions, permitting a personally satisfying performance to come to fruition.

Some aspect of your game was being executed as planned, uncluttered with the short-circuiting effects of distractions making the game complicated and frustrating. With a scarcity of resources available to help golfers learn strategies and methods to control negative influences and distractions, it is not surprising that a small percentage of rounds conclude with satisfying results.

The good news is that your personally satisfying rounds or gratifying periods of play were real events, representing real golf and real scores. Most golfers hope to re-experience this level of play every time they tee up the ball on the first hole. Being aware of their better performances, coupled with the inability to repeat this level of play more consistently is a recurring concern of most golfers. Frustration is derived from not being able to play at better performance levels, despite already demonstrating capabilities equal to or higher than this mark. Golfers have difficulty with the wide fluctuations they see in their scores, which only adds to the turmoil they feel in getting their games on track.

Section 3 - Golfers and Mind State Issues

If golfers were collectively surveyed to identify concerns associated with their play, the result would be an unlimited variety of wishes or hopes to resolve a litany of issues. These issues and concerns restrict opportunities for even mid-range performances from occurring. Superior playing levels feel like an anomaly to most golfers as a result. The variety and sheer number of issues and problems raised by golfers is daunting; "I wish I could drive the ball more consistently into the fairway" - "if only I could make more of my putts from within six feet" - "I would love to play a round of golf without scoring a big number on a hole". The variety of issues being faced is limitless.

Even the problems or concerns faced by an individual golfer vary widely. Sometimes the driver is the most disappointing club in the bag, and a month later, the putter is the new nemesis. In other instances, the problems are unchanging or somewhat static in nature. "Almost every shot I take curves off to the right", having to deal with the constant frustration of a chronic slice. Whether it is improvement in iron play to increase the number of greens hit in regulation, or being petrified when having to execute a bunker shot, every golfer has their own specific problems, issues, or concerns with their game. Exploring the issues and concerns facing golfers and their satisfaction levels regarding their progress and improvement, it became increasingly apparent the source of these issues and problems is primarily the golfer's mind state.

The insatiable hunger for solutions to the issues and problems golfers have faced, often for years, is indicative of the shortage of resources and exposure to techniques for addressing mind state concerns. The shortage of resources on this topic will manifest itself as a strong demand to be provided with implementable means to develop and maintain a mind state conducive to superior golf. Golfers are seeking the means to remedy their inability to break 80, or overcome their fear of the sand, or perhaps to overcome the issue of missing extremely short putts. These issues and problems are mental issues golfers are unsure how to remedy.

Many of the issues and problems being faced are long standing concerns that have not been remedied for years and have solidified as mind state issues. Golfers also have phobias chronically affecting performance, which also consolidate as mindset concerns. It becomes overwhelmingly apparent the concerns and problems faced, more often than not, relates to psychological or mind state issues.

Golfers soon realize their mind state is ultimately affected by their own actions and thoughts. Golfers constantly struggle to take control of, or shape their mind state to enhance the likelihood of a career performance, but feel poorly equipped to create a mindset conducive to superior play. Golfers are not able to inventory mindset conditions during better rounds to serve as a reference to aid in repeating these superior performances. They can't capture or simulate factors causing these rare outstanding periods of play. As a result, they become victims to playing at levels well below their capabilities, with superior play remaining elusive. Identifying the conditions or factors for these rare occasions of superb play is difficult, because most golfers do not experience them with enough frequency to formulate strategies promoting their reoccurrence. It is understandable why golfers have struggled with this elusive aspect of their games.

It is clearly apparent the primary obstacle to achieving this equilibrium or ideal state of mind is being equipped with strategies and tools designed to achieve this purpose. The absence of strategies and tools leaves the mind vulnerable to react in ways that often destroy or prevent the establishment of a healthy positive mindset. In many cases golfers implement strategies they believe will support and cultivate a favourable mental attitude, but these end up having limited or no effect. In some cases even having the negative effect of inadvertently worsening playing conditions. Golfers constantly contend with emotions and distractions creating less than favourable conditions in the mind at the time of shot execution, which sabotages hopes of achieving top performance. Fear, cockiness, embarrassment, anger, sympathy, negative events, stress, anxiety, poor results, bad luck and a wide array of other factors can quickly alter the mind's state, destroying confidence and faith of one's abilities as a golfer.

For example, consider the negative thoughts and anxiety that arise for the player standing on the seventeenth tee considering the possibility of achieving a record best score. Far too many golfers fall victim to the "too good to be true" scenario when in this situation. In too many cases, the achievement of a milestone score raises mind state issues or problems that in many instances come as negative distractions that compromise a positive mindset at a time when self-assurance and confidence are essential. How often has a golfer been on track to achieve a personal best, or better score, only to have it destroyed by negative or distracting thoughts becoming an obstacle to achieving a milestone event? How often have you found yourself or been a witness to a fellow competitor in this situation? In the majority of cases, the negative outcome of the final two holes ruins a possible record performance, and tarnishes the quality of play exhibited during the first sixteen holes. Even more detrimental are the reinforced negative effects that must be dealt with following yet another perceived failure.

Millions of golfers experience the same negative results, in similar situations, repeatedly over their careers. The fact that it is so frequently repeated indicates the need for golfers to be given the opportunity to learn how to establish, develop, and maintain a healthy and positive mindset to prevent these opportunities from slipping away. In other words, when pressure situations arise, it is possible to be armed with strategies to control, mask or eliminate the effects of negative influences and distractions, greatly improving the likelihood of a successful and satisfying round of play.

CHAPTER 2

Golf's Changing Paradigm

"What we need most is not so much to realize the ideal as to idealize the real."
Francis Herbert Hedge

Section 1 - The Nebulous Nature of Mindset

To define the processes, strategies and methods directed at establishing a healthy positive mindset, or to answer how the mind is psychologically altered are difficult questions to answer. The nebulous nature of arriving at a practicable and sound answer to these questions is the primary reason why golf improvement publications and resources are limited in the area of golf psychology or mindset development. The difficulty associated with trying to put to words the ideas and concepts required to create and constructively develop a golfer's mindset could be a major reason why so few resources exist in this area, relative to the physical aspects of the game.

A comparison or analogy to convey the difficulties encountered with articulating mindset concepts would be similar to trying to describe "red" to a blind person. Simply stated, it is much more difficult to articulate the development of a strategy, or define the methodology for a process of managing something that is not visible or tangible, as compared to visually addressing obvious errors evident in a golfer's physical swing. Most resources that presently exists to assist golfers in the area of golf psychology or mindset development are generally limited to valid listing of independent suggestions and tips, but lack the activities and tools permitting the golfer to nurture and build upon these skills. Despite most of these tips or strategies being valid and sound suggestions for improvement, golfers want to know what they are trying to achieve and be provided the strategies and tools necessary to be able to do this independently, in a personalized manner. Golfers are seeking the tools to nurture and improve their mental approach to the game to confront these distractions and remedy concerns that have persisted over time. Achieving this ability ensures the golfer has the capability of implementing a comprehensive ongoing customized improvement project tailored specific to their needs.

The obscure nature of golf psychology has left golfers in a vacuum searching for practical solutions or a methodology to address this highly influential aspect of the sport. Given the importance and brevity of the impact of a golfer's mental state on performance, it is astounding the discrepancy between the resources devoted to the physical game, like swing analysis and instruction, as compared to the mental or psychological aspects of the game. Even in the media, there is very limited and surface discussion related to the mental aspects of golf and a barrage of in-depth aids and dialogue in the area of physical swing analysis and improvement.

The limited availability of mind state development resources is certainly not limited to the amorphous nature of the topic. Many of today's resources related to golf psychology are desultory tips that have proven to be effective and successful in specific situations, but fall short of instilling any tangible permanence for developing a resilient healthy mind state. Golfers want to see tangible, real, and permanent results, permitting them to personally address a range of mind state issues.

The implications of arming golfers with tools addressing their greatest nemesis will certainly create amazing changes in confidence. This immediate impact on confidence will inevitably have an indeterminable positive impact on performance, but it is the ability to develop mind state competencies tailored to the needs of individual golfers that garners the greatest benefit. Every means has been incorporated to provide a practical solution for golfers to gain control of the mental aspects of the game, but be warned this comes at the price of changing your approach to the game, and being diligent in your efforts to implement sound and valid strategies to develop as a complete player. Strategizing the development of an effective resource providing achievable competency based outcomes related to mind state issues requires the defining of attainable learning outcomes inclusive of the mental approach to the game. Defining these outcomes opens the door for golfers, through a series of achievable steps, to introduce, develop, and fully incorporate activities to gain competencies for maintaining a healthy positive mind state. There are simple activities you can master providing the framework for a mindset development methodology delivering real positive performance changes. It is the culmination of the experiences offered through these activities and strategies that provide the total summative effect of your efforts, creating a playing environment tailored to perform at your best.

The establishment of a goal setting plan providing achievable and incremental steps in physical or mental skill development fosters an environment where confidence levels are continuously being raised by the positive reinforcement and motivation associated with goal attainment. Whether there is intended development in physical or mental skills, there must be associated target performance statements defining the skills to be met, creating an improvement initiative where positive reinforcement and subsequent confidence growth become the norm for both the physical and mental aspects of the sport.

Setting easily implementable performance targets defining mindset skills creates a whole new dimension to the development of a player. I was excited with the prospect of making available to golfers a means of personalizing and incorporating mindset strategies to deal with or control the negative influences that constantly emerge during play. A required premise of golfers seeking a greater degree of control of their play is the realization and acceptance of the simplicity of what is to be achieved. In other words, golfers must extinguish self created thoughts and notions that overcomplicate the game and prevent them from performing at levels they are more than capable of achieving.

The primary difficulty facing most golfers is resolution of mental issues having a detrimental impact on scoring. Golfers generally have some aspect of the sport that creates fear or anxiety affecting performance. Whether its the fear of water, bunkers, a tight driving hole, long iron concerns or an inability to get a lag putt close to the hole, most golfers have an aspect of their play adversely affected by their mental state of mind and are unable to control or resolve these issues.

Golfers feel lost and bewildered because they are unaware of practical and easy ways of gaining control of these detrimental thoughts and notions. Golfers need to create a more stable and favourable mindset better equipped for promoting superior and more consistent levels of performance. Another hindrance to meeting this goal are the years of negatively reinforced bad habits and methods that have victimized golfers. Following years of unguided and poorly planned practice sessions, coupled with few strategies to deal with mental distractions, it is understandable why a large percentage of golfers have seen their handicaps descend little over the years, with consistency of performance remaining sporadic. It is possible to play a round of golf and control factors that overcomplicated the game, but how you approach the game, and how you react to circumstances and situations may have to change.

Golf is a simple game, but golfers through self-created means, make it much more difficult than it really is. Despite all the effort and money spent to improve, the progress experienced by many golfers certainly does not meet their expectations. Far too many golfers experience long-termed minimal handicap improvement, erratic levels of overall performance, stalled skill improvement and a wide variety of re-emerging issues, concerns, and problems, often with no resolve. Fifteen years ago, when I was trying to attain a scratch handicap, I was the aspiring golfer desperately looking for resources to address my own mind state issues. Following an extended period of research seeking solutions to my own mind state issues, it became apparent resources in this area were extremely scarce, relative to the physical and visible aspects of the sport. The resources I sought to permanently instill and develop a mind state personally able to confront and address the negative influences encountered during play were never found. As I approached a scratch handicap, I was well aware of the increased dependency a golfer has on mind state issues as they improved. It was clearly evident as my handicap improved, reliance on controlling mind state issues was increasingly more important to maintain consistency of play and improvement. Maximized success of any golfer is dependent on his or her ability to deal with the mental aspects of the game. I searched the internet and libraries for useable ways to improve consistency, and discover aids or remedies to deal with stressful playing situations that often come up in the form of "pressure". The paltry resources I managed to assemble in my quest for help were a series of desultory tidbits of information, providing suggestions pertaining to narrow and specific aspects of the game. The resources suggested remedies to specific mind state situations or circumstances in the form of isolated antidotes, but lacked an underlying unifying approach, methodology or system providing real tools for golfers to personally hone skills solidifying and strengthening a mind state maximizing performance. The resources I managed to compile lacked the strategies or a system of implementation developing a sustained ongoing positive mindset.

It is unfortunate there has been a longtime scarcity of practical mind state development resources, but as golf's paradigm changes, new opinions, beliefs, and methods will emerge reflecting the influence of the times. Recently, there has been a gradual re-emergence and reaffirmation of the importance of mind state regarding performance, which should result in new resources becoming available on this topic. Unfilled golfer demand for resources dealing with mindset issues, and the relative scarcity of these resources is unfortunate, but golf's instructional paradigm will undergo changes that should see this problem resolved in the future. The peaking of longstanding golfer demand for mind state development resources, coupled with the recent resurgence of the importance of mind state regarding top caliber play should initiate the emergence of resources filling the void in this area. From the time this publication was originally started back in 1993, until its completion in 2016, there has been a relative scarcity of golf psychology resources specifically directed at ways golfers can personally develop and improve mind state competencies.

More golf psychology publications will become available with the widespread recognition of the practice of including mind state performance objectives as a regular component of golfer growth. Golf's instructional paradigm will shift in response to recognition of the strong positive impact of developing and instilling a positive mind state on performance and improvement.

As a golfer and educator specializing in competency based training of occupations dealing with hands-on psychomotor skills, it was immediately apparent the mental part of the game must be an experience-based environment permitting the measured evaluation of acquired skills as a means of verifying and validating progress. In other words, it is possible to set goals, objectives and challenges for the mental aspects of the game, just the same as the physical side of the game.

It was as if fate brought my working career in learning resource development and instructional design, and my own struggles to maintain a scratch handicap on an inevitable collision course. As a professional educator specialized in training program development, coupled with maintaining a scratch handicap, I saw an opportunity to invest my time developing a learning or coaching resource, specifically directed at creating an all-inclusive integrated approach to golfer development. There is nothing holding any golfer from developing both physical and mental skills on a continual ongoing basis.

The Golfer Mindset is a direct result of a merging of my life work in learning, coaching and training and the articulation of my experiences to achieve a sub-par level of play. I took the liberty to record my needs and thoughts as a golfer to identify and define the issue to provide insight into possible solutions. As a professional educator, I identified targets of achievement to be met applying valid and sound methods and tactics for confidence building and distraction management. The integration of mind state skills initiated my desire to create an instructional resource specifically outlining actions and activities any golfer can engage in to successfully instill mind state skills, promote confidence, and successfully provide capability to ward off or avoid negative mental thoughts during competitive play. After all, it is the negative distractions and influences causing golfers to either question their abilities, or create disruptions affecting shot execution. In either case, having the means of avoiding the blemishes on the scorecard caused by these issues is a luxury most golfers will relish.

The struggles I went through to get to a sub-par level of play primarily dealt with mind state issues. I wanted to take advantage of the ability to articulate the development of both mental and physical skills into a single process. Utilizing my coaching, training and education background, I set the target of integrating the development of mindset skills as a regular component of golfer growth, to create a resource directed at complete player development.

Without the benefits gained through mind state development, a player's improvement remains stagnant. Perhaps this is why so many golfers hit the "wall of limited improvement". Is it possible that the periods of time when a golfer experiences questionable play and can't make any headway lowering their handicap due to deficiencies in controlling mind state issues? Thousands of golfers hit an imaginary barrier where their handicap Index changes little for extended periods of time, despite having opportunity to improve over a number of years. What is preventing so many from achieving more satisfying levels of growth?

Providing golfers the opportunity to systematically enhance their ability to deal with mind state issues and reap the benefits this brings could be a major contributor to a return to constant, continuous progress in confidence levels and a movement to more satisfying levels of improvement and play. In addition, the degree of overall player development will not be realized until mental skills improvement becomes an integrated part of practice and play. To reach your true potential, it is essential to integrate mind state improvement initiatives into regular play and practice sessions to provide adequate opportunity to utilize and develop mental skills in playing situations.

Section 2 - The Progressive Benefit of Instilling Mindset Competencies

Providing golfers with the competencies to nurture mind state to support and improve control over negative influences will have a compounded beneficial effect on scoring and confidence. The ability to reduce the effects of negative influences and distractions through the acquisition of mind state competencies provides the ability to greatly reduce the frequency of poorly executed shots. The instilling of mindset development as a means of reducing the frequency of poor shots has the immediate benefit of eliminating the strokes for these poorly executed shots, however, the gains are far greater than the stroke or strokes initially saved. It is obvious there is an immediate positive effect of the stroke(s) saved by avoiding the costly shot, however, there are many possible additional strokes saved as the result of not being placed in these comprising situations. After all, it is the number of subsequent recovery shots that seriously affects the numbers on the scorecard and results in a big score on a hole.

The compounded advantage of nurturing mind state skills is the avoidance of the additional shots and newly created distractions arising as a consequence of not having to recover for so many errant shots. Avoiding these additional distractions and situations potentially saves many additional strokes by eliminating the devastating effects these circumstances have on a golfer's confidence. Keeping negative influences to a minimum is essential because they have the potential of becoming a disastrous scoring meltdown.

Finally, the elimination of all these possible additional strokes will have a supplemental positive effect on confidence levels. The ability to eliminate or mask negative distractions provides new potential to improve scoring in many new ways greatly enhancing performance and improvement. Golf's paradigm will shift toward honing both physical and mental skills to ensure complete and comprehensive development of the golfer. The value of instilling mindset skills as a means of reducing the shots causing grief for golfers cannot be overstated. The diversity of mindset issues plaguing golfers is limitless, however, through the implementation of mind state improvement strategies to confront them, accelerated improvement, enhanced confidence and superior performance will result. It is possible for golfers to easily nurture and develop a mind state promoting superior play.

CHAPTER 3

Setting The Demeanour

"We have to learn to be our best friends because we fall to easily in the trap of being our worst enemies."
Roderick Thorpe

Section 1 - Golfers Have The Greatest Intentions

Commitment to improve and the refinement of abilities require effort and motivation for planned growth to occur. This must not be equated to merely identifying the type of player you wish or hope to become. Wanting something is certainly not the same as committing to it, but many golfers do not differentiate between the two. Wanting to be the player you envision is merely fantasizing or hoping to play at the levels of a tour player, whereas commitment is a promise to act to achieve the goal. Greater overall rewards will come to those promising to implement actions to fulfill this end, as opposed to merely wishing or hoping to get there. Commitment and perseverance for improvement must include a dedication to fully implement the necessary strategies, methods or processes needed to maximize the benefits of initiatives directed at skill development and improvement. Commitment to the implementation of proven strategies for improvement is the first step that must be taken to realize maximum gains in performance. The reading of this book coupled with the willingness of learning ways to aid in controlling negative influences indicates your keen interest to take command of factors adversely affecting scoring and performance.

Initially, many golfers see the value of activities associated with a sound golf skill improvement initiative, but conveniently avoid or drop them. To avoid this, golfers must first make a real commitment to improvement and strive to maintain the motivation to keep their improvement activities ongoing and habitual. Golfers must constantly search for new and interesting ways of creating and enhancing motivation to maintain devotion to their improvement initiatives. The proven value of some improvement initiatives often avoided by golfers are too valuable not to ensure they are carried out and completed. Examples of indispensable tools not implemented by golfers, but having a huge impact on improvement levels include goal setting and planning, practice sessions planning, skill benchmarking and monitoring, performance data gathering and game management.

A golfer's improvement can slow or become stagnant for many reasons. In many cases, they are aware of sound and valid strategies for improvement and performance enhancement, but never implement or maintain them, despite being aware of their value. There is a range of proven tools specifically geared to enhance skill development, but golfers elect to sidestep them, failing to realize or care about the potential improvement gains being lost.

Golfers are notorious for aspiring to play at the levels of a tour player, but their methods and good intentions are often suspect. This is because many of the shortcomings or issues affecting golfer development are due to feeble and ineffective attempts to improve, or conscious and outright refusal to action items designed to greatly enhance superior performance. Golfers want and hope for the benefits these activities promote, while having the greatest intentions of taking the steps necessary to reach their aspirations. Their lack of conviction, motivation and perseverance results in their efforts being casually dropped or never being given the priority to pursue the goals they hoped to achieve.

Another issue arising is golfers maintaining the motivation to carry out activities viewed as boring or mundane, but required for real and satisfying levels of improvement to happen. For example, activities associated with any improvement program will require organization, planning and paperwork. These preliminary administrative types of activities are essential to a development program being effective and cannot be overemphasized regarding the rate of improvement experienced. Numerous improvement strategies and methods require administrative tasks to be performed to realize their benefit. For example, it is impossible to monitor progress without measuring performance. This entails the golfer to be in possession of information regarding their performance skill level for all clubs in the bag, for a variety of shot types. The golfer has no alternative but to constantly monitor progress by collecting and managing performance data to determine when performance has reached specified targets, indicating progress has been achieved. To achieve this outcome, administrative activities must be carried out to take advantage of the benefits. Ironically, the measurement of improvement or performance increases is only possible when there is an ability to compare performance with another criteria. This provides a point of reference to determine if progress has been achieved.

It is clearly evident that administrative tasks like organizing, planning, information gathering, data management, and record keeping, along with the associated paperwork, have caused golfers to avoid or shortchange themselves of many extremely valuable and effective improvement initiatives. The immediate loss to golfers by avoiding these supportive activities is slowed improvement and inconsistencies in performance. Improvement is compromised and performance is inconsistent because of an unwillingness to put into place organizational tasks permitting the measurement of skill development and the associated confidence increases this brings. It is essential to have a means of measuring skill development to determine if it has occurred. A system for improvement must include mechanisms permitting the ability to assess gains in skills, which promotes growth in confidence and motivation to excel. Notwithstanding the point that improvement presumes a measured advancement or refinement of a skill, the reluctance to pursue those activities associated with personal skill benchmarking, goal and objective setting, and planned improvement causes developmental activities and initiatives to be disorganized, ineffective and aimless. The result is a total lack of unity and direction guiding the golfer's efforts. The valued tools most quickly sidelined and discarded are activities normally associated with the details of a plan for improvement requiring constant monitoring and the recording of skills.

Perhaps golfers view these activities as extrinsic and having little influence on improvement and performance. Maybe they feel the value or benefit of these methods and strategies are not worth the time and effort required to implement them. Whatever the reasons to consciously negate or omit a proven and highly beneficial strategy, it is essential golfers realize the value of these strategies and actively insure they are implemented or skill achievement and maximized improvement are adversely affected.

Section 2 - Essential Commitments

Before the introduction of the Positive Competitive Mindset Model and its associated strategies and activities it is essential the golfer pledge to commit to a few fundamental underlying bases supporting it. Commitment to these initial basic concepts is a precondition of the model's implementation. These commitments may be contrary to your current practices and habits, but a strong effort must be made to instill them as a basic conviction to your goal to build a healthy and positive mind state. The success and rewards you realize are directly dependent on unconditionally adopting and instilling these commitments. The advantages gained implementing and adopting these basic principles are primarily based on the consistency with which they are used. Partial implementation or the occasional exception not to support them will detrimentally diminish their effectiveness. Commitment refers to their habitual support in every possible instance. They are essential to the effective establishment of a healthy Positive Competitive Mindset.

Later examination of the strategies and activities related to each of the major components of the Positive Competitive Mindset will clearly indicate the benefits and value of a habitual dedication to the commitments to be presented. Your ability to unconditionally adhere to each of the commitments will have far reaching effects establishing a mindset specifically directed at obtaining superior performance, and enhanced improvement. The decision to support these founding elements precipitates a positive on-course demeanour and a more constructive attitude, leading to enhanced improvement rates, effective on-course play, reliable growth in self-confidence, and a renewed and optimistic enthusiasm for the sport.

Commitment 1

The first underlying commitment to foster to develop a Positive Competitive Mindset is the unconditional acceptance of each and every shot you make on the golf course. Unconditional acceptance refers to eliminating any emotional attachment to every shot you make.

The avoidance of emotional reactions to shots eliminates negative influences or distractions creating mindset instability leading to inconsistent shot execution. Through their own actions, golfers often inadvertently and unintentionally place the burden of pressure on themselves. Golfers are often unaware of how damaging their reactions to shots may be during a round of play. Golfers respond to individual shots in a variety of ways, with far too many reactions negatively affecting performance, leading to disastrous results. Even the reactions many golfers make toward better shots can have a negative effect on their ability to perform at an optimum level. You may ask, "How can a golfer's reaction to a superbly hit shot possibly create negative influences on their performance level? Unwittingly, golfers can place themselves in pressure situations following a wonderfully executed shot.

The choice of the following example is to extinguish the notion negative influences or distractions only originate from emotional attachment displayed by displeasure with unfavourable shot results. For example, consider a golfer on a par three placing the tee shot to within three feet of the hole and casually commenting to the rest of the foursome "It looks like I will get a stroke back here". The casual statement reflects an emotional attachment with the shot through the presumption a birdie will be the result. The distraction created emerges when the golfer attempts the birdie putt with the fear his bold prediction of a birdie may have been a little presumptuous, thus creating an anxious filled attempt to put the ball in the hole. What is more important is recognizing the potential for all the possible additional negative influences created, if the birdie putt is missed. You have witnessed the reaction many times, the disgust, anger or disbelief that is displayed. This often manifests itself as a façade attempting to camouflage the embarrassment for missing a putt, following a presumption bordering on cockiness.

Devotion to the unconditional elimination of any emotional reaction to every shot must be instilled and cultivated for building and maintaining a Positive Competitive Mindset. It's important to realize is that the disgust and anger felt are real emotions and feelings, creating new negative influences and distractions. These new distractions include anger, embarrassment, pride concerns and a range of ego concerns. The negative distractions contributing to poor shot execution can have a progressively negative effect on a golfer's game because unsuccessful shots are a major contributor to the creation of new negative distractions.

To emphasize the concept being illustrated, let us more closely examine the above example. In the case that the putt is missed, the emotions attached to this can have seriously devastating effects on subsequent holes. For example, negative distractions created as a result of the missed putt, could manifested as an effort to over aggressively gain back the lost stroke to save face for the embarrassment it caused. The golfer often lets emotions overtake their mindset in an attempt to reassert their confidence and re-justify their competencies, not only to themselves, but their playing partners. Most importantly, the distractions created produce a state of mind no longer conducive to superior play. It is imperative to take any steps to avoid the creation of negative influences because of their potentially devastating effect on confidence levels and performance.

Negative influences interrupt a golfer's clarity of purpose and shot execution, often leading to negative shot outcomes, creating new distractions putting additional strokes on the scorecard. What is ironic in the above example is despite paring the hole; many golfers in this situation beat themselves up for not making the birdie putt. Taking a slightly different and objective view of this example, it seems absurd and ironic there is potential for disaster to occur when scoring a par on a hole. This is just a simple example of where the inadvertent creation of a distraction can easily escalate to where the mindset is in disarray, seriously affecting performance.

Committing to unconditional acceptance of every shot free of any emotional attachment is more conducive and supportive of superior play and enhanced improvement because this more positive approach to the game inherently avoids negative distractions that are detrimental to self-assuredness and confidence. The avoidance of negative distractions that detrimentally affect performance permits the golfer to perform without contending with confusing, mental issues that create shot execution concerns. It is important to remember the golfer not only benefits from the original strokes saved by controlling the original negative influences, but is spared the subsequent barrage of distractions generated if the original negative influence is not controlled.

Keeping your emotions in check following every shot will be integrated and supported as a fundamental commitment or condition supporting the development of an effective Positive Competitive Mindset. Its value cannot be overemphasized. To further extend the positive effect of avoiding negative distractions following every shot is to use this time to assess of the shot, comparatively reflecting on the feelings associated with the swing and the actual shot result.

Implementing the practice of shot assessment following every shot serves as a productive substitute activity avoiding the disastrous implications of overzealous shot expectations or poor shot results. The elimination of emotional attachment to individual shots permits the golfer to objectively evaluate the causes of mishits and ingrain the feelings or sensations associated with better shots. Rather than the negative reactions to shots having a detrimental affect on later shots, the golfer can be more constructive in rectifying mishits, providing a much more positive environment where improvement is a primary motive or objective. This valuable practice of shot evaluation can be extended to include other integrated and valuable activities further extending the development of a Positive Competitive Mindset.

In addition, following a period of assessment of the shot the mind is then free to begin to determine a strategy for the next shot. In short, the implementation of this practice allows you to deal with each shot on an individual basis without residual influences affecting subsequent shots. This is an advantage that will help eliminate poor shots resulting from thoughts originating from other events.

There are other examples where a golfer's actions or words results in negative distractions seriously affecting performance. For example, Colin Montgomerie experienced an extended period where undue pressure was placed on him as the result of emotional responses he made regarding comments from a few members of the gallery. His emotional attachment to the incident and his wish to express his views to hecklers in the gallery only worsened his playing circumstances, by extending and escalating the issue. If Colin had kept his emotions in check and avoided his verbal comments, the issue would have ended and the subsequent negative distractions would never have developed. What's ironic is that Colin has never played well in the United States since the incident. It has only been since becoming a senior joining the Champions Tour that he has experienced any real successful play in the United States. We may never know the mindset effects of this event on Colin, but the evidence suggests the negative results were greater than originally thought.

Implementing the unconditional acceptance of every shot as a part of your game will allow you to detach yourself from the unpleasant behaviours resulting from emotional outbursts and embarrassing situations, making you a golfer that is much more enjoyable to be with. In addition, the strength of character you demonstrate in controlling your emotions will better equip you to deal with pressure and distractions that are out of your control. The importance of demonstrating this trait cannot be overemphasized. You must make this a priority, if you are to realize the full benefit of a healthy Positive Competitive Mindset.

Finally, the adoption of this trait will permit execution of a shot without fear for what the result will be. If you unconditionally accept the results of your shot execution, then the fears, anxiety and negative thoughts that come into your mind just before and during the execution of a stroke will be eliminated, allowing the shot to be freely executed.

It is difficult to eliminate your normal patterns of behaviour because they have been a part of your mental processing for a long time, however, your awareness of the benefits afforded this trait will make you conscious of your efforts to make it an engrained part of your approach to the game. When you slice a ball into the woods, it will at first be difficult to control your emotions, but through discipline and effort you will be able to control your emotions and realize the benefits of this commitment. Instead of your normal reaction, take a couple additional swings to help determine what caused the slice and create a learning opportunity for yourself. The game of golf is challenging enough, without beating yourself up and creating new obstacles that are of your own creation.

Your ability to let this emotional detachment become a part of your being will greatly improve the enjoyment you get from the game because your only concern will be the game. Relish the good shots you make appreciating the satisfaction of the ball racing to its intended target, but don't let your good fortune become cockiness, its an emotional attachment that will only cause you grief, as illustrated earlier.

Commitment 2

The second underlying premise or commitment you must foster to develop a Positive Competitive Mindset is the establishment and consistent utilization of planned measurable skill based performance achievement guiding golfer development

If a golfer has any intention of making skill improvements and experiencing consistent growth in performance then there is no alternative but to include the setting of target statements defining what it is you are going to achieve to serve as a beacon to strive for. Without some means of quantifying skill development, then there is no way of determining whether improvement has even occurred. The skill performance targets you set for yourself clearly define a quantified measurable performance level to be achieved for easily determining when the target has been met, with a new measurable performance level determined to continue progress. The golfer using this process is provided the reward of attaining a skill and the satisfaction associated with its attainment, providing the motivation to repeat the process. After all, it worked the first time, what is preventing it from occurring again, or even repeatedly. The golfer's awareness of their skill achievement being a real measured and tangible target reveals they are seeing real tangible growth in areas they have defined, which then creates experienced based confidence growth. Confidence growth is based on real and justifiable skill improvements creating an attitude of expected success with the knowledge it can be achieved. In addition, the consistent quantification of skills that are measured keeps the golfer intimately aware of their capabilities and tendencies; essential to playing at top levels.

Commitment 3

The third underlying premise or commitment you must foster to develop a Positive Competitive Mindset is the establishment and consistent utilization of a specific planned repeatable pre-shot assessment and pre-shot execution routine for every shot executed.

Every shot requires the opportunity to consider all shot variables to be decisive and committed to what is to be executed, where the repetitive nature of the process promotes consistency. This is achieved by eliminating any possible negative distractions because of indecision or noncommittal, permitting an effortless and unaffected swing to occur. Before the execution of any stroke, you must decide on a course of action and be committed to what you intend to do with the shot. Indecision and noncommittal to an action reflects uncertainty for what must be achieved, and are two states of mind that must be avoided at all costs. Being unsure of what to do and attempting shots without an envisioned commitment causes a flood of questions and concerns impeding the brains ability to successfully execute an envisioned shot. Without visualization of the intended shot there has not been any opportunity for the brain to assimilate this information.

The brain is an amazing part of the human body that continues to reveal new secrets pertaining to its functions and complexities. We have all experienced activities or events related to brain processing that have left us gob-smacked in awe of its power, precision and reliability. Whether its photographic memory, the capacity to store information, intuitions, musical genius, mathematical brilliance, exceptional artistic talent or extraordinary psychomotor skills, the brain continues to astonish and confound us with its staggering capability. We have all had experiences regarding its function providing clues on how to better utilize its capabilities. Unfortunately we have only scratched the surface of understanding how the brain works in relation to thought processes and controlling physical psychomotor activities, but we have witnessed incidents and events providing hints to ways of utilizing its capabilities.

You have probably personally experienced situations where you have made those occasional superb shots where you experienced an above average clarity of purpose for what it was you wanted to achieve, with the shot being executed exactly as planned. These are the experiences accompanied by a "just do it" feeling at the time of the stroke that is so strong, the result is the exact shot you envisioned. I am referring to experiencing a spontaneous clearly determined shot objective accompanied by a fleeting but precise shot visualization that includes the shot's intended flight, bounces and roll. It is important to always visualize a shot before execution to provide the brain with an opportunity to rehearse and assimilate the actions required for an intended shot. Visualization of a shot's outcome greatly enhances the likelihood of a shot being executed as planned. These rare instances of focused shot clarity do not occur often, but with enough frequency to determine conscious thought is completely absent during great shot execution, usually preceded by a fleeting clear image or notion for what is to be achieved.

The brain is wonderfully incredible in its ability to unconsciously execute psychomotor skills replicating a clearly visualized shot outcome. As a parallel example, a basketball player does not score field goals from varying distances on the court by consciously thinking of the force and trajectory of the ball as each shot is executed. The basketball player recognizes or re-experiences the distance from the basket as visually perceived, and lets the subconscious brain use its ability to accurately control psychomotor skills based on the experience and repeated trial and error of numerous shots taken over time. The basketball player merely replicates the process repeatedly based on a visually perceived distance from the hoop. There is no conscious thought relating to the force and trajectory with which to throw the ball, but rather a strong reliability on the instinctive and automatic execution being guided by what is immediately perceived just before the shot being taken.

When you settle over the ball and are ready to trigger a shot, the mind must be completely free of any second-guessing that occurs when you have not committed to a precise idea of what you hope to achieve. It is imperative that you make a specific shot decision that allows you to swing the club in an unimpeded manner, without the short-circuiting effects of distractions caused by a tentative reluctance to execute a shot. Taking the extra time necessary to come to a point of decision and commitment will repel the formation of distractions caused by the discrepancy of not being able to visualize what it is you wish to achieve. Making a judgment and committing to a specific shot may not always be successful, however, habitually instilling this approach into your game will greatly reduce the number of disappointing shots experienced.

Consistent application of an effective pre-shot assessment routine, guiding the determination of the shot to be executed will always ensure all the pertinent variables are considered before committing to a shot. Developing a routine for shot assessment will insure the golfer consistently considers all pertinent factors required to decide on a course of action, with full committal to attempt a shot having a desired or planned outcome. Shots are made more confidently because golfers have an action plan reflecting what they hope to attain, greatly increasing the likelihood of experiencing success.

Likewise, the ongoing and repeated application of a shot execution routine provides numerous benefits. Consistent use of a shot execution routine could be the single most important action you can take to improve consistency of play and eliminate distractions. The shot execution routine is a replicated sequence of actions occurring between the time a shot making decision has been made and the triggering of swing execution. Implementing a shot execution routine will have an astonishing affect on improved shot consistency, simply based on the benefits that come from the repetitive nature of the process creating some degree of comfortable familiarity for every shot taken. The shot execution routine will greatly enhance your ability to eliminate or mask mental distractions just before and during shot execution. Your conscious preoccupation with the routine developed for every shot inherently suppresses negative influences because of the diversion of the mental fixation caused by the routine itself. The mind becomes dominated by execution of the routine, which eventually becomes an automatic process, leaving the mind inactive to freely execute the shot.

Routine also provides the added benefit of improved shot consistency due to the improved efficiencies of unaffected brain activity as a result of repetition. Simplified, repetition of complex psychomotor actions improves the communication efficiency of pathways in the brain that are utilized in carrying out the action. The result is improvement in brain processing to more efficiently execute the action. The result is improved repeatability, equating to improved consistency. The above 3 commitments are simple actions the golfer can incorporate into their games to see marked changes in performance and improvement. In addition, support and conviction for these commitments directly enhances and promotes positive development of a golfer's mental approach to the game.

Section 3 - Focusing Efforts

When it comes to hitting perfectly executed golf shots, there are countless and widely varying diversions that can culminate as disruptions to the smooth flow of a shot's execution. After all, when you consider the distance the club head is moved during a swing, there is always the danger of slight inconsistencies resulting in a questionable shot result. With each swing, also consider the repetitive precision required to accurately achieve successful clubface approach and alignment with the ball to attain a successful ball strike. The ability of a golfer to repetitively and successfully execute a swing every time is extremely difficult to achieve. The many problems and issues facing golfers create similar type phobias and fears having different origins, but emerge as mental issues golfers struggle to control, but with little success.

Diversions or distractions can manifest themselves as a tee shot that ends up snap hooking sharply to the left, as the result of overexertion to gain extra yardage on a drive or it could appear as a golfer with a paralyzing fear of sand shots, always leaving the first attempt out, in the bunker. Diversions or distractions cause minor disruptions to an intended or envisioned swing, resulting in suspect or detrimentally affected shot execution. This causes frustration, only worsening performance, resulting in deterioration of confidence, which regretfully could repeat. No wonder scores positively affecting the handicap index are a limited occurrence, when it is a constant battle to get over those costly parts of the game that make a golfer feel defeated every time a troublesome scenario repeats itself.

Distraction can be conjured up internally within the golfer's mind, like the fear of playing out of bunkers or can originate externally, like the distraction caused by a family emergency or financial crisis. It is important to be able to differentiate between the internal and external categories of distraction or diversions because the means with which the golfer deals with each type may be different.

Internal Distractions

An internal distraction is a diversion originating in the mind of the golfer, as a result of internally self-created thought processes. The diversion or distraction usually takes the form of a thought or thinking which impedes the ability to freely execute a shot. Examples of internal distractions include anxiety when a golfer is placed in specific situations where fear, stress and a wide range of other emotions arise as the result of a preoccupation of failing to achieve a desired result. A golfer becoming nervous when hitting over water or always tightening up to execute a three to four foot putt for fear of missing are prime examples of internal distractions.

External Distractions

This type of distraction manifests itself in the mind of the golfer, but originates from an external source. An external distraction can be thought of as a diversion entering the golfer's mind as a result of an event, action, comment or other outside influence. The loss of a job, or the death of a family member are examples of an external distraction that could divert the golfer from the normal execution of a shot. Like internal distractions, external distractions impede the ability to freely and successfully execute a shot.

Both internal and external distractions can have the same devastating influences on shot execution. The only difference between the two is the source of the golfer's frustration. The reason for the differentiation between the two types of distractions relates to the methods a golfer has at his or her disposal to control them. It is also important to realize that many external diversions or distractions encountered do not relate to golf. A golfer's personal life can have a major impact on the distractions they must deal with. Family issues, finances, work, health, and a range of other personal factors can all create external distractions having potentially huge negative effects on the mindset of the golfer. Golfers striving to excel at the game must minimize these personal external influences and take steps to insure they do not act as distractions affecting improvement and performance. For example, getting your financial house in order will go a long way having this external distraction extinguished as a source of anxiety.

A practical and implementable solution to control negative influences, distractions and other mind state issues has been elusive due to the nebulous nature of the topic, and the diversity of the issues associated with a golfers mind state. Recently there's been greater attention on the mental aspects of the game, which may be driven by the increased number of highly skilled and talented young professional golfers reliant on improving in this area to remain competitive. Recognition of the influence of mind state or mental psychology on performance has been a topic of discussion for years, with some of golf's greatest players expounding on its importance, and offering valued information and advise in this area.

As a teen with a yearning to play golf well, I read numerous books seeking the wisdom and advice of a number of PGA players. Arnold Palmer was the source of my belief that greater consistency of superior performance is directly dependent on mind state stability and the ability to deal with personal shortcomings. My enthusiasm and intrigue with the mental aspects of golf have a life-long link with his reference to the words; "But we've still-remembered those words of my father? - got 90% of the game to go. We've arrived at the most important part of the game, the most interesting, the most inspiring, the part that really separates the men from the boys. We've finished with the checkers and ready to start on the chess. We will discuss, in the rest of the book, how to play golf from the shoulders up."

Mr. Palmer emphatically purports the importance of the mental aspects of golf, referring to numerous instances of mind state influencing shot execution and tournament outcomes. His 90 percent emphasis on the mental game is indicative of his belief that success is inherently tied to a golfer's ability to manage mind state. The importance of a golfer's mind state for superior performance has been emphasized by many noted coaches, players, and other golf authorities, but tangible resources instilling and fostering strategies and activities developing these skills are extremely limited.

Positive Reinforcement And Confidence

Henry Ford's words, "Obstacles are those frightful things you see when you take your eyes off your goal" is so true when it comes to the game of golf. When the golfer is goal focused a positive mindset is much easier to establish and maintain. Despite the mental interference distracting golfers from executing shots capable of attainment, the ability to repel these negative influences and execute shots as planned can become a reality for any golfer. The integration of mindset skill development as a component of complete golfer growth introduces a wide range of new strategies, methodologies and approaches for instilling these skills. These new initiatives make necessary some fundamental changes to a golfer's normal or typical development activities, often requiring attitudinal changes with respect to their approach to the game. The importance of golfer's adopting specific mind state improvement practices into their day-to-day repertoire is paramount in realizing the untapped potential of becoming a "master" of the mind game.

Confidence can be viewed as a measure of a golfer's perceived ability to successfully execute a specified action. It is natural for confidence levels to change positively when success is achieved and diminishes when positive reinforcement is nonexistent or negative outcomes begin to dominate. Confidence building is dependent on a golfer's perceived ability to successfully execute an action, therefore, the ongoing identification and achievement of incremental skills or performance targets within a Goal Setting Plan is an absolute necessity for confidence levels to be elevated. Without a Goal Setting Plan opportunities for confidence building become limited and performance suffers. Any initiative or strategy providing opportunities to achieve measured goals or objectives is an opportunity for confidence building, through the associated positive reinforcement, and motivation of skill achievement. I reiterate a Goal Setting Plan with inclusion of incremental performance targets is essential for measured improvement to occur. The successful attainment of progressively more rigorous targets is representative of incremental improvements in skill development.

A necessary prerequisite to the identification and monitoring of progressive target performance statements is the initial benchmarking of current skills. Before determining if any improvement has been achieved, it is absolutely necessary to initially benchmark current skills to establish a starting point for measured skill development. It is essential to have an applicable knowledge of current capabilities to effectively identify the new target performance statements defining your intended plan for improvement.

Building positive influences requires the golfer to provide ample opportunity for success. To facilitate overall positive reinforcement of your abilities, then the majority of shot outcomes must meet with success. Simply, this means that greater than 50% of your shots must meet your expectations or be viewed as successful for an overall positive influence on the mindset is to be achieved. If the majority of your shots are meeting your expectations, then this entails being positively reinforced or successful for the majority of them. For an overall improvement in self-confidence, then the level of expectations must be such that success is achievable the majority of the time. The golfer is obligated to benchmark their abilities for all clubs in the bag. Obtaining a good working knowledge of your present shot making capabilities goes a long way in initially establishing some confidence regarding your abilities, while at the same time providing a starting point for your improvement program. Knowing your present abilities lays the groundwork for having a Goal Setting Plan, with a measurement component associated with skill acquisition. Improvement becomes a planned and progressive activity always directed by targets of achievement, bringing about continuous improvement and consistency of performance that is substantiated, validly raising confidence levels.

Knowledge Application

It is essential the golfer be in constant pursuit of possessing an up to date knowledge of their skill capabilities and tendencies, and applying the best known practices to maximize improvement efforts.

Failure to use the best methods, information and knowledge available to guide an improvement initiative will shortchange the positive results the endeavour intends to achieve. Golfers should always be searching for the information and knowledge that provides maximum results for their efforts. Utilizing the best information and knowledge available will always ensure the golfer is maximizing their opportunities for growth.

CHAPTER 4

The Positive Competitive Mindset

"Give me six hours to chop down a tree and I will spend the first four hours sharpening the axe."
Abraham Lincoln

Section 1 - Foundational Elements

MODEL: Functionality

A priority for the success of any new approach or methodology of golf improvement is the value and credibility of the strategies and activities supporting it, second is the ease of implementation and maintenance of methodologies sustaining it, and third is the applicability of the approach to meet the wide ranging needs of golfers. My quest was to provide the tools a golfer needs to instill a Positive Competitive Mindset as a methodology for enhanced performance and accelerated improvement.

The success of any improvement initiative must have all the above characteristics to be successful and a valued resource that can to be used by any golfer. Special effort has been made to ensure any strategies and methods employed meet all three of the above criteria. Ensuring this promotes and supports both the efficiency and effectiveness of your efforts.

The Positive Competitive Mindset Model is based on a simple premise providing structure and guidance to easily conceptualize and organize the activities, strategies and practices implemented to support the model. A great deal of care has been taken to provide an approach to game development that permits the golfer to readily internalize and foster concepts based on a sound and valid approach to golf.

MODEL: Considerations

It is imperative the strategies and activities supporting the model be easily adopted to insure the versatility and effectiveness of the approach. Another precondition of the model is the ability to measure and monitor progress. This requirement insinuates goal setting and goal achievement as the means of monitoring skill improvement and progress. Where the methodology diverts from conventional golfer development is the added focus placed on the mental aspect of the game, creating a resource specifically directed at a more comprehensive or complete approach to improvement. Taking this avenue provides the golfer with the opportunity to grow in a more comprehensive manner, by developing both physical and mental skills. The model raises the profile of mind state issues and concerns as a means of accelerating improvement and achieving greater consistency of performance by providing golfers access to a means of developing a more effective mindset better able to address negative influences confronted during play, taking on each shot with a justified confidence of being successful.

MODEL: Foundation

The model lays the foundation for the organization and utilization of strategies based on three premises. These foundational principles are designed to guide and support the integration of all supporting strategies and activities to promote a unified approach integrating the relationships of these activities, to culminate in a competitive playing environment better geared for accelerated growth. The gradual implementation of the complementary activities and strategies supporting the model causes a strengthening of the mind state as a result of the reinforcing effect of the interrelationships of newly introduced strategies, culminating in greater focus on what you hope to attain. Each newly added strategy solidifies the mindset further, through the reinforcing linkages and supports garnered with every improvement activity introduced.

An important aspect of the model is the equal emphasis placed on each of the premises and the necessity to consistently address all three components. The premises can be viewed as the three legs supporting a stool. Like a stool, if one leg of the model is not adequately addressed, then the stability of the model is compromised. This analogy stresses the importance of equally addressing all three premises of the model by using strategies and activities supporting each. The effectiveness and stability of the mindset model is based on all component premises being addressed to facilitate the stability of the mindset established. Building a stable support for a highly effective improvement initiative with a focus on mind state development is essential to providing a long lasting developmental environment to initiate, establish, and build a healthy Positive Competitive Mindset.

The Positive Competitive Mindset Model

Let us more closely examine the premises for establishment of the Positive Competitive Mindset. Lets look at a basic overview of its structure and the supports the model provides to nurture a mind state providing new found opportunities to excel.

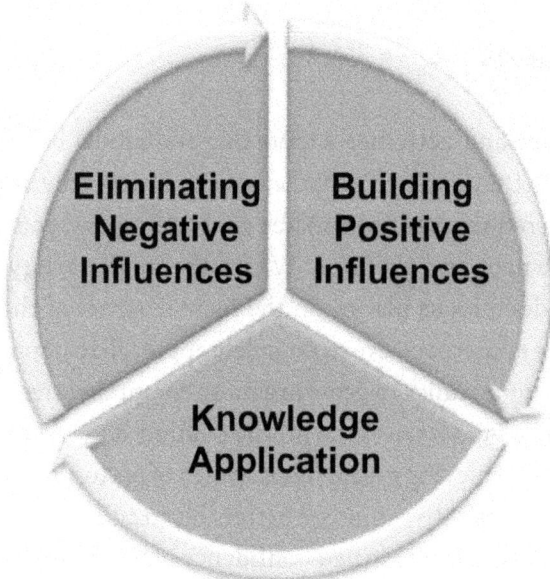

Positive reinforcement, distraction management, and targeted knowledge acquisition are the three primary components forming the basis of the establishment of the Positive Competitive Mindset. The Positive Competitive Mindset model or frame of reference is based on the foundation that development of mind state skills is enhanced by, first, creating numerous opportunities for positive reinforcement, second, destroying negative influences or distractions that divert attention from achieving desired outcomes, and third, acquiring he best possible knowledge base directly supporting clarity of purpose for the objectives a golfer desires or hopes to achieve.

It's these three basic ideas that constitute the three primary components or founding premises of the Positive Competitive Mindset. The approach can be viewed as a complete golf performance and improvement approach using an integrated regimen of strategies and activities, which together provide improved mindset stability, for improved competitive play, and the ability to address pressure situations more effectively. If a golfer takes the necessary steps to insure activities and methods implemented build positive influences, eliminate negative influences and are based on sound and valid information as relates to improvement initiatives, then the ideal conditions for development of the Positive Competitive Mindset will be fostered and established.

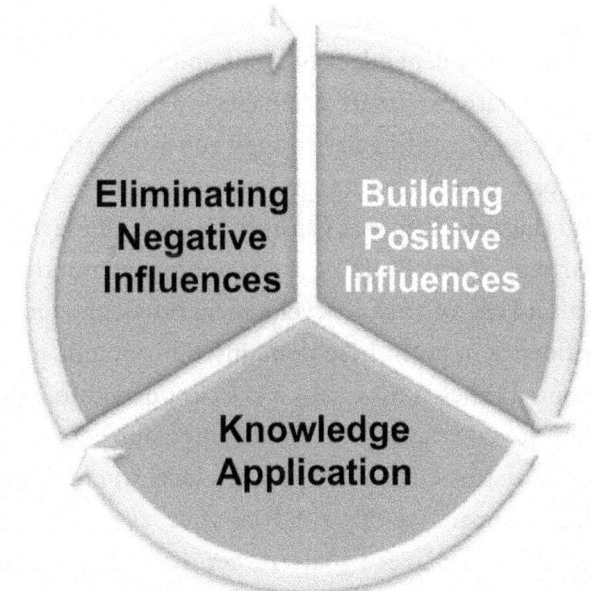

PCM MODEL: Premise 1 – Building Positive Influences

This premise promotes strategies elevating the profile, frequency and impact of positive reinforcement for the purpose of enhanced confidence building. Building Positive Influences presents the strategies, methods and tools to provide maximum opportunity for the positive reinforcement of competencies gained or achieved, spawning a corresponding rise in confidence.

Your confidence level must be based on real and proven capabilities that have been demonstrated, giving credence to the belief of attaining a challenge being faced. Confidence gains are realized as the result of an awareness of increases in abilities. The achievement of set targets or goals serves as the fuel for a powerful tool ensuring knowledge of capabilities is captured to facilitate and substantiate confidence growth. The most successful and rewarding experiences that create the greatest gains in confidence are those achieved under the most adverse conditions. There is greater satisfaction, pride and promotion of self worth that manifests itself in these more rigorous types of circumstances. There precipitates an embellished reaffirmation of the self-perception for being successful in more challenging circumstances or situations.

Your ability to show measured improvement in scores or in statistical aspects of your game raises belief in what is achievable. Your confidence level should never be based on your best guess of what you perceive your abilities to be. Confidence is a reflected belief in your abilities to be successful. The measurable increases in abilities are driven by a performance standard or criteria being reached or attained. Confidence is a trait that is strengthened through successful experiences. Personally believing you can improve something puts into motion a series of events and a state of mind motivated to find the best methods and strategies for maximized improvement. The only way you have to determine the level of trust or confidence you have in your capabilities is to base it on measurable and observable behaviours you have demonstrated.

Always establish goals, targets and positive thoughts based on a confident ability to successfully execute actions permitting you to experience these goals and objectives being achieved. Since your performance is primarily based on your ability to execute successful shots, it is clearly advantageous to set goals which are consistently being achieved and adjusted upward to boost confidence levels. Your development as a great ball striker is dependent on your ability to effectively adjust your goals and targets in a manner that sets expectations that are attainable in a timely manner. This fosters motivation, excitement to excel and improves self-confidence through consistent and successful goal achievement.

This is why goal-setting plan must be an integral part of a golfer's development. By establishing performance goals and monitoring achievements, you have a basis for the level of conviction you can place in yourself to perform at a particular level. Building psychomotor and mind state competencies through strategies directed at physical and cognitive skill development provides ongoing positive reinforcement, promoting increases in confidence in both these domains. This entails playing at a confidence level where you can perform to your abilities. This is why it is so important to know what your abilities are. Confidence level is reflective of your capabilities solidifying your personal knowledge that you can succeed in most shot-making situations. You must play at a level where there is a realistic expectation to achieve or be successful. It is imperative that you base your level of confidence on achievement of observable and measurable skill performance goals, rather than dead-end accomplishments like the number of tournaments won, scores and awards. The number of tournaments won is not a measure of a quantified attainment of a skill. It is important to always keep performance statements in your plan defining standards of skill level performance, rather than the setting of milestones in the form of trophies and other awards.

Planning and Goal-setting provides the mechanism for the golfer to consistently experience positive reinforcement, essential to elevating confidence levels. More importantly, how is it possible to raise confidence levels through positive reinforcement without quantitative validation of skill improvement based on real skill development? Skill target setting is one of the few ways true confidence building can occur. By setting measurable goals, achieving them, setting new goals, achieving them, and so on, you prove or demonstrate your abilities to yourself. You are able to gain re-assuredness in yourself to perform and achieve effectively. You will experience, recognize and enjoy your achievements, and feel real self-worth as a result. By knowing what you can achieve, you are not setting yourself up for unwanted surprises and failures because you have a reasonably accurate assessment of what your abilities really are. Also, assessment of your abilities is not clouded by ego or totally unfounded self-justified guesses.

The emphasis placed on goal achievement, and the methodologies for practice are specifically directed at creating enhanced occurrences for positive reinforcement, which fosters justified feeling of having the ability to accomplish something. Taking ownership of a goal-setting plan builds self-confidence as targets are reached and improvements in performance are achieved. As the golfer acquires the reward of new competencies, these skills raise overall expectations and confidence to meet the next step in the progression of the plan. As skills and competencies are acquired self-confidence in one's ability flourishes proportionately with the rate of positive reinforcement occurring.

Improved self-confidence permits the golfer to take what would be considered to be greater risks, because of the improved confidence in their abilities to perform at a level bringing greater rewards. In short, a golfer's perceives less risks and greater opportunities for reward as self-confidence is enhanced. In order to play the game at a highly skilled level, a commitment must be made to maximize opportunities for measured skill attainment to provide the positive reinforcement driving confidence building.

Ultimately, the achievement of mastery or excellence in golf, to which your plan aspires, demands the highest level of commitment. Your level of commitment to the sport of golf is the single most influential decision you will make in determining the level of play you hope to achieve. It is obvious the time commitment made by a golfer aspiring to play professionally will be far different from the weekend golfer playing the game for the enjoyment of the outdoors and the social aspects of the game. The level of commitment will again differ for the new golfer and another aspiring to win the club championship. The golfer having adequate time devoted to improvement will have a plan of greater complexity than a golfer having limited time available for play and practice. No matter the complexity or detail of a plan for improvement, dedication, perseverance and resolve must characterize the commitment made to attain the goals to be achieved. There is no room for apathy, laziness, and excuses regarding the commitments you make. Your plan must be realistic from the start, reflecting your lifestyle, free time, work schedule, family obligations and other competing activities, so you can be confident the targets set in your plan are reachable. Commitment and persistence to being steadfast in pursuing your plan is crucial to realizing the full benefit of your efforts. Whatever your hopes, wishes or dreams, the degree of commitment to getting there becomes the reality of what you aspire to achieve.

Confidence Considerations

Under-confidence

There are cautions to watch for concerning self-confidence. To perform at an optimum level, under-confidence and over-confidence must be thwarted off at all costs. Under-confidence will prevent you from taking risks when there are opportunities for reward. When there are drops in self-confidence levels, this opens the door for negative thoughts and distractions to manifest themselves causing a further deterioration in confidence. When under-confident, you will experience fear of failure or reluctance to engage, preventing you from strategically taking risks. Doubt in your abilities and a deterioration in your ability to focus or concentrate will also affect your mental processing. You will also start to conjure thoughts of seeking blame for faults, misfortune and unfortunate circumstances, which originate elsewhere or are completely unfounded. You will also experience less enjoyment for the sport when you play under-confidently.

Overconfidence

On the other hand, overconfidence can cause you to take risks that should never have been taken, or results in failure to put in the work and effort necessary to improve, missing out on the benefits you would have earned from your efforts to excel. Overconfidence may be the result of misleading or pushy friends, family or coaches not fully understanding of your abilities, but can also be caused by vanity or ego issues. Just as complacency can lead to letting under-confidence manifest itself, cockiness or smugness are equally damaging. Overconfidence creates negative situations, as the result of not having the abilities to achieve what you hoped or believed was attainable. Overconfidence is a confidence level that is not based on your abilities, but rather on a self-perception of what you think they should be, or what you believe them to be. On a purely rudimentary level, overconfidence is usually caused by overzealous and hopeful expectations for shots, which are not backed up by attained capabilities you have demonstrated in the past. This often creates additional negative circumstances leading to further declines in self-confidence, which only leads to further deterioration of performance.

Another benefit underlying adopting a methodology stressing occurrences of positive reinforcement is the internalized permanence or resiliency of confidence levels when exposed to experiences having a higher frequency of positive reinforcement in similar situations. The frequency of being successful in past endeavours serves to minimize the questioning of your capabilities in different situations. Increasing the frequency of positive reinforcement is a foundational premise for maximizing improvement due to its direct and immediate effect on confidence levels.

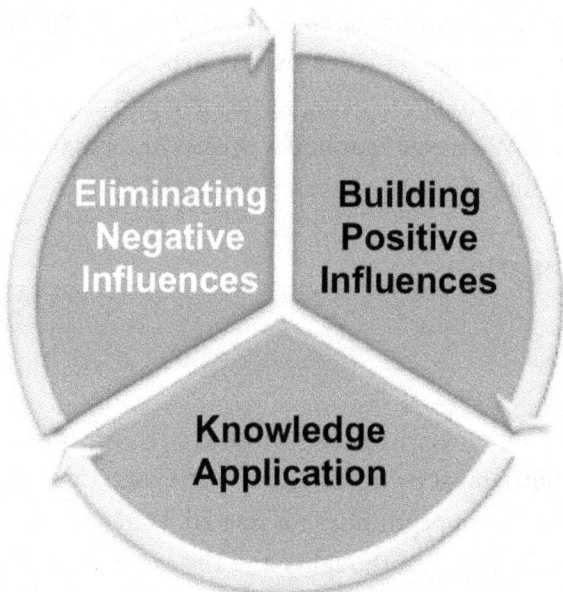

PCM MODEL: Premise II – Eliminating Negative Influences

This premise promotes strategies instilling the ability to eliminate or control negative influences and distractions.

Lets more closely examine the second of three premises defining the model for the Positive Competitive Mindset. The Controlling Negative Influences premise supports implementable strategies, methods, and tools providing opportunity to acquire the skills to eliminate or repel distractions that so often lead to errant shots and inflated scores on holes. Having the opportunity to adopt strategies avoiding circumstances leading to potentially demoralizing events is an indication of the untapped potential for stroke reduction through this premise. Eliminating high impact negative events will stop extreme confidence swings, by avoiding the wasted time required to rebuild confidence levels, which inherently take longer periods of time to build. Being willing to engage in strategies controlling the distractions met during play is a powerful option to have for the potential rewards offered.

The importance of controlling the negative influences during play is essential to establishing an effective Positive Competitive Mindset. Fundamental to controlling negative distractions are the commitments alluded to earlier in the previous chapter. Promoting initiatives extinguishing or eliminating negative influences is critical for superior performance and improvement. The commitments expressed earlier are essential to the establishment of the Positive Competitive Mindset and directly support the model. They foster a mind state having a sound foundation directed at extinguishing mental issues these commitments help to eliminate. In addition, golfers are aware of how easily negative influences can lead to devastating periods of play, crushing confidence, causing performance to fall well below capabilities. This obviously raises the flag for the golfer to implement any steps necessary to avoid negative influences and distractions.

The strategies specifically directed at minimizing negative influences and distractions are unique because they are specifically directed at the mental side of the game and provide impetus for new possibilities in golfer development. The potential value for development of skills controlling, masking or eliminating negative influences is limitless and an overview of the strategies is a window into the impact this premise of the Positive Competitive Mindset model can have on your improvement rates and overall performance. The full presentation of methods and the activities outlining the implementation of each strategy are examined in upcoming chapters.

Golfers soon realize rebuilding confidence is a slower process, compared to how quickly it can be deflated following a demoralizing negative event. It's ironic that despite golfers being knowledgeable of the crushing effects these negative influences can have on confidence, golfers contradict this basic premise based on shot expectations that are consistently overzealous.

It is extremely difficult to provide positive reinforcement for shot-making expectations that are nothing short of unreasonable. Unrealistic shot expectations negates the golfer from experiencing positive outcomes the majority of the time, resulting in negative reinforcement, and reduced confidence. This usually precipitates negative influences creeping into the game reeking havoc with performance. How can a golfer rebuild confidence levels, if high expectations limit opportunities of success? It is a formidable challenge to control all the negative influences confronted during a round of play, but to compound the difficulties by being unnecessarily demanding on yourself does little to build a mindset promoting superior performance.

Golfers are helpless to deal with the many mental obstacles met because of not having the ability to deal with the many negative influences that precipitate additional distractions, which is a primary reason why "in the zone" performance is rare and short-lived. If you are a golfer with expectations that are overbearing, then you are probably one of your own worst enemies, impeding your own growth as a great ball-striker. It is a natural tendency for the golfer with excessively zealous expectations to create negative influences as a result of falling short of anticipated goals and targets. In other words, most golfers create the unnecessary generation of negative distractions by setting personal expectations with little tolerance for error, resulting in few shots having a successful result. This is a negation of the principles of positive reinforcement, and an example of how easy it is to be misled, or make an inaccurate assumption that can seriously affect performance.

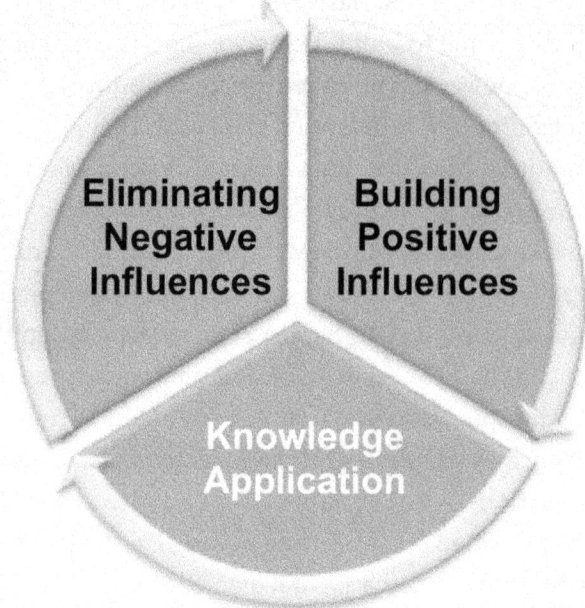

PCM MODEL: Premise III – Knowledge Application

This premise promotes strategies that effectively use and appropriately apply the best knowledge and information available.

Over a career, the golfer will access a variety of information or knowledge to tackle numerous issues associated with improving their games. It is important for golfers to ensure the information guiding their efforts is current, validated, and through fair assessment, provides the best guidance available. For any improvement initiative, the golfer must utilize the "best" knowledge and information available to maximize the benefits and returns for their effort. Using the appropriate and best knowledge and information available, before any decisions related to development is essential to maximizing competency growth. Always seeking to acquire pertinent knowledge and information equips the golfer with the prerequisites necessary to maximize the likelihood of achieving success and enhancing results, but is also pivotal in raising the effectiveness of the strategies and activities employed.

The importance of the "best" knowledge cannot be overemphasized. It is the quality of the knowledge and information employed that raises the likelihood of meeting goals, objectives, and challenges identified in your goal-setting plan. It is understandable that pertinent leading edge knowledge is utilized to maximize the advantages of any developmental plans undertaken. For example, knowing the effects of grain or incline of the green on your putts, or the effects of side-hill lies on how a shot will react is "knowledge" that improves the scores you put on the scorecard. Knowing methods for achieving desired results for different bunker situations, how elevation affects the distance shots travel, or how different types of shots react when they hit the green are examples of how knowledge of the game will enhance performance.

Maximizing the effectiveness of the knowledge you have regarding your own capabilities and the insights learned regarding tendencies in you performance is critical to raising confidence levels and maximizing the results of improvement efforts. The Knowledge Application component of the Positive Competitive Mindset Model is based on the idea - if information or knowledge is needed to support any improvement initiative, then using the best information enhances the effectiveness and efficiency of the golfer's efforts. The scope of the knowledge and information utilized by golfers to meet their goals and objectives will widely vary. The concerns, issues and shortcomings encountered are based on the constant assessment of the knowledge required to address them. This requires the golfer to access the knowledge and information to best address numerous changing factors influencing performance and developmental growth on an ongoing basis.

Strategies, techniques, activities and tools are introduced to specifically target practice sessions, course and game management, on-course assessment data gathering, and comprehensive golfer development. It's even more important to ensure the strategies supporting the Knowledge Application component are reflective of wise use of information; after all, this is the very basis for this premise supporting the Positive Competitive Mindset.

CHAPTER 5

PCM Implementation

"Before everything else, getting ready is the secret to success."
Henry Ford

Section 1 - Strategy Integration

Overview

During my own struggles of achieving and maintaining a scratch handicap, I knew the constantly changing issues and problems I faced with my own golf game were similar to those faced by thousands of golfers. During the quest to reach my goal it became increasingly apparent mind state related issues were my primary concerns, rather than issues related to my physical capabilities. The commonality I recognized, based on the wide range of issues faced by golfers, was their inability to effectively deal with the psychological aspects of the game stemming from personal problems and concerns they confronted. When I undertook this project it was apparent the ability to have some way of moulding mind state was the essential element required to address the unique and wide ranging issues confronted by all golfer's. This emphasized developing a universally practical approach equipping them with the capacity to specifically address a wide range of mind state concerns. This entailed the methodology must be easily understood, effortlessly applied through simple implementation, readily instilled as a component of any golfer's demeanour, and valued as an effective mind state management tool. Additionally, the approach had to provide the individual the ability to incorporate their own ideas, providing flexibility and ownership to a methodology viewed as being adaptable, and easily tailored to anyone.

A key element of an improvement initiative is seeing value and reward in its purpose. If golfers take an approach to the game specific to their own issues and concerns, and taking their own steps to adopt additional strategies, then the approach provides the flexibility to be universally applied. The golfer can then take the things learned, and by making personal contributions, further strengthen the supports and integrity of their personal development.

Integration

An underlying precept of the Positive Competitive Mindset Model (PCM) is for easy employment by golfers, with its effectiveness originating from the interrelated and supportive relationships of its strategies and activities. A consideration when implementing a new strategy or activity supporting the model is seeking ways for it to have a unifying and reinforcing effect on mind state growth. This permits the golfer to individually introduce new strategies and methods shaping mind state, and adopt additional ways of supporting the intent of the model. Examining what integration of strategies represents, and what it means, provides the golfer with the basic essentials for extending these concepts to include their own personal contributions, by adding additional strategies to the arsenal fortifying their ability to deal with mind state concerns.

The effectiveness of the approach is the integration of tangible strategies and activities specifically designed to reinforce and complement each other, creating a consistent familiar playing environment that eagerly embraces competition, through improved readiness and motivation. The model conceptualizes the basic requirements for establishing and maintaining mind state development, however, the activities implemented also introduce linkages and unique relationships promoting a fusion of all strategies that instill and reinforce a permanent and complete attitudinal approach to the game.

Golfers are urged to consider other activities, aids, or methods falling under any of the three premises of the PCM Model. Even after setting up a plan for improvement, always look for new ways of promoting positive reinforcement, better information utilization, or improved ways of avoiding distractions. Any valid strategy strengthening and reinforcing the health of the mind state should be considered for implementation. The integration of activities, aids, and other tasks fortify the links and connections of related strategies, strengthening and reinforcing consolidation of the mindset, and your efforts to achieve superior performance.

For example, the On-Course Assessment strategy is primarily directed at providing the golfer with on-course performance information supporting the Knowledge Application premise of the model, but additional benefits come from the activity also supporting the Elimination of Negative Influences premise, by serving as a supporting activity following shot execution aimed at stopping distractive negative reactions to shots, and dwelling on negative results. This strategy also supports the Building Positive Influences premise, by utilizing the information gathered for goal and target setting, which is specifically directed at a plan for positive reinforcement. The simple introduction of a data-gathering tool for information purposes creates new opportunities for positive reinforcement through the introduction of target performance statements related to the on-course performance data collected, while at the same time controlling negative influences, as a result of the process serving to block out external distractions. On-Course Assessment is an example of a strategy aimed at one premise of the model, but as a result of implementation creates interlinked connections, enhancing the cohesiveness of the mindset, by further entrenching a mind state shaping the golfer's perceptions and reactions during play.

In another example, Benchmarking is a strategy directed at the Knowledge Application premise due to the valuable information learned by the process, but confidence levels are also raised as a result of becoming more knowledgeable of personal capabilities, resulting in support for the Building Positive Influences premise of the model. Likewise, the Elimination of Negative Influences premise is also supported through the information learned and its immediate confidence benefits affecting play. Here again is another strategy primarily directed at an activity supporting one premise of the model, with the result being support of all foundational components.

A strategy or activity introduced can support one, two or all three of the foundational components of the model. Feel free to introduce any tactic supporting premises of the PCM Model, always looking for new ways of reinforcing interrelationships to further entrench the Positive Competitive Mindset being created.

As each of the strategies and activities supporting the model are introduced it will quickly become apparent how each contributes to the fostering of an approach to the game, increasingly providing confidence in your ability to remain focused for every shot you execute. Familiarity with the strategies presented, coupled with an increased understanding of the purpose or intent of each, will permit golfers to add new initiatives, strengthening their mind state's resiliency and shot execution. The strategies more specific to distraction management will be of special value to golfers having specific phobias or long-standing concerns over an extended time. Real confidence growth and control of negative influences places the golfer in a playing environment where achievable results will be more regularly attained and a golfer's personal demons can be confronted.

Positive Competitive Mindset Model
Strategy Support Levels

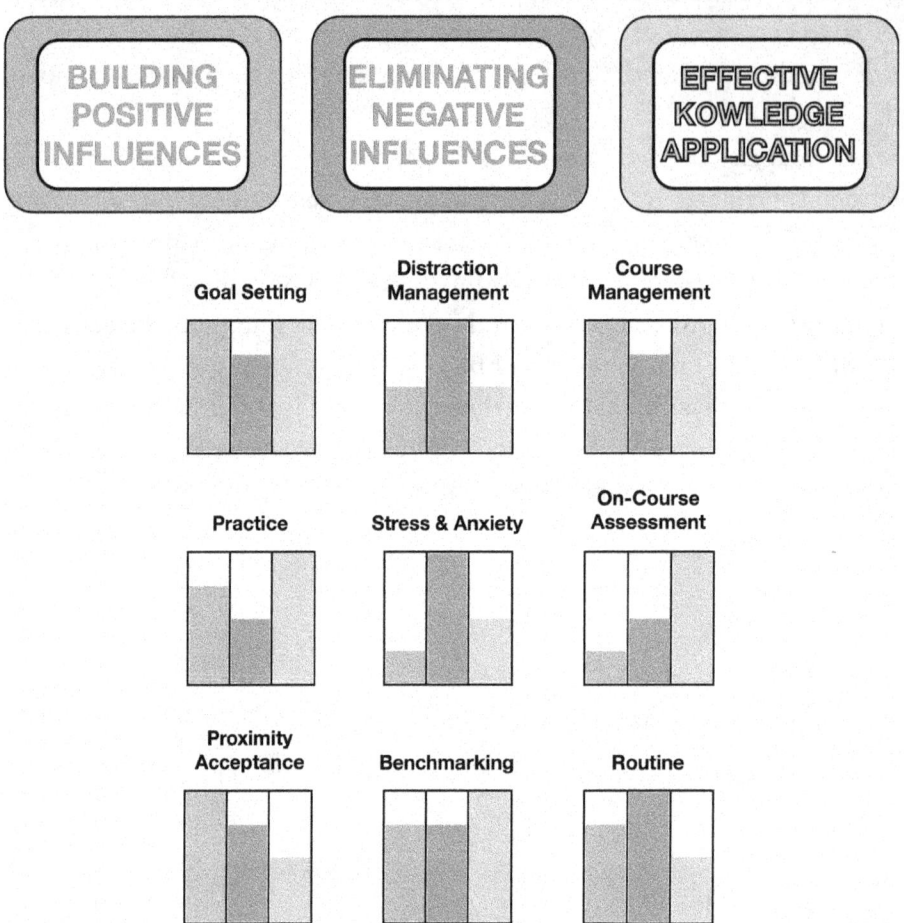

The illustration above provides a quick and easy way of determining the support each strategy has for each premise of the model.

Identifying the level of support each strategy has for each foundational premise helps the golfer to individualize their own program for implementation, with provision for introducing strategies in a fully customized manner, reflective of any golfer's different circumstances or inclinations. There will be recommendations made and suggestions to put into place, but the golfer chooses and selects the order and combination of strategies to incorporate for mind state development. The golfer is able to strategically emphasize any single premise of the Positive Competitive Mindset Model to personalize their areas of concern. Whether the emphasis is positive reinforcement for confidence building, distraction management or more effective utilization of the knowledge available for improvement, the golfer can emphasize growth for any one of the three foundational premises.

Adding Complementary Strategies

A means of identifying new activities strengthening your mind state is to examine new actions supplementing the strategies presented. Another great way is to explore and determine other activities solely supporting just one premise. This isolates and specifies the primary focus of potential strategies, making it much easier to determine tangible contributions to add. Whatever the source of a strategy or activity considered for inclusion, each new addition fortifies mindset stability, by improving the resiliency of mindset in pressure situations, or when confronting negativity affected confidence levels.

Strategy Implementation

The impact, or overall benefit of each strategy presented varies dramatically. This entails certain strategies having a greater overall impact on mind state development than others. In a few cases, there are strategies having the attraction of requiring little effort and time to incorporate, but having huge rewards for the effort entailed. This makes these activities attractive to golfers, due to their easy implementation, and rapid positive influence on play. There are also a couple strategies considered essential or paramount to the functionality of the PCM model, and the establishment of sound confidence growth. Due to the relative effectiveness and importance of strategies some additional insights are presented to help the golfer better determine the strategies to initiate. Recommendations and assistance regarding strategy implementation better equips golfers with making informed decisions, regarding the order or combination of strategies used in their improvement plan.

Failure to include Benchmarking, Planning and Goal Setting, and Routine as implemented strategies would be missing on benefits of three activities that cannot be overlooked. I am confident golfers will agree with the reasoning differentiating these strategies from the rest as having greater significance, or a more pronounced effect on building The Positive Competitive Mindset. The primary reasons for the Goal Setting and Routine strategies being given greater significance is the necessity of any improvement proposal to provide a mechanism for continuous positive reinforcement to foster confidence growth and the untapped value of having the ability of warding off negative influences, thus preserving confidence in situations that have been demoralizing in the past. These two strategies are essential supports of the PCM Model and must be included in the golfer's intended execution plan.

Based on assessment of the strategies and activities presented, the golfer can determine the areas to emphasize, choose the order they are implemented, customize how they are used and add some of their own unique strategies to address personal issues and concerns. After all, as indicated earlier, a key characteristic of an improvement initiative being successful is to ensure a degree of flexibility, providing the golfer with some personal ownership in controlling and influencing the outcomes of their efforts. Getting the golfer to see value in planning for improvement and understanding the effects of their efforts is a primary objective when starting any new initiative, the second is doing those things that will make it happen.

The strategies presented in each of the remaining chapters are stand alone information packages, providing background and information specific to their implementation, supporting activities, benefits, and positive effects on performance and improvement. I apologize for the sometimes repetitive nature of the material and terminology presented, but this is made necessary by the intent of having each strategy presented independently, providing all essential information in one location. Reference to the linkages between strategies and activities also creates circumstances adding to the repetitiveness or redundancy of terminology and phrasing.

Mindset Stability

This section examines the relationships of strategies and activities implemented and their integration in supporting the effectiveness, permanence and resiliency of the mind state you cultivate. Lets explore some of the considerations for certain strategies and how implementation of each will affect the overall effectiveness of the demeanour you create.

Always be aware that your confidence level can only be based on successful attainment of a level of performance you believe you are capable of achieving. This means your confidence level must be based on experiences of having had a level of success accomplishing what it is you are trying to achieve. Without these positive experiences, where an accomplishment has been consciously witnessed, confidence will never be elevated. Confidence is not something you can just decide to have because there is no basis upon which it has been acquired or created. Confidence can be thought of as a firm feeling or belief in your ability to accomplish a task, or with anticipation to action what has to be achieved.

All the strategies and activities falling under the Building Positive Influences component of the PCM Model are based on the achieving of goals and objectives. This provides the mechanism for the experiencing of accomplishments through continuous confidence building experiences. Every target a golfer sets and achieves, no matter its significance, raises confidence. This is a commonality of all the strategies and activities under this component of the model and is essential for a mind state having stability and permanence.

Equally important to maintaining confidence growth and mindset stability is the frequency of success in goal accomplishment being the majority of the time. Experiencing success must be more than fifty percent of the time. Failure to ensure this fifty percent minimum requirement is being met will result in negative reinforcement becoming dominant, causing deterioration in confidence levels. It is important for golfers to devote a portion of their improvement programs monitoring for effective levels of positive reinforcement. The stability of mind state is dependent on experiencing success in the majority of cases.

Mind state stability is also enhanced when experiences simulate reality and make provision for being diverse and varying, better simulating actual on-course play. Mindset stability comes from having experienced the trial and errors, and the successes and failures in different situations. Hitting shots out of wet sand, on excessive sidehill lies, from "fried egg" lies, or other challenging situations, stabilizes confidence levels, as the result of providing some security in believing " I'm capable of accomplishing a particular shot". Expanding experiences by mimicking reality is the catalyst for a more broadly based or stable mindset. The ability to demonstrate successful responses in extenuating circumstances is extremely effective in establishing a resiliency to adversity in real conditions, by providing the belief anything is achievable.

Having confidence to successfully execute a particular shot in a peculiar or unusual set of circumstances has a stabilizing effect on mind state, by expanding and validating the golfer's sources of confidence. This creates a sort of resiliency to mindset, where new and additional positive reinforcement from these less common situations, broadens confidence in your ability to be more versatile, and raises overall self assuredness, by extending the belief of being successful with more difficult challenges. This also avoids the destructive negative influences emerging as a result of the distractions and anxiety caused by the doubt of being successful, due to inexperience executing a particular type of shot.

The solidification of links and connections created by activities associated with the strategies introduced creates interrelationships and associations further engraining or cementing the mindset. With the passing of time, the permanence and effectiveness of strategies are enhanced by the complementary effects of the strategies, reinforcing and supporting each other. With the passing of time, the interrelationships of the strategies and activities introduced to fortify your Positive Competitive Mindset will solidify, with everyday supporting tasks becoming "second natured" and habitual, losing their aura of being laborious inconveniences. They will become an everyday component of your regular demeanour or approach to the game, improving in efficiency, drastically reducing the time and effort required to administer them. Moreover, the strides in improvement you witness will provide new found motivation to maintain the positive gains in your performance, causing the maintenance and management of your initiative to be valued and welcomed. The golfer is fostering an approach to the game that becomes easier to maintain and more effective with the passing of time.

Comprehensive Development

The distress, uneasiness and trepidation experienced by golfers today creates phobias, apprehension and indecisiveness emerging as mental issues golfers struggle to change, but with little success. This causes frustration, only worsening performance, resulting in deterioration of confidence, which can cause this cycle to repeat. No wonder scores having a positive effect on handicap index are a limited occurrence, when it is a constant battle for the golfer to get over those costly parts of their game making them feel defeated every time the scenario repeats itself.

Establishing a mood or demeanour similar to when superior performance is experienced is an aspect of mind state that is promoted or mimicked. The established mind state must be stable and free of any events or occurrences that are out of the ordinary, where nothing dramatic or emphatic is experienced to disrupt the tranquility of the moment. This is the realm we wish to create; this is the same realm that golfers relish when they are playing well, where it seems there was nothing that could disrupt the perfection of the moment. To more frequently experience "in the zone" type of play, where a greater number of superior level performances are experienced is to maintain a stable, familiar and an uneventful mindset, which is more conducive to consistency of play.

The state of mind at the time of shot execution is the single most important factor influencing a golfer's performance. Creating the conditions helping to ensure the creation of a tranquil, familiar, focused mind state prepared for the unhindered execution of an envisioned shot is ultimately the impetus behind the PCM Model. I set the goal of providing golfers with an understandable, implementable and effective means of putting into place a number of activities and strategies, which together provided a cohesive easily managed means of growing or developing, both mentally and physically, as a complete golfer.

Many of the ideas presented in the strategies in the following chapters are not new, and others are unique, however, the system or approach for applying these ideas is what distinguishes The Positive Competitive Mindset from other golf improvement initiatives. At this point, feel free to address any of the following strategies making up the remainder of the book, but it is strongly recommended to become familiar with all strategies before creating your Positive Competitive Mindset implementation plan.

- Goal Setting & Planning
- Distraction Management
- Game And Course Management
- Practice
- Stress and Anxiety
- On-Course Assessment
- Benchmarking
- Proximity Acceptance
- Routine

CHAPTER 6

Benchmarking

"A man should look for what is, and not for what he thinks should be."
Henry Ford

Section 1 - Prerequisite of a Goal Setting Plan

Despite benchmarking being a supportive aspect of Goal Setting and Planning and other strategies, the radical improvement in performance resulting from the activity warranted it being considered a strategy on its own. Golfers will be pleased with the immediate positive effects the benchmarking process has on ball striking and overall performance, as the result of confidence gained by the process. With confidence congruent to the belief of having the ability to accomplish something based on the experiences of already having attained it, then benchmarking will have an immediate positive effect on confidence level. The confidence gains are spawned through the reaffirmation or awareness of the skills or abilities demonstrated as a result of the process. Golfers completing benchmarking activities will show immediate improvement in performance simply based on this activity. This is because benchmarking provides essential information regarding a golfer's capabilities and inclinations, increasing confidence levels based on actual demonstrated shot-making results.

A sound knowledge of your shot-making capabilities and inclinations serves as a starting point for the identification of the initial target performance statements guiding improvement. In addition, an intimate knowledge of your capabilities, tendencies, strengths, weaknesses, and characteristics of play is essential for guiding the areas of improvement to be emphasized. Superior performance during competitive play demands having an accurate and intimate knowledge of your game, and is also pivotal for confidence levels to be realized and affirmed. The more effectively and accurately skill levels are determined, the more successful the golfer will be with shot execution.

For the sake of this publication, benchmarking is viewed as the establishment of a standard of proficiency serving as a starting point for the quantitative monitoring of change. Benchmarking permits the comparison of initial shot-making proficiency levels to changes in performance, easily determining if measured improvement has occurred. Benchmarking provides a reference point for the development of newly acquired capabilities and is an essential activity before starting the goal-setting process. In short, diligently and accurately benchmarking your abilities facilitates effectively establishing the first set of target performance statements guiding improvement. The Challenges guiding practice established during Goal Setting and Planning originates with this first set of performance statements defining the skills to be achieved.

Benchmarking Information

	Full Shot Data						Proximity Acceptance Data
Club	Total Shots	Shots Long %	Shots Short %	Shot Left %	Shots Right %	Shot Length Average	Tolerance Distance
Driver							
3 Fairway							
5 Fairway							
Utility							
3-Iron							
4-Iron							
5-Iron							
6-Iron							
7-Iron							
8-Iron							
9-Iron							
P Wedge							
G Wedge							
S Wedge							
L Wedge							

Benchmarking Information

	Partial Shot Data						Proximity Acceptance Data
Club	Total Shots	Shots Long %	Shots Short %	Shot Left %	Shots Right %	Shot Length Average	Tolerance Distance
L Wedge - 7:30							
L Wedge - 9:00							
L Wedge - 10:30							
S Wedge - 7:30							
S Wedge - 9:00							
S Wedge - 10:30							
G Wedge - 7:30							
G Wedge - 9:00							
G Wedge - 10:30							
P Wedge - 7:30							
P Wedge - 9:00							
P Wedge - 10:30							
9 Iron - 7:30							
9 Iron - 9:00							
9 Iron - 10:30							

Without a sound and accurate determination of your capabilities it is not even possible to establish a valid target performance statement. Following the benchmarking of a skill, new standards of performance or definitions of competency can be identified, facilitating continued development of that skill. As long as the improvement plan is maintained by creating new achievable performance statements, as others are achieved, puts into place a guaranteed vehicle for ongoing skill development, with the added bonus of being fully aware of your shot execution strengths and weaknesses.

Benchmarking quantifies your progress through the targets identified in your Goal-Setting Plan, but also includes key information related to the implementation of the On-Course Assessment, Proximity Acceptance and Game and Course Management strategies, which all collectively support the premises of the Positive Competitive Mindset Model. Due to the similarity of the data collected for the Proximity Acceptance strategy and convenience sake it has been included on the sample Benchmarking tool illustrated above. It is suggested the Proximity Acceptance strategy is reviewed prior to benchmarking data in this area. The benchmarking process is required of these strategies because of their reliance on the identification of a golfer's capabilities before their implementation. For example, how could a golfer be expected to adopt a Game or Course Management strategy without some idea of their shot-making capabilities and tendencies, or identify the initial performance targets in their Goal-Setting Plan without some knowledge of their initial skills. Some of the benefits Benchmarking include:

- immediate confidence gains
- ongoing awareness of capabilities, weaknesses and inclinations
- making better or more sound shot execution and game management decisions based on the best and most up-to-date information available
- enhanced performance as a result of benefits above
- accelerated improvement as a result of benefits above

Creating New Areas of Growth

The golfer needs a way to introduce newly benchmarked skills into their practice sessions, providing opportunity to develop these competencies. The benchmarking of new skills to be developed is completed during the experimental portion of a practice session, which will be discussed in detail later in the Practice strategy. It is during this experimental portion of a practice when different shot types are introduced and new performance statements are established. Benchmarking is incorporated into practice in this manner to provide an avenue for taking on new skill development, thus increasing the repertoire of shot execution skills being developed. It is during experimental portion of a practice session the golfer gets to explore the new shot making skills to be monitored for improvement. This provides the benefit of introducing new skill development in areas having the most positive impact on scoring and performance. The process ensures the most up-to-date and accurate skill information is used when making shot execution decisions and that you are providing yourself the greatest number of opportunities to expand your experiences of achieving success for a wider range of shot types.

Establishing On-Course Assessment for Benchmarking Purposes

Along with the benchmarking activities being a part of every practice, there must be a means of gathering or recording on-course capabilities and tendencies. This is essential to providing an accurate means of benchmarking aspects of play directly related to competitive play. You will be introduced to an on-course, data gathering tool providing the appropriate information for benchmarking your on-course abilities and tendencies during competitive play. An on-course assessment tool is presented that can be used as presented or be modified slightly to better monitor different aspects of play. The value of benchmarking greens in regulation, fairways hit, saves, and other on-course performance indicators provided through an assessment tool is ability to establish performance statements in the goal setting plan directly related to factors being monitored during competitive play.

Through diligent recording of on-course performance data, the golfer can establish target performance statements measuring changes in performance related to data specifically collected during regular rounds of golf. The golfer will be able to set performance targets related to any of the factors monitored during the data gathering process, and can alter the data gathering tool to suit their personal needs. Implementation of a data gather tool permits the benchmarking of this data to establish the challenges for the skills needing to be addressed as a result of the information gained. For example, based on the compiling of data comparing the last five rounds to the previous five rounds shows a noticeable drop in save percentage. This could initiate the setting of challenges for practice sessions directed at short game skills within 30 yards of the green. This could include chipping, varied short pitch shots and bunker shots.

On the other hand, a challenge can also be established identifying a target to be achieved during upcoming play. For example, a golfer wishing to improve their greens hit in regulation could base a challenge on achieving a level of performance in this area over the next five rounds. The ability to establish challenges in a Goal Setting Plan specific to on-course play provides the golfer with the valued experience of consistently attaining goals directly related to competitive on-course play. Its value comes from the confidence growth and the experience of consistently having opportunity of taking on challenges to get the experience of being successful in competitive circumstances. Experiencing ongoing success in competitive situations has a emphatic boost to confidence and on-course performance due to the frequency and consistency of past successes being experienced.

Utilizing the benchmarked information from every practice and round of golf played provides the golfer with a valid and sound knowledge of on-course abilities, and an intimate knowledge of their shot making tendencies and inclinations, leading to enhanced confidence growth, and more effective course and game management. In addition, the knowledge learned about your game will better equip you to maximize improvement during practice, as a result of being more aware of those aspects of your game having the greatest impact on improvement.

Every golfer should include an overall benchmarking assessment in their early season preparation activities. What better way to start off the season than to have an accurate and recent knowledge of your ball-striking abilities and weaknesses?

Establishing Benchmarks for On-Course Assessment

Through implementation of the On-course Assessment tool it is also possible to benchmark playing data to establish performance targets specifically related to common performance indicators. The ability to quickly and accurately determine areas of concern helps ensure the effective use of practice time for correcting or improving in areas showing signs of deterioration. The illustration below shows some performance areas that can be monitored for the establishment of a benchmark. Once a benchmark has been established for a specific performance indicator, the consistent monitoring of past and more recent performances provides immediate and accurate feedback to pinpoint areas requiring attention.

BENCHMARKING - On-Course Assessement
Sample Use Of Data - Remediation

Maintain two Averages of each Assessment Variable listed below; one for the last 5 rounds, and the other for the previous 5 rounds. Variations of what rounds intervals are included to determine Averages influence the sensitivity to performance change and dependability of the information being provided.

Base practice session Challenge identification on the largest negative Variable Differences of the 5 round segments. This permits prompt attention to specific issues or problems focusing remediation in areas having the greatest impact on improved performance.

Sample On-Course Assessment Variables Monitored	Areas of Practice Influenced
Percentage of Fairways Hit	Challenges related primarily to accuracy of the Driver.
Greens in Regulation Percentage	Challenges related to the accuracy of mid-long irons.
Sand Saves Percentage	Challenges related to bunker play.
Save Percentage	Challenges related to short iron and wedge play.
# Putts Per Round	Challenges related to putting improvement.
Penalty Strokes	Challenges related to driving accuracy and experimental practice.

CHAPTER 7

Goal Setting And Planning

"Obstacles are those frightful things you see when you take your eyes off your goal."
Henry Ford

Section 1 - The Essential Element

You probably believe you know where you stand regarding your golf game. You have an idea of what you consider to be the best parts of your play, and believe you are aware of those aspects of your game requiring improvement. Most golfers base assessment of their performance on an impromptu subjective impression of their on-course play, which lacks objectivity and a formalized form of measurement to accurately assess skills or abilities. This is the case with the majority of golfers. Not having a mechanism to quantify capabilities leaves the golfer truly ignorant of what can be achieved and totally lacking the ability to track their development.

Despite golfers guessing at what aspects of play require improvement, they fail to even address their perceived weaknesses. Far too much time is spent on questionable aspects of their game, rather than focusing on activities reaping much greater return for their efforts. Golfers don't have a good grasp of their true abilities because they have never put in the time and effort to accurately measure and record them. Without knowing the full range of your abilities, how can it be expected to monitor and witness improvement.

It is understandable why many golfers experience longstanding plateaus in levels of play that become impenetrable barriers, progressing very little, and remaining developmentally static for years. Haphazard practice methods that are aimless, disorganized and unproductive, and a host of other bad habits cause improvement to suffer and stagnate. It is common practice for thousands of players to spend limited time practicing, emphasizing poorly targeted aspects of their game, and then immediately diving into play on the golf course. This routine becomes entrenched for years, contributing to frustrating levels of improvement.

How can a golfer expect to experience satisfying levels of improvement, or enjoy the success of superior performance, when there is no connection between measuring past and future performance? The lack of a Goal Setting Plan is a major contributing factor to why guesswork, static improvement, bewilderment and frustration confront so many golfers. Golfers can effectively fill this vacuum with a goal-setting plan including goals, objectives, and challenges defining demonstrable abilities and performance standards to be achieved. You have the option of creating a blueprint maximizing the benefits of the time available for improvement, while providing relevance to a course of action suiting your personal circumstances.

A Goal Setting Plan will define achievable, measurable targets based on lifestyle, time restraints, abilities, physical condition, or any other personal circumstances to be considered. It is also important the plan remain current and easily managed. The plan must be used on an ongoing basis to provide the mechanism for determining target attainment and performance improvements, which are necessary for promoting positive reinforcement and confidence building. Diligently monitoring your performance objectives will not only keep you intimately familiar with your skill development, but provide the motivation to re-experience further successes.

Before entering into any plan and identifying goals for improvement, you must have a starting point. The foundation for a developmental plan must include an initial assessment of your abilities to provide a starting point for your endeavour. The continuous monitoring and readjustment of the goals and objectives driving the plan becomes the catalyst for continuous improvement, and the subsequent building of self-confidence so necessary for a healthy mind state. Failing to benchmark your performance or abilities leaves you hopelessly unable to measure or monitor progress.

In many cases, golfers know where they would like to improve, but the game of golf, with all its variables, sometimes leaves them bewildered when determining the aspects of their game to address and how to approach areas of weakness. For a golfer truly seeking accelerated improvement, a plan must be implemented and continuously monitored to insure target attainment and appropriateness of the goals and objectives to be achieved.

This ensures progress is being maintained and that attainment of targets is a regular and consistent process. A plan will provide direction to your endeavours and give meaning and relevance to the steps you make to improve. A plan's focus and personalized significance creates motivation to meet the measurable performance targets you want to achieve. Ultimately, goal setting and planning provides focus on achievable target attainment, where success and positive reinforcement, motivates you to achieve newly readjusted targets.

The value of Goal Setting and Planning is often overlooked because of its association to the drudgery of paperwork. The diligence you devote to your plan and its upkeep will cause a range of benefits well worth the efforts to keep the plan current and relevant. If you ignore the creation of a thoughtful plan, you shortchange yourself of the most powerful means of becoming the golfer you hope to be. Planning is an essential step to creating a framework to build a positive mindset supporting top-level performance and accelerated improvement. A plan will serve as a map to help you reach a desired destination. Without one, you will move aimlessly, never knowing where you are or where you will end up. To leave on a journey with no plan also causes you to waste valuable time, and leaves you lost and bewildered.

This is characteristic of so many avid golfers today. How many players do you know that have participated in the sport for a number of years, showing little or no significant improvement over that time? They aimlessly practice for hours, playing numerous rounds of golf, with their games often remaining relatively static from year to year. They are the travellers without a map, unable to evaluate their progress, wasting money and time on the range and ultimately reinforcing a mindset that locks them into their current level of play, without any significant signs of improvement.

Realizing the benefits of a well thought out plan for improvement and performance enhancement will validate the value of a system, where progress is accurately monitored and well planned, justifiably raising confidence levels. Goal setting and planning provides the golfer with the ability to quantify improvement, insuring skill progress is being maintained, emphasizing areas having the greatest impact on performance and improvement levels.

A goal-setting plan is simple in nature, but the commitment to sustain it requires the effort to consistently set and maintain realistic targets, monitoring progress and modifying the plan as the need arises. The most influential action you can take to realize maximized improvement in your ability to play the game of golf is to diligently administer the plan. You will equip yourself with a powerful tool permitting you to measure improvement in your game, while promoting greater consistency in achieving satisfying levels of performance.

You will be presented with the guidelines and procedures for the creation of your plan. You will learn how to structure your plan, write effective target performance statements, and be introduced to methods for establishing your Goal Setting Plan. You will gain the expertise for building a blueprint guiding and guaranteeing your growth as a competent player. With the ability to write good target performance statements you can easily add new targets as others are achieved. In addition, you will acquire the ability to easily and quickly modify target statements when they are too easily achieved, or if they are too rigorous, modify them so they are attainable. This flexibility in modifying targets strongly boosts the effectiveness of your plan, by providing the additional benefit of immediate and continuous feedback, and eliminating periods of stagnant improvement. Ensure all statements identified in your plan are accurately written to ensure appropriateness and measurability. Having a sound knowledge of how to write performance objectives arms you with a skill that not only simplifies the process of establishing your plan, but also, significantly improves the effectiveness of the targets you are trying to achieve.

Your plan is the foundation upon which all the activities, strategies and methods are based facilitating measured incremental improvements in both the mental and physical ability. Accomplishment of your goals, objectives and challenges are the building blocks to becoming the player you want to be. In addition, consolidation of a plan and the processes needed to maintain it, increases motivation through the successes achieved, and builds confidence when targets are met. Through goal setting and planning, you are able to identify changes in performance, setting numerous possible ways for you to progress skills, while reaping the benefits of the positive reinforcement as targets are attained.

Section 2 - Process Overview

Lets explore an analogous example providing a brief overview of the entire planning process before examining its components and relationships. The example provides an analogous overview of the components of the planning process, giving insights into the interrelationships between them. The analogy will provide a simplified clarity of the activities associated with the goal setting and planning process before formally learning how to formulate your plan.

Your entire plan inclusive of all the goals you set for yourself is synonymous to reaching the summit of a mountain, or the final desired destination. The goals are the major hurdles you must overcome on your ascent to the top. Before the ascent, you will choose a route that will most easily allow you reach the destination of your plan. This entails identifying the intermediary goals that will lead you to the summit. The goals are the targets you must achieve representing the actions and activities you have defined as being required to enable your ascent to the top. Goals guiding your plan identify or represent the overriding areas of focus for the plan. The obstacles you overcome on your path of ascent to reach a goal represent objectives, which define the activities and actions you must successfully achieve to meet each goal. After identifying all your goals, it is necessary to determine the objectives enabling each goal to be met. The river you must cross, the heavy forest you must pass through, and the major cliffs you must climb represent the objectives that must be overcome to meet the goals necessary to reach the summit. Similarly, Challenges have the same supporting relationship to objectives, just as objectives have in supporting goals. Continuing with our example, the objective of crossing the river will have a number of activities that must be completed to meet this objective. Finding a location where the river is shallow and the water is flowing more slowly, or having to build a raft to permit the crossing are examples of challenges requiring attainment before the objective of crossing the river is completed.

During your climb you may be forced to change your route due to unforeseen or underestimated difficulties. Likewise, you may have to change your plans by modifying some of the challenges to reach an objective. Remember that your identified objectives and challenges are not unchangeable. It may be advantageous to use slightly different challenges to meet an objective, or different objectives to reach a goal. As you progress on your journey, you are able to judge when modification to objectives or challenges is required to continue the ascent. Deciding to modify a goal could result in changing an objective or two, which could also entail changing a number of the supporting challenges. Ultimately, to reach the summit, attain all challenges to achieve all your objectives. With all objectives met, successful goal attainment is achieved, taking your plan to exactly where you want to be.

Section 3 - Reaping The Benefits Gained

The Goal Setting and Planning strategy distinguishes itself from other strategies supporting the PCM Model, by providing the greatest impetus for assuring all aspects of what you wish and hope to achieve is attainable, and applicable to your specific situation and circumstances. The benefits and advantages of implementing and administering Goal Setting and Planning are provided below to emphasize the importance and impact this strategy has on the establishment and growth of a healthy mind state and performance.

1. Rewards of Achievement

The structure of your goal-setting plan requires the identification of targets to be achieved. The success and satisfaction gained meeting your goals, objectives and challenges has a confidence building effect regarding your abilities. This creates motivation to attain newly established targets to re-experience the satisfying feelings positive reinforcement brings through target achievement. In most cases, the satisfaction gained achieving targets intrinsically provides motivation to repeat the process, based on the positive effects of the personal satisfaction and reward, resulting from target attainment. In cases where the targets achieved are personally more significant or more personally satisfying due to the additional effort to attain them, always be sure to provide yourself an additional reward for your efforts.

Being true to efforts to identify what is to be accomplished, and being diligent identifying and attaining targets to get there, creates a golf improvement environment intrinsically motivating the golfer to experience the addiction of success and new found confidence. A "Success Breeds Success" environment is created, becoming a regular and routine process, while promoting enthusiasm and inspiration for consistent growth. The reward and satisfaction of achievements becomes measurable and real, but diligence in pursuing your goals is essential for this to occur.

2. Increased Confidence

When you attain an objective or target, you have improved some aspect of your game, which will make you feel more positive about your abilities, consequently leading to new found confidence in meeting new challenges. Ultimately, a Goal Setting Plan creates enhanced occurrences for positive reinforcement, which foster improved self worth leading to elevated self-confidence and improved performance.

3. Increased Motivation

The regular positive reinforcement and affirmative feelings experienced, as a result of meeting your goals and objectives, will renew the positive feelings associated with success. The want for renewal of the experience will manifest itself as increased motivation. Goal attainment may be motivational, but seeing consistent progress is inspirational, which creates additional ambition for your efforts.

4. Springboard For New Goals

When you have reached a goal, just as when you reach the peak of the mountain, you can scan the horizon and see that there are higher peaks to be conquered. The experience of achieving one goal reinforces your conviction that another goal is attainable. You are also awarded with the benefit of knowing what it takes to achieve a goal, causing you to feel better equipped to fulfill your next aspiration.

5. Creates Awareness of Strengths and Weaknesses

The process of formulating and monitoring your goal setting plan will inherently permit you to assess your capabilities on an ongoing basis. The fact that the goal setting process requires you to constantly evaluate your abilities, there is the resulting benefit of becoming aware of what you do well and what requires improvement.

6. Improved Effectiveness of Practice

It is logical to conclude that the largest gains in your ability to score better will be realized by strengthening your weaknesses. These are the areas where the largest performance gains will reap the greatest reward. An enhanced awareness of your weaknesses, resulting from the ongoing evaluation associated with the goal setting process better equips you to identify specific areas of your game requiring remediation. More effective practice sessions will be the product of your efforts. You will be assured the aspects of the game elevating your performance will be the priority for practice sessions.

7. Improved Scoring and Consistency

If the logic pertaining to the improved effectiveness of practice is sound, then a rate of improvement in scoring will be another product of the goal setting plan. Moreover, an increased rate of improvement infers accelerated performance increases. Not only will superior performance levels be achieved but consistency of play will also improve.

8. Reduction of Anxiety and Stress

Experiencing a satisfactory rate of improvement, coupled with performing at a higher level of play will extinguish much of the stress and anxiety caused by being in the dark about your capabilities. Also, the dissatisfaction you feel during periods of time characterized by little or no improvement will end.

9. Reassurance of Addressing Mind State Issues

Knowing your goal setting plan includes activities and tools, specifically addressing mind state issues helps reduce the stress of dealing with shortcomings, long standing issues and phobias.

10. Enhanced Enjoyment of the Sport

All the benefits listed above will provide you with greater enjoyment and satisfaction for the game. The strategies and activities presented in this book will result in the elimination or reduction of experiences creating negativity, resulting in a much more positive attitude toward the game. Your new demeanour will also make the golfing experiences of your fellow competitors more enjoyable. Golf may be a difficult game to master, but this element of difficulty precipitates correspondingly greater feelings of satisfaction for objectives being achieved. Golfers get great satisfaction seeing their games improve.

11. Appreciation for the Principles Maintaining a Healthy Positive Competitive Mindset

Your Goal-Setting Plan is the mechanism establishing the interface to the strategies and actions you will use to build, support and maintain your development as a player. These tools will provide a catalyst for rapidly building self-confidence, eliminating negative influences and motivating the acquisition of knowledge and information driving your plan. You will gain an appreciation for the connections of your plan to the strategies and tools employed to foster the development of a Positive Competitive Mindset.

Section 4 - Considerations and Pitfalls

Before creating a plan, it is essential to take the time to identify the areas of your golf game you hope to address. It is also important to insure the plan addresses each of the primary components of the Positive Competitive Mindset. Having goals pertaining to each of the components of the Positive Competitive Mindset ensures your developing as a complete player where both physical and mental aspects of the game are extended. Once you have determined the key areas to focus on, you must take the time to identify goals directed at working toward your intentions. The goals you identify are the skeleton upon which the remainder of the plan is based. All objectives and challenges are simply a reflection of actions you take to fulfill you goals.

It should be obvious that the goals for your plan are stated in more general terms than the objectives and challenges supporting them. Likewise, the time required to fulfill a goal is much longer than required to attaining a supporting objective. This is also true of the relation of a more general objective to a more specifically stated challenge. Insuring all challenges are directed at achieving objectives, and all objectives are directed at achieving goals, results in a plan that successfully achieves the development you hope to gain through your efforts. In addition, assuring all target statements define an attainable standard of performance that is achievable, paves the way for a methodology promising success for your efforts.

The management of a goal-setting plan is the single most influential action you can take, of all the strategies presented in this publication, having the greatest impact on your growth as a golfer. Your goal-setting plan is what drives all the strategies and activities outlined in this publication. Failure to devote the time to build and maintain a goal-setting plan is to shortchange yourself of a tool having a dramatic affect on your improvement, and your ability to achieve higher levels of proficiency and competence in your golf abilities.

All goals, objectives and challenges identified must support the overall plan and have the characteristics outlined above. The Goals for your plan are all identified before identifying the objectives and challenges supporting them. Following the identification of goals, then the objectives to achieve each goal are determined. Finally, all Challenges supporting each Objective are then identified. This ensures your plan is built from the top down, with an initial focus on the major areas you hope to improve.

1. Ensuring The Plan Fits

It is not necessarily the case that all your goals and objectives specifically relate to golf activities. As a part of your goal-setting plans, it is often appropriate to include non-golf related goals, due to the many benefits they may provide by their inclusion. For example, you may have factors in your life requiring some balancing or concessions to be made before focusing on your planned golf improvement. Work, family and other competing activities may have to be included in your plan to have the greatest benefit to your golf game. Another example could be the inclusion of an objective related to a fitness program designed to support your efforts to improve as a golfer. You could have plans for a full training schedule of aerobics and weight training to supplement your efforts. It would be appropriate in this case to include a goal specific to your training initiative.

Do not create your plan in a vacuum. Ensure you include in your goals all aspects of your life affecting golf. Failure to do so could very quickly undo all the work you put into setting goals and establishing a plan. Include all factors affecting your plan from the beginning. In this way you ensure your plan is inclusive of all considerations having an influence on it. There are things you can do proactively providing the best circumstances for your plan to come to fruition.

It is essential to regularly visit your Goal Setting Plan to monitor your progress and make the necessary changes to the plan as required. With completion time ranging from 2-4 weeks for objectives, and less than 2 weeks for challenges, plus considering the number of performance statements to be managed, it's essential to monitor your plan at least twice per week. Of course this regularity of monitoring may be less, if less time is devoted to improvement. Monitoring your plan twice weekly will maintain a regular focus on your growth as a golfer, but what is more important is providing the time necessary to properly gauge your progress and create or adjust objectives as others are attained.

2. Identify Performance Outcomes Rather Than Personal Goals

Do not get into the trap of identifying outside personal achievements or goals instead of improvements in standards of performance. In other words, don't write or identify performance outcomes that include things like:

- Winning a Particular Tournament
- Breaking a Score
- Winning a Particular Amount of Money
- Bettering or Defeating an Opponent

Ensure the targets you set in your plan are directed at skill development rather empty hopes of winning a certain number of tournaments or breaking a particular score. The achievements you make should reflect attainment of real and actual skills showing measurable improvement.

3. Setting Goals That Lose Relevance

One of the primary mistakes golfers make regarding a goal setting plan is setting goals, objectives and challenges that lose relevance, due to the time being required to attain them. Remember one of the most powerful effects of goal, objective and challenge identification and achievement is the positive reinforcement and confidence building associated with their attainment. In other words, if you set a target that requires a year to achieve, positive reinforcement and the positive effects associated with the target's attainment provides little benefit to the golfer.

4. Inaccurate Appraisal Of Performance

Another pitfall golfers get trapped in following the establishment of performance targets is being too lenient or too charitable in their assessment of the achievement of performance targets. Remember the goals, objectives and challenges you identify in your goal-setting plan are very specific regarding the standard of achievement you have set for yourself. If you are excessively tolerable or have a slightly skewed perception of a performance targets attainment, then you could get yourself into a situation where it is next to impossible to attain the new target you set for yourself. This leads to the eventual dropping of your goal-setting plan, due to feelings of guilt or long periods of time without being successful. Remember you can quickly and easily adjust the rigour of a performance target, so it should be easy to ensure targets are being adjusted to allow for continuous improvement.

5. Not Using The Means & Tools To Monitor Goal Achievement

The maintenance of a goal–setting plan and an on-course information-gathering tool are two essential ways of monitoring improvement and enhancing confidence building. Remember that improvement is impossible to quantitatively monitor if you have no means of measuring against a standard or benchmark. In addition, you have no accurate means of determining the areas of your game requiring improvement, nor the ability to address those aspects of play requiring the greatest attention. Without a means of benchmarking your on-course play there is no reliable way of determining the areas of your game adding strokes to the scorecard. Without reliable tools to ascertain this information, your efforts are merely an unfounded guess to address the problems you hope are benefiting your play. Failure to put a system in place to provide sound information regarding your play or abilities makes it very difficult to monitor and promote improvement.

6. Charting Accomplishments and Implementing Rewards

For the golfers that put in a serious effort to improve and have made the sacrifices that are necessary for maximized improvement, accomplishments will start to be realized with the achievement of the first performance target. With new targets immediately replacing successfully achieved targets, the accomplishment of goals, objectives and challenges is ongoing, offering an unlimited source of positive reinforcement and confidence building. As a component of your improvement plan, you will monitor or track your accomplishments to provide a quick ongoing look at trends developing in your game. It is also highly recommended that a system for rewarding your accomplishments be implemented providing a mechanism to "give yourself a pat on the back" for the effort required to meet your targets.

7. Target Performance for All Aspects of Your Game

An effective Goal Setting Plan is a summary of your intended actions based on a manageable number of goals, each supported by an appropriate set of Objectives, with each Objective being supported by a more specific stated set of Challenges. This means a Challenge defines a more specific action than an Objective, and that an Objective defines a more specific action than a Goal. It should also be apparent that the time to achieve a Challenge will be shorter than that required to meet an Objective. Similarly, the time required to fulfill an Objective will likewise be shorter relative to the attainment of a Goal. Based on this structural relationship, the majority of performance targets identified will be at the Challenge level.

All the Challenges identified in your plan are the specific target performance statements that either guide practice sessions or identify performance targets for on-course performance. In the first case of guiding practice, the target performance statements for day to day practice sessions could be expressed as the Challenges that can be grouped into basic divisions falling under Objectives related to different shot types like driving, fairway woods, long irons, mid irons, pitching, chipping, lag putts, makeable putts, and specialty shots. In this case, the golfer simply identifies the appropriate Objectives related to driving or mid-irons, then defines the Challenges to meet the Objectives identified. This means target performance statements guiding and quantifying all aspects of practice are seamlessly integrated into Goal Setting.

As stated earlier, Challenges also identify performance targets for on-course performance. This other set of Challenge level performance targets statements identified for on-course performance are established following the benchmarking of on-course performance data and deriving Challenge performance target statements for Objectives directed at variables like greens in regulation, driving, fairways hit, saves, sand saves, putting and other benchmarked aspects of on-course performance. In Summary, all the Challenges identified in your ongoing plan collectively are all the specific improvement targets related to practice and on-course performance identified to achieve the overriding Objectives and Goals of your plan.

The writing of performance target statements with standards defined with two variables will be introduced later in the book to provide flexibility adjusting the rigour or difficulty of target performance statements. The ability to quickly redefine performance standards in 2 variables readily permits the quick modification of practice session's targets to maximize practice time effectiveness.

Also introduced in <u>The Golfer Mindset</u> are the factors and methods for defining target performance statements in the area of mind state development. You will be able to establish specific performance targets at the Challenge level representing definite improvements in mental skills through the elimination of negative influences and the building of confidence.

8. Ensuring Links Between Goal Setting & Commitments

Golfers often make the mistake of setting their plan for what they hope to achieve, but fail to consider the limited time and resources available, or previous commitments seriously limiting the ability to achieve the goals set. A plan created in this manner is doomed to failure simply because of the inability to meet set goals and objectives because of circumstances not being considered when the plan was originated. Whatever the playing level or aspirations of the golfer, the plan must be reflective of realistic expectations that can be accomplished within the opportunities provided. This means that no matter the competency a golfer has for the game, or the limitations they may have restricting exposure to practice and play, a well-developed plan created using sound learning principles will facilitate the improvement desired.

GOAL SETTING & PLANNING - Cautions and Pitfalls

Let us examine some of the planning process pitfalls and cautions to avoid. The following is a list of commonly overlooked guidelines or errors when a plan is being formulated or created.

- Keep your performance statements achievable and realistic.
- Do not set lofty performance statements taking long periods of time to achieve. This results in becoming apathetic and depressed over the lack of success in meeting the targets you have set for yourself.

- Do not create performance statements so easy to achieve that you are not being challenged and lose the benefit of the satisfaction for meeting your targets. The satisfaction you get from achieving targets is the mechanism building self-confidence. Easily achieved objectives can hamper your rate of improvement.
- It is recommended that you work with as many performance statements as you feel are effectively guiding your improvement program. As long as you feel confident with keeping a plan updated and current, then the number of actions or performances you are monitoring is appropriate.
- Consistently monitor your plan's currency and effectiveness to oversee progress and ensure success of your plan. The regular monitoring of progress will instill the process in a short period of time, resulting in the process becoming habitual, losing its laborious nature.

Section 5 - Basic Principles and Concepts

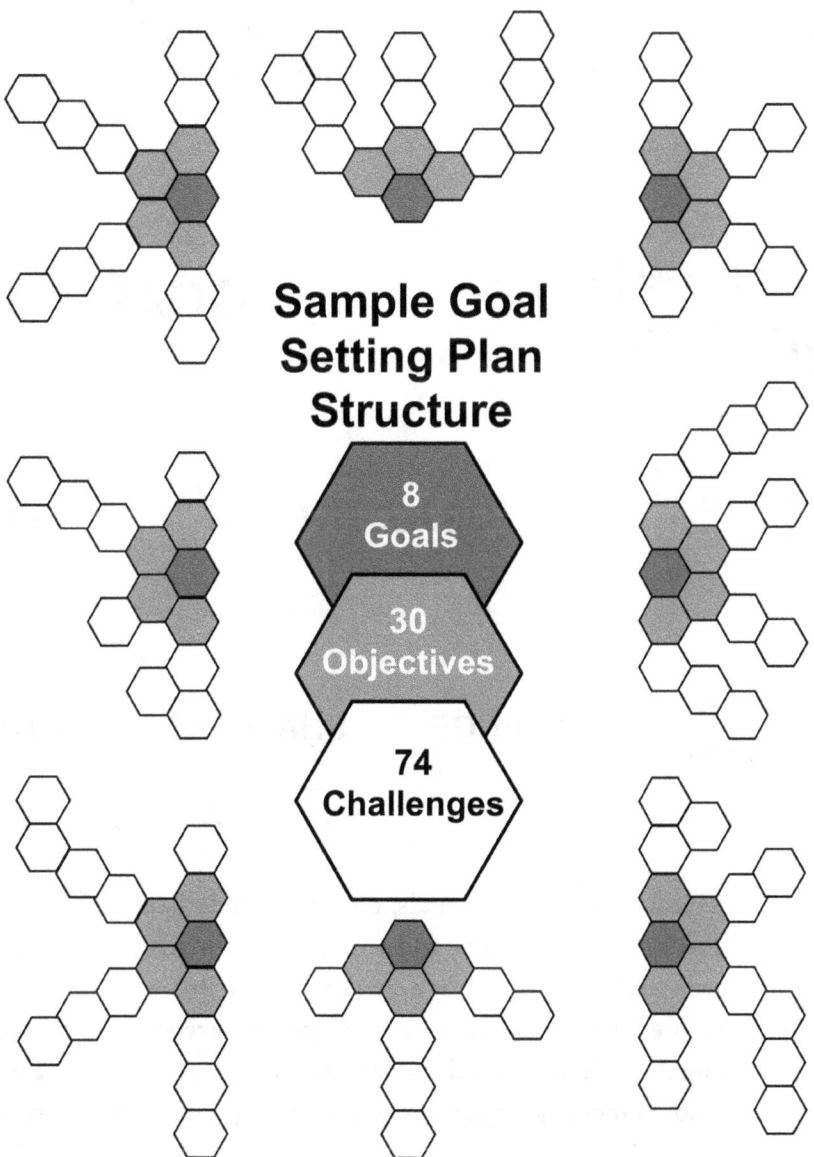

Overview of Plan

The illustration above shows a goal setting plan directing all goals towards the intended accomplishments for a season, with the alignment of all challenges supporting the objectives to attain these goals, providing an overview of a typical plan's structure. In this example, 74 challenges have been identified to meet the 30 objectives, which must be completed to achieve 8 overriding goals. The principles of administering the plan are simple, but the effects are amazing. Just the sense of having some control over where you would like to take your golf game builds motivation, revitalizing an eagerness to excel, immediately creating a performance enhancing playing environment or demeanour. Empowering the golfer with the tools needed to guide progress along a path of skill development, inclusive of fostering supportive strategies for building a Positive Competitive Mindset, opens the door to golfer's individually adopting a more comprehensive approach to golfer growth.

Let's explore the terms and definitions associated with Goal Setting to become familiar with interrelationships existing between aspects of the process, insuring the golfer can effectively create the target performance statements becoming the goals, objectives and challenges of their plan.

Target Performance Statements

An important aspect of Goal Setting is that goals, objectives and challenges are all written target performance statements identifying measurable and achievable actions defining a desired outcome. All target statements, whether a goal, an objective, or a challenge are written in a similar manner, and have the same component structure. I have reserved the term "target" to be representative of any performance to be achieved. This allows the term to be used synonymously with goal, objective or challenge. This proves advantageous in more quickly grasping the goal setting process and interrelationship of the terminology adopted.

If you can write an excellent objective, then you can write an excellent goal or challenge. The difference between these three types of target performance statements is the level of specificity of each. The specificity of a defined action increases or is more detailed as we move from Goals to Objectives, then to Challenges.

Target Performance Statement Essentials

All target performance statements (Goals, Objectives, and Challenges) must include these 3 basic components to adequately and accurately define an outcome to be achieved. The statements must include an action, conditions governing the action, and a criterion or standard defining what must be achieved.

Target Performance Statements

3 Essential Elements

	Condition	Action Or Performance	Standard or Criterion
Goals	For the 2016-17 season,	implement an aerobics conditioning program	by planning and participating in 2 – 90 minute conditioning sessions per week.
	By the end of season	improve present save percentage	from present level of 39% to 50%
	During the season	participate in planned practice sessions	a minimum of once per week.
Objectives	Between Aug 1 and end of season	reduce the occurrences of 3-putt greens	from the present level of 28% to 20%.
	Between season start and June 1	Increase GIR percentage	from the present level of 41% to 50%.
	Between June 1 and Sept 30	Improve driver accuracy	from the present level of 32% to 40%.
	Prior to season start	develop and practice a shot execution routine	to be used for all shots during competitive play.
	For the entire season	participate in planned practice sessions	at least 5 times per monthly period
Challenges	Given 10 shots and the time desired	execute 8 full L Wedge shots	finishing within 15 feet of hole.
	Given the required number of sets of 12 - 4ft putts equally spaced around a hole on a slope	sink 10 of 12 putts	twice consecutively.
	Provided 40 balls distributed randomly on the fringe of the green and using an 8-iron	chip 30 of the balls	to within 4 feet of the hole.
	Over the next 5 competitive rounds	Improve FIR percentage	from present 31% to 50%.

Attaining challenges leads to the meeting of objectives, with objective attainment leading to goal achievement. In short, once you can write a sound target performance statement defining an attainable outcome with a measurable performance level, while describing the conditions under which the outcome must be achieved, you are able to write effective goals, objectives, or challenges. Following are some guidelines for writing target performance statements. Let us more closely explore some of the characteristics and requirements that must be inherent in all target performance statements. We will first examine what is common, and later we will explore the structure of a plan by more closely examining the differences and relationships of goals, objectives, and challenges.

Writing Quality Target Performance Statements

All target performance statements, whether identified as a Goal, Objective or Challenge should meet the following conditions, or have the following characteristics. Care should be taken to ensure all target performance statements making up a Goal-Setting Plan meet the following criteria.

Action Oriented

All target performance statements have a component specifically devoted to identifying a particular action or demonstrable skill that must be executed or performed. Having well defined and accurately described actions that are clearly identifiable is essential for all target performance statements. The statements you create must clearly indicate the action to be performed to insure the appropriate skills are displayed to provide the ability to clearly determine target achievement or attainment.

Measurable Performance

As stated earlier, all action performance statements include an action or description of a performance, the standard or criteria to determine attainment and any conditions under which the action or performance will be executed. The standard or criteria you attach to a performance statement or action provides the measure for determining when the target action performance has been attained. Ensure the target performance statements you write have a criteria or level of competency that is easily identifiable to facilitate easy determination of achievement. It is merely the comparison of a previous measured performance level to a newly set performance level that provides an indication of the rigour or ease with which a performance target statement is achieved, and defines the minimum standard of performance to achieve the next target. All target performance statements must have this measurability characteristic, not only to determine "when" an objective or challenge has been met, but also to acknowledge and record the level of achievement for the establishment of the next performance level or competency to be set.

Inclusions of Conditions

All target performance statements also include the conditions under which the action or performance will be executed. Any aspect of the action to be displayed should be stipulate in a manner to ensure the skill being assessed is evaluated in an objective manner. For example, to improve iron accuracy during windy conditions, it would be mandatory for the skill to be demonstrated under the same windy conditions. It would be impossible to determine if you are making progress playing in windy conditions unless you measure your performance in the same specific conditions. To accomplish this, you could have challenges defining practice sessions indicating strong cross wind conditions existing to complete a particular target performance statement. The condition of a performance statement defines the circumstances under which the action must be performed. In those cases, where the conditions are not stated in an target performance statement it is normal convention for this to mean, "attainable at any time under normal conditions".

Conditions for a target statement could also refer to variables like time, frequency, percentages or accuracy as a control or trigger to advance to a higher competency level. For example, Within 15 minutes successfully execute 6 tee shots in a row, using the driver to within 10 lateral yards of a designated target. The condition of 15 minutes could be used to provide a degree of pressure when completing a challenge during a practice. The condition under which a target statement must be achieved provides the golfer with an easy means of varying the rigour of actions to be demonstrated, providing a great deal of flexibility in changing the instructional intent of the target being set. By changing conditions it is easy to emphasize accuracy, consistency, or difficulty levels.

Achievable

Create target performance statements that provide an immediate feeling of being able to meet the standard defined. Create statements you are confident of being able to meet. Whatever targets you set for yourself, insure each is achievable to provide positive reinforcement and a sense of accomplishment. Target performance statements should be challenging enough get your engagement, but not so easily achieved they lose their purpose.

When attempting to meet an objective, you may realize the standard of performance to be achieved in a two-week period is too aggressive, causing excessive time needed to meet the outcome. It would be appropriate to reduce the standard of performance to shorten the time for attainment. This strategy provides greater opportunity for experiencing success and the resulting confidence gains, while still maintaining improvement. Likewise, a challenge statement that is going to be too easily achieved should result in a statement change having more rigour. Be sure that performance target statements provide enough effort to provide the satisfaction of achievement that leads to confidence building. As the manager of your plan, be aware of keeping targets achievable, but at the same time, generate enough satisfaction to build self-assurance in your new abilities. Be constantly aware of the performance actions you are attempting to achieve and your ability to quickly alter their rigour. This greatly improves flexibility for maintaining continuous positive improvement with all practice challenges, consequently improving the efficiency and effectiveness of practice time.

Relevant

Your target statements must be relevant to the plan you have established, with every Challenge working toward its parent Objective, and every Objective working towards its parent Goal. This insures all action or target performance statements are working to fulfill your goal-setting plan. Taking care to accurately identify the goals you hope to attain, the objectives supporting those goals, and the challenge statements defining them, creates the blueprint for exactly where you wanted to take your game.

Time-Framed

A target performance statement must indicate the amount of time for it to be accomplished. After all, it would be pointless to have a level of performance to be attained without a time limit. The attainment of a level of performance is certainly going to be dependent on the time available to accomplish it. The time it takes to achieve a target can be easily adjusted by the standard of performance you have defined. You will have to give yourself more time for objectives having more rigour, or less time for statements that are easier to attain.

Do not create action performance statements requiring unreasonable amounts of time and effort to achieve. Remember to set the rigour for achievement at a level that allows you to attain the target in a reasonable time. Goals generally take longer to achieve than objectives, and likewise, objectives generally take longer to achieve than challenges. This is inherent in the way challenges support objectives and how objectives support goals.

Stated Positively

All action performance statements must be stated in a manner that has a positive connotation. For example you should define a standard to be successful 70% of the time rather than unsuccessful 30% of the time. There is no need to have negativity in a statement, when the statement can be phrased positively.

Awareness of Specificity

Ensure all target statements have the appropriate level of specificity. This means ensuring all target statements detail three important components; the action you will perform, the conditions under which it is carried out, and the specific criteria or standard of performance for determining when it has been achieved. Depending on the target statement being written, there is a degree of flexibility regarding variations of these components to easily identify exactly what you want demonstrated and achieved. Specificity also refers to having the appropriate structural relationship of challenges supporting objectives, and objectives supporting goals. Challenges will be more specific target statements than objectives, and objectives will be narrower in scope than goals.

Differentiating Goals, Objectives And Challenges

Guidelines for Establishing The Goals of Your Plan

A Goal is a general long-range target performance statement indicating what you would like to achieve over a time ranging from 2 months, to a full season. Collectively, all your goals together identify where you want to be at the end of the playing season. The sum of the goals you identify for a season defines what you feel you can accomplish, considering your circumstances, and all factors having an influence on the plan.

Goals identify the general categories of broader actions you are able to implement and achieve to see your plan meet its purpose. Goals could include, weight training, aerobic training, flexibility sessions, knowledge acquisition sessions, and other areas golfers view as being important to their plan. It is important to include all factors having an influence on your aspirations. A goal could also be a target performance statement defining a level of achievement for different aspects of your game. Goals could include performance target statements relating to long irons, short irons, putting, sand play or any other general facet of your game.

A goal could be a target performance statement specific to your scrambling ability, with performance statements identifying saves and sand saves targets set at the objective level, with skill development specific performance statements creating the challenges driving your practice sessions. In another example, a goal could be set regarding tee shot accuracy, with the objectives supporting this goal related to performance statements regarding "fairways in regulation" (FIR), and greens hit in regulation on par threes. Supporting these objectives would be the challenges identifying specific accuracy related target performance statements driving portions of a practice session.

The number of goals included in a plan is dependent on your circumstances and what you're hoping to accomplish. Considering the time to reach goals, if you live in a climate with a shorter playing season, keep goals to a 2-month completion period. This will enhance positive reinforcement for confidence growth and provide greater flexibility compiling your plan,

Manage only 4 to 8 active goals at any single time during a season. The number of goals taken on is dependent on familiarity with the process, time availability, depth of focus, and motivation. If this is a completely new process to you, then dealing with 3 – 5 goals at any single time may be appropriate, but for a player with the ability to dedicate more time, or having a strong conviction to improve, 10 goals could be managed. Be cautioned, too many goals will make your plan cumbersome to manage causing it to lose focus. This can eventually lead to abandonment of a sound plan guaranteeing development in areas you took the time to assemble and compile. Having a realistic plan appropriate to your time availability, motivational drive, and commitment level will strongly support the plan's success and effectiveness.

A great way to implement this strategy is to take from 1-3 three goals only, and be diligent ensuring monitoring of skill attainment and progress. As you become more acquainted and gain proficiencies streamlining the process, new goals can be added with a comfort level for their management. Take on what you are comfortable handling to ensure the process of goal attainment is engaged and there is monitoring of improvement. This approach will help ensure implementation of this strategy and provide time and practice in becoming more efficient working with the performance statements guiding the progression of all skills, while reaping the benefits of the confidence earned for your efforts.

Guidelines For Identifying Objectives

An objective is a more specific medium-level target performance statement, supporting a goal that describes an action to be performed at a measured level or standard of performance under specified conditions. Objectives are usually at a level identifying general aspects of your game you would like to develop or improve. This could include, short game play, putting, long irons, or statements related to driving the ball off the tee. Objectives could also be stated with targeted improvement based on achievements related to on-course play like saves, greens in regulation, fairways hit and other similar statistics related to on-course performance.

When you achieve an objective, you are a step closer to achieving its associated goal. When all the objectives identified under a specific goal are successfully achieved, then the respective goal has been accomplished. All objectives must be associated with a goal, to ensure all objectives support your plan for improvement.

Objectives define accomplishments ranging from 2-6 weeks to complete. If your golf season is only 6-7 months in length, it may be advantageous to keep the time range to complete an objective to 2-3 weeks. This adjustment is made to enhance the positive effects of increased frequency of positive reinforcement in a shortened season.

There are usually from 1 - 5 objectives supporting each goal. Having an excess number of objectives will cause a loss of focus for what is to be accomplished, plus causes the plan to be more difficult to manage. In addition, too many objectives will result in the compounded problem of having to deal with an unmanageable number of challenges.

Guidelines For Identifying Challenges Supporting Objectives

A challenge is a more specific target performance statement supporting an objective that describes an action to be performed, at an identified level of performance, under specified conditions. All challenges must be directed at an objective, to ensure they support your plan for improvement. When a challenge is achieved, you are a step closer to attaining its associated objective. When all the challenges identified under a specific objective are successfully achieved, then the respective objective has been accomplished.

Challenges are short termed target statements defining accomplishments taking less than 2 weeks to complete. Keeping the time to achieve a challenge less than two weeks provides many opportunities for experiencing success and positive reinforcement, leading to enhanced motivation and improved self-confidence. This time allocation is appropriate considering all target performance statements at the challenge level, either define actions to be performed during a practice session, or are short termed performance targets for on-course play. Challenges directing practice sessions will often require just a single practice period to complete, making it necessary to identify new targets statements for the next practice session. As eluded to above, challenges can also be target performance statements related to statistical information gathered through On-course Assessment. The statements could relate to targets associated with greens-in-regulation, fairways hit, saves, sand saves and other measured statistics.

Challenges identify very specific skills you are working to improve. This could include, shaping of iron shots, distance consistency of short irons, accuracy of long irons, sand shots, chipping, or statements related to actions prompting pressure situations for development of mind state skills.

A plan usually becomes unmanageable losing its focus primarily as the result of identifying too many Goals, or secondarily, because of establishing too many Objectives to meet the Goals identified, but any number of Challenges can be identified to meet an Objective. Since Challenge achievement is short termed, it is inappropriate to limit the number of Challenges required to meet an Objective.

The identification of up to eight Goals collectively supported by 30-40 Objectives, and driven by in excess of a hundred Challenges, provides a snapshot of a typical plan, inclusive of all target performance statements set for a season. As indicated earlier, goals can be introduce gradually to get a feel for the strategy and its benefits. With the introduction of each new goal, the golfer will appreciate and enjoy achievements being made, while reaping the benefit of being familiar and comfortable with a process that can be expanded to a full plan.

Section 6 - Supports and Linkages

Goal Setting & The Positive Competitive Mindset

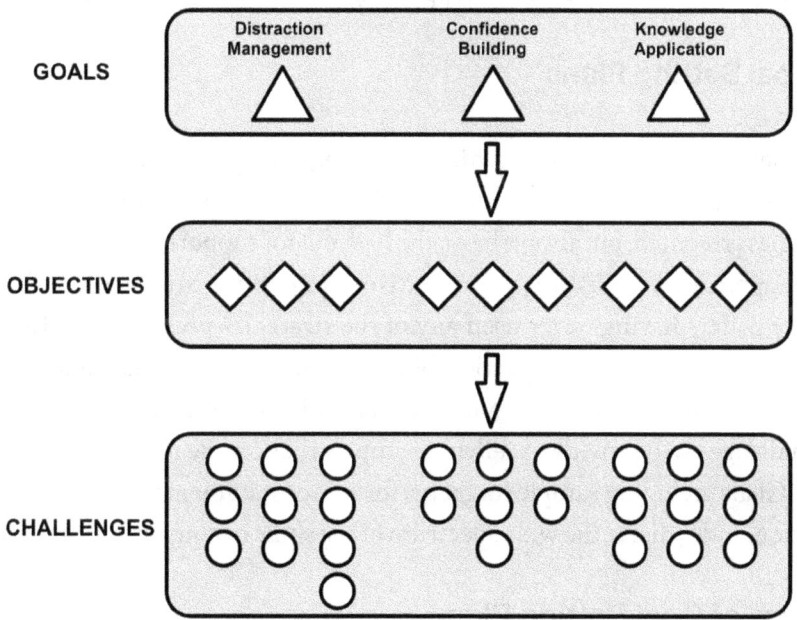

Goals Supportive of the Positive Competitive Mindset Model Ensure Complete Golfer Growth Inclusive of Mindset Skill Development

The Goal Setting Plan is based on definitions, principles, and relationships providing organizational structure and a definition of purpose, while serving as a frame of reference for organizing and simplifying concepts. The Goal Setting Plan depicted above shows how the plan's overall implementation is immediately linked to the establishment of a Positive Competitive Mindset.

Components of the plan and the initiative to foster a Positive Competitive Mindset are merged, by fine-tuning the Goals to also be supportive of the foundational premises of the Positive Competitive Mindset Model. All improvement then supports Elimination of Negative Influences, Building Positive Influences and ensuring efficiency of Knowledge Application; all foundational premises of the Model are supported.

Integration of the three components of the Positive Competitive Mindset into the Goal-Setting Plan is designed to ensure linkages and supports are created promoting complete golfer growth through mind state development, plus assimilate and reinforce the solidifying cumulative effects of the mind state development strategies presented for integration.

The golfer is exposed to a range of activities to personally address mind state issues and concerns through the implementation of strategies helping address distractions, building experientially based confidence, and possessing the best information available when making improvement decisions. Golfers will recognize they can address their personal demons, plus feel real and actual, heightened levels of confidence. What is being introduced is not magic, but sound and valid principles coordinated in a focused manner to maintain an ongoing, stable, and comfortable playing environment, specifically directed at providing the conditions for enhanced performance and accelerated improvement.

For example, the section regarding Practice describes in detail how practice session targets are an integral part of the Goal Setting Plan. For all practice sessions, objectives describing the targets of improvement for shot making are the basis for all the challenges specifically outlining the activities and strategies to be carried out for a practice session. The strategies presented for the challenges identified for practice sessions have been specifically structured to minimize the time required to maintain them, while incorporating a methodology directly supporting the Positive Competitive Mindset Model.

Diversity of Goal Setting Plans

The initial Goal-Setting Plans of golfers will vary widely in rigour and complexity, based on past improvement practices, personal time restraints, and time availability. You may be comfortable adopting many of the strategies presented, but always be on the look out for supporting strategies, or enhancements to customize your approach establishing your Positive Competitive Mindset.

For the sake of golfers having never used any of the strategies presented for the establishment of a Positive Competitive Mindset, a fair portion of a Goal Setting Plan has been compiled to provide suggestions to strategically enhance the outcomes of an initial or startup plan. The sample goals, objectives and challenges will provide excellent examples that can be modified to suit your own plan. There are sample Goals including sample target performance statements, to illustrate different aspects of statement creation, and indicate the wide spectrum of the skills or competencies that can be measured.

Sample Portions of Goal Setting Plans

Reference to various portions of goal-setting plans illustrates different aspects of the planning process, with numerous sample Goals, Objectives and Challenges providing examples of the flexibility and relative simplicity in constructing Target Performance Statements. Modifying the target performance statements and the final structure of the plan as desired to suit your individual needs.

The sample below is specifically directed at the implementation of the Pre-Shot Assessment Routine and the Shot Execution Routine as actions or tactics specifically supporting the Elimination of Negative Influences premise of the Positive Competitive Mindset Model. This is an excellent example of implementing a Positive Competitive Mindset Model driven Goal to specifically put into place actions supporting mind state skill development activities. There is also another supportive objective in the example directed at exploring aspects of Game and Course Management for implementation into routine.

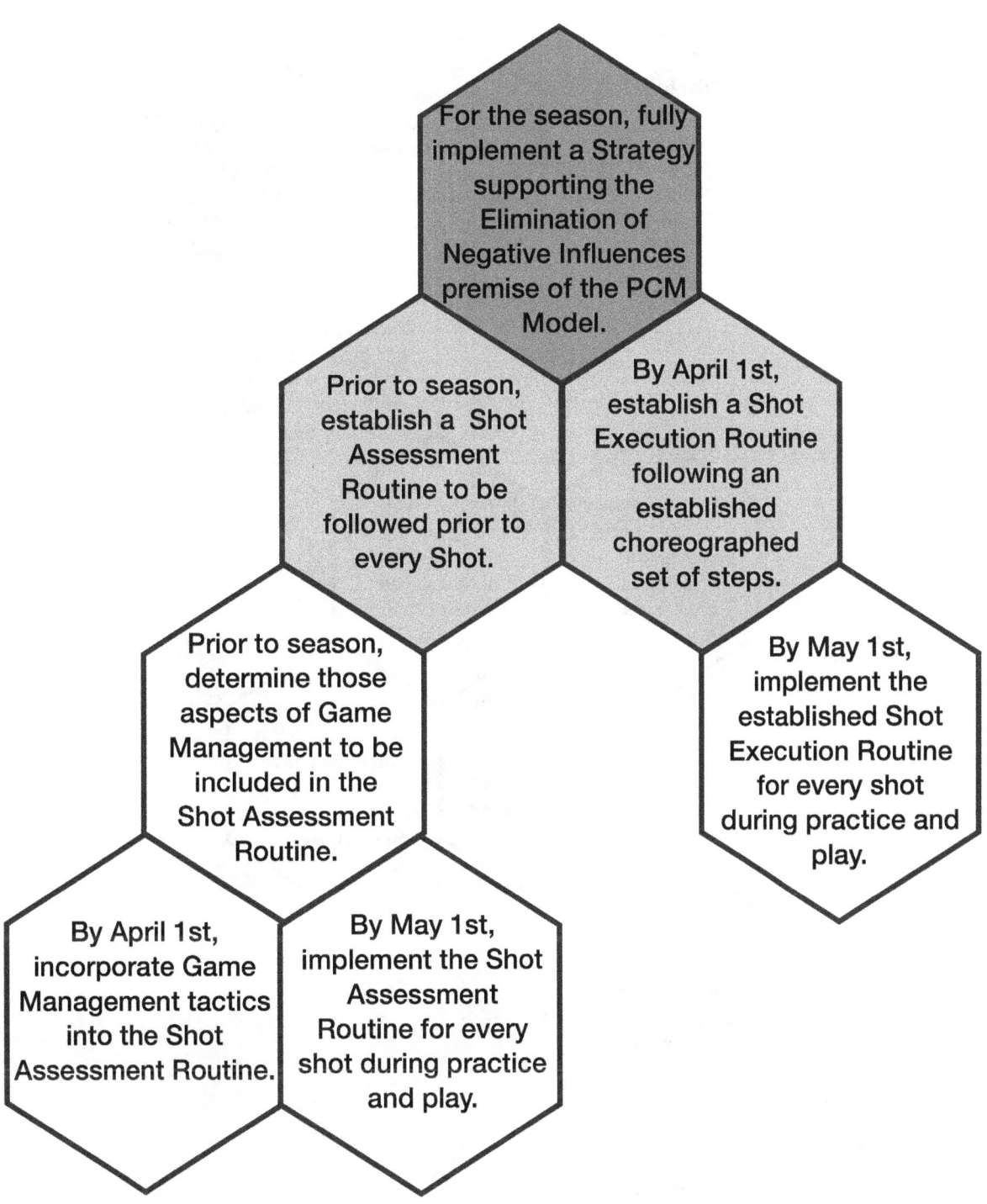

The following set of target performance statements are specifically directed at putting into place the actions necessary to action the Benchmarking of on-course performance and individual club shot execution data required before establishment of a Goal Setting Plan and implementing steps for the management of Challenges specifically identified to guide practice session activities.

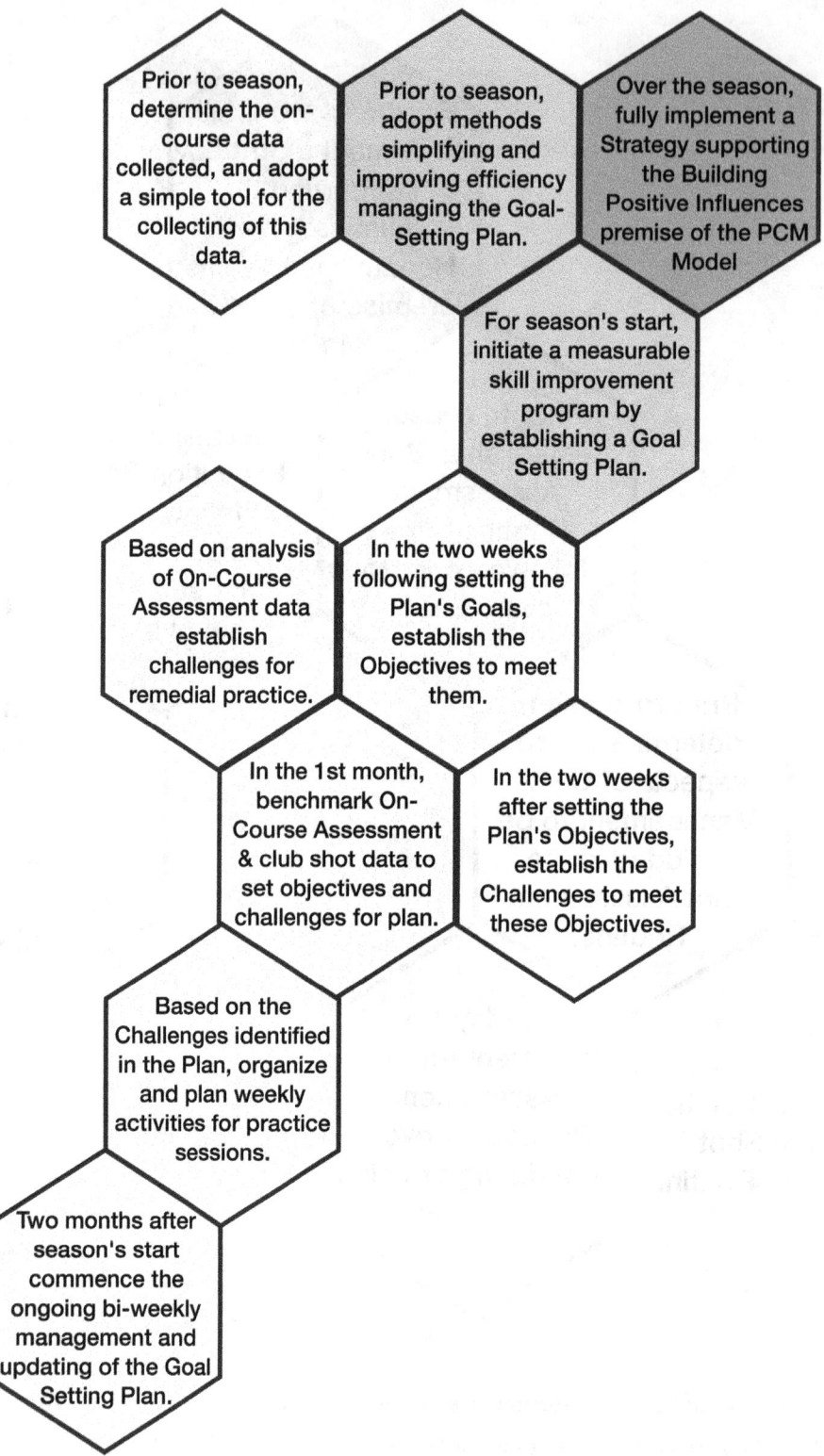

Having a clear understanding of the components of target performance statements, a grounding in the relationship between them, and ensuring they meet certain criteria, provides the golfer with the ability to map their own measured improvement and skill progression customized to their personal needs.

Superimposing the premises of the Positive Competitive Mindset over the sound basic principles of a goal setting plan in no way restricts the areas of improvement a golfer wishes to emphasize. Introduction of the Model simply adds strategies or methods of implementation specifically directed at stabilizing mind state through positive reinforcement, an intimate knowledge of skills, and access to tools and tactics helping to control personal demons affecting performance. Application of the Positive Competitive Mindset Model to Goal Setting simply alters the approach taken to greatly enhance mind state development by including strategies like On-Course Assessment, Routine, Proximity Acceptance, Stress and Anxiety, and Game and Course Management, which as integrated establishes and progressively instills a playing environment geared to improve consistency and enhance performance.

In the next example, a Goal pertaining to an improvement in accuracy of fully executed shots, and includes an Objective directed at the improving the accuracy of shots taken with the driver.

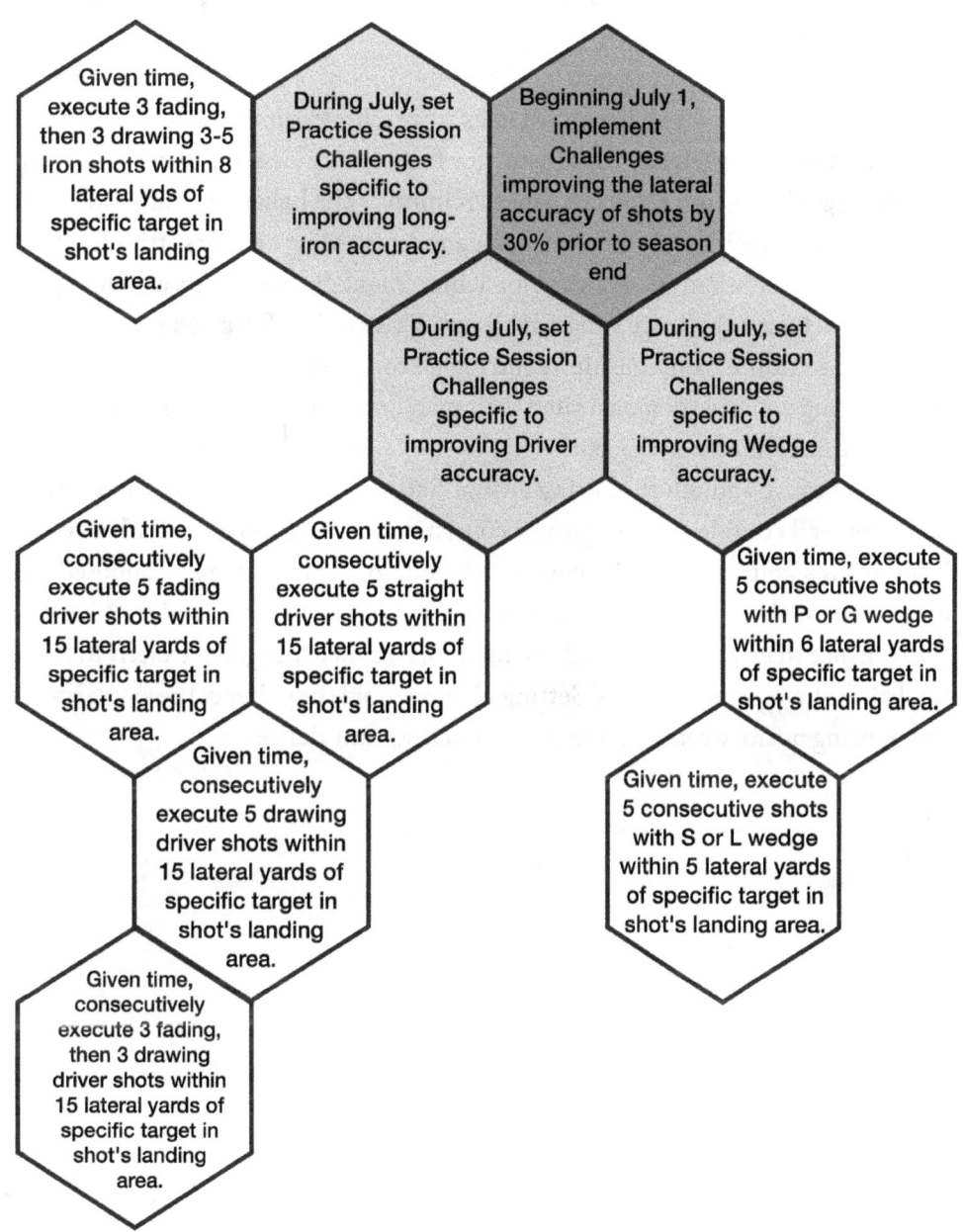

All Challenges supporting this Objective directly support actions improving not only the accuracy of shots taken, but note that the "condition" attached to each statement indicates, "Providing the Time Needed". This condition has the added intent of not only improving driver accuracy, but to potentially increase the pressure associated with the activity, because its completion may require a number of attempts to complete. This naturally increases the pressure to achieve the criterion set. These types of challenges provide a quantitative way of measuring changes in variables to reflect mind state development. For example, in this case, if a golfer were to progress from 5 to 10 consecutive driver shots to within 10 yards of each shot's originally intended target line", there is evidence of real measure improvement in accuracy, but the times the golfer is in the position to hit the final drive to complete the activity, or miss and have to repeat it, creates the same stress and anxiety felt when needing to hit a good drive on the final hole to win the Club Championship. This is just a simple way of indicating growth in the area of mind state control of stress and anxiety by illustrating measured improvements in skills under increasing pressure.

Ultimately the greatest benefit or reward for the establishment of a Goal-Setting Plan is the ongoing and consistent experience of overcoming obstacles to reach a desired outcome. The regularity of consistently achieving target performances instills or fosters confidence any challenge is achievable. Constantly meeting goals, objective and challenges reinforces the belief; any future obstacles can and will be met. This creates a significantly different demeanour regarding a golfer's attitude toward reaching desired outcomes. The conditioning of reward for achievement greatly boosts a golfer's prospects and expectations a random future challenge will be achieved. This random future challenge could be playing the final round of the Club Championship requiring a score you have achieved many times before. Confidence in knowing you have demonstrated the capability to achieve numerous targeted outcomes greatly increases the likelihood it will occur.

There is a direct cause and effect of using a Goal-Setting Plan, which translates into guaranteed improvement, improved confidence, and greater consistency of performance. With a system virtually ensuring the progress a golfer hopes to achieve, it is mandatory this strategy be adopted to ensure the improvement efforts of the golfer are maximized. All strategies to be introduced have measurable aspects of performance that can be identified and monitored to take the golfer exactly to the level of play they aspire to. Failure to implement a Goal Setting Plan will void the golfer of the single most important means of experiencing positive reinforcement and building confidence.

CHAPTER 8

Practice

"Difficulties mastered are opportunities won."
Winston Churchill

Section 1 - The Building Blocks of Practice

Practice is a supportive strategy of the Positive Competitive Mindset Model and can be viewed as merely an extension of the Goal Setting and Planning strategy. Practice could have been included with Goal Setting and Planning, but the differences and nature of the topics presented, plus the need for greater detail of methodology regarding practice warranted its own status as a strategy supporting golfer mind state development.

In the previous chapter, the basics necessary for the establishment of a development plan identifying the goals, objectives and challenges guiding improvement were closely examined. The essentials of target statement development were discussed to insure the plan is driven by measurable criteria, providing the ability to monitor and assess the measurable progression of skills. The defining of goals, objectives, and challenges, plus the relationship of one to the other was also explained. In this chapter, a much closer examination of the challenges specific to practice in the goal-setting plan will be examined. The setting of challenges in the planning stages becomes the driving force guiding practices and performance targets set for competitive play. Practice methodologies introduced in this chapter also provide opportunities to experience measured improvements in areas of mind state development. This more detailed look at the target statements driving practice is necessary to share ways of attaining greater flexibility adjusting the rigour of targets at the practice level, and introduce ideas providing easy management of the range of challenges defining practice activities. In addition, the examination of practice as a separate strategy better accommodates topics related to how it should be approached and provides insight for the inclusion of mind state development into practice.

Practice: An Extension of Goal-Setting

As indicated in the Goal Setting and Planning strategy, Challenges are the third or most basic level identified in your goal setting plan and represents the targets set to be achieved during practice time. Your practice time is extremely valuable, due to the positive reinforcement derived from the achievement of all challenges associated with practice. With Practice viewed as an extension of the goal-setting plan, getting the greatest benefit from practice time requires the regular preparation of a practice session plan outlining the activities and challenges to be completed. Each challenge is merely an identified incremental step describing the skill that must be demonstrated before moving to an ensuing or new challenge identified for attainment. Each challenge achieved represents a small incremental step of improvement. The positive reinforcement and satisfaction experienced for every accomplishment makes practice a primary source of confidence building and motivation.

It is important to note that other than challenge attainment during practice and those set for on-course performance, the golfer has no source of regular positive reinforcement, which is essential to confidence building. Unless a golfer implements other strategies like Proximity Acceptance or Benchmarking, there is no way of promoting growth in confidence. If a golfer is limited to recognizing skill improvement based on a few intermittent revelations of possible improvement, then positive reinforcement will be almost nonexistent. The golfer's positive reinforcement experiences must be ongoing and continuous, or they are unable to discern when progress has occurred, totally missing any opportunity to build confidence. Analogously, it is much the same as not really noticing you have lost weight, but a friend not seen for a time would notice it immediately. The golfer is blind of their own progress in much the same manner, unless there is continuous monitoring of achievable targets. As a result, positive reinforcement is totally lost, seriously affecting confidence.

Section 2 - The Cost of Inaction

The compilation and regular updating of challenges identified in the goal-setting plan is the guiding material for all practice sessions. As previously indicated, it is usually this aspect of plan management that causes abandoning of goal setting by most golfers, as a result of the work associated with maintaining the plan. Failure to recognize the detrimental affect this has on golfer growth and development cannot be overstated. The achievement of challenges guiding practice is the primary source of confidence acquisition for the golfer, therefore eliminating the time and effort required to administer practice session planning is one of the gravest errors a golfer can make affecting growth and development. It is ironic that despite the value of maintaining an organized and goal-centered approach to practice, golfers seem to casually dismiss its importance to improvement and performance enhancement. The failure of most golfers to maintain a goal-centered approach to skill development is unquestionably a leading cause of lackluster improvement and dissatisfaction with performance.

One of the major reasons why practice time is at a premium is because, in most cases, the average golfer will elect to play a round of golf, as opposed to partake in a practice session. Generally, when golfers have time available for the game, they elect to play, rather than practice. Practice is not a priority. They could believe playing is the best form of practice. If a golfer truly wants maximized improvement, then a greater proportion of time dedicated to the game must be devoted to practice. The developmental benefit acquired from the time devoted to practice far exceeds that gained from an equal amount of time playing a round of golf. Simply devoting some time to practice provides the first opportunity to cause pause identifying skills and provide permanence to the skills acquired.

Despite this, the majority of golfers prefer an additional round of play, rather than making time available for a practice session. Through the introduction of mind state development activities into practice, adding greater realism and challenge, a greater portion of golfers may begin to participate in regular practice sessions to explore mindset development. Comparatively, it is commonly accepted in other sports that practice is a welcomed and expected activity. If practice sessions were eliminated from football, basketball, hockey, and soccer, most participants would feel an essential element of playing the sport had been lost. The same would be true for individual type sports like skiing, swimming, tennis, gymnastics and track and field. Practice is a time when the golfer is free to hone a skill and be focused on areas of improvement having the most positive affect on play and development. Validation of ongoing skills and opportunity to experience new obstacles through newly developed skills are also products of effective practice.

Many golfers must be under the impression that simply playing round after round is the best source of practice time for the sport, because they spend little or set no time specifically aside for practicing or remedying problems. Golfers may not have had opportunity to experience effective and challenging practice sessions, where improvement is quantitatively measured showing real and true rising of competency levels related to shot making and performance. The establishment of a planned approach to growth, with skill attainment the impetus for meeting new targets for both physical and mentally related skills, could result in more golfers seeing the value of setting aside time specific to practice

I reiterate my concern for golfers often avoiding steps toward improvement, due to the nature of the activities associated with some initiatives. Your Goal Setting Plan includes all targets to be achieved during practice and during on-course play, which must be updated and maintained to realize the benefits of your efforts. If golfers wish to include challenge performance statements related to on-course performance, it would be appropriate to have some challenges related to Proximity Acceptance, and other on-course targets following implementation of the On-course Assessment and Benchmarking strategies. Measured improvement, enhanced confidence, brand new motivation, superior performance and a rekindled love for the game will be the result of the commitment to administer your improvement plan. The positive changes of managing practice within a plan specifically aimed at the benefit of continuous positive reinforcement will have a profound influence on performance. The impetus comes from the direct positive effect on confidence levels as the targets are achieved.

With most golfers electing to play with little or no real significant time set aside for practice, it is easy to see why performance is inconsistent, and improvement hampered. It also clarifies why real improvement is elusive, and why so many have instilled some extremely poor habits since taking up the game. Golfers that rarely practice, or not taking the time for periodically scheduled practices are constantly trying to make adjustments and corrections during play, for issues that should be addressed during practice. The result is widely varying levels of performance, lacking any direction for growth, while instilling or fostering a methodology that is totally non-supportive of the building of confidence and a sound mind state.

Knowing that a practice session provides real evidence that skills and abilities are being achieved may be different from your experiences with practice. Many golfers seem to view practice times as ball bashing sessions, with the intention of winning a prize for the greatest number of balls hit, or a race to empty the basket as quickly as possible. In most cases, there are no remedial activities attached to practice time to address the issues affecting performance. Being assured practice sessions are directed at issues offering the greatest return for improvement, in a manner that is inspirational to take on new challenges, creates a new practice environment much more supportive of improvement and skill progression. The effort of managing and maintaining practice session performance statements is very satisfying when real gains in confidence and measured increases in skill development are quickly and tangibly seen.

Section 3 - The Outcomes of Practice

Practice must become a true reflection of those areas of your golf game, not only requiring remediation, but also having the greatest affect on the rate of improvement. Moreover, the primary source of material or information determining the plans and establishing the challenges identified for practice sessions must be based on actual on-course performance. For example, if your on-course play indicates a dramatic negative change in driving accuracy, this knowledge must trigger remedial practice to rectify the issue. Practice time must be reflective and responsive to current issues and problems to maximize the effectiveness of your efforts and prioritize activities making up your practice sessions.

To maximize the benefit you obtain from your practice time, each session must be viewed as your next opportunity to benchmark, correct, improve, or experiment with aspects of shot making having a significant influence on performance. Breaking your practice time into these areas of focus provides needed variety for maintaining interest and motivation, and assures a number of key aspects of golfer development are addressed with every practice. In addition, these different areas of emphasis provide ample opportunity for confidence building, and better assists developing a Positive Competitive Mindset, by better supporting each of the foundational premises of the model. This serves to better integrate practice as a regular component of an approach to the game specific to maximizing improvement. Let's more closely examine the four different aspects or components of practice that should be inclusive of every practice session.

Types of Practice Activities

Remedial Practice

Remedial practice outlines methods for improving on course weaknesses identified through data gathered during actual on-course play. Corrective practice activities specific to on-course performance are essential to avoiding regressions in improvement and declines in confidence. By using the information gathered under actual playing conditions, weaknesses can be immediately determined, permitting specific action to be taken to strengthen any newly arising concerns.

The activities normally associated with remedial practice are usually related to current issues having the most dramatic influence on scoring, or relate to issues potentially becoming a major confidence issue. Remedial initiatives immediately address current issues and concerns experienced on the golf course and correcting them before becoming an emerging mind state issue. Remedial practice is getting the opportunity to correct or remedy some of your more recent difficulties as identified through On-Course Assessment, Proximity Acceptance, and Benchmarking activities. After all, it is these strategies that are providing you with the information that is the basis upon which your remedial practice is based. There will be days you are losing the ball to the right and on a different day there is a tendency to roll over the shot with a more left to right ball flight. Perhaps the past two rounds have shown there has been a noticeable decline in the number of fairways hit in regulation, immediately initiating steps to address this issue. There could be a substantial increase in the number of putts taken over the last few rounds triggering an analysis to determine, if the issue is the acceptability of approach shots into the green, or is the issue strictly limited to putting concerns.

Through the analysis of information gathered, it is possible to focus on creating incrementally attainable challenges for skills you know will combat the issues causing recent drops in performance. Remedial practice pursues any aspects of your game that are costly and damaging or showing negative shot execution trending changes. These are the areas of improvement undertaken during remedial practice.

General Practice

General practice addresses the establishment of general consistency in shot making. Every practice session must include specific areas of skill progression for development and improvement of general shot execution. Session activities directed at consistency, accuracy, and distance control are examples of general shot execution characteristics that could be addressed.

Activities falling into this area of practice are directed at an organized inventory of improvement across the board; for all clubs in the bag. Partaking in session activities geared at improved shot execution for every club is emphasized during general improvement activities. For example, you may not be having any particular issue with your driving off the tee, but a component of practice time is devoted to improving your driving accuracy. This type of practice is directed at improving general shot making skills, not addressing an issue or concern. Another good example of a practice activity falling in this category is the establishment of a well articulated and ingrained pre-shot routine. Again this is not addressing a particular concern, but is directed at a general overall improvement of shot execution.

Experimental Practice

Experimental practice is open to all shot types not yet benchmarked and not included in General or Remedial Practice. Experimental practice provides the golfer the opportunity to experiment and experience a wide array of different shots not yet quantified as challenge performance statements. In order to identify and quantify the new challenges addressed during Experimental practice activities, include the initial benchmarking of the skill and the formulation of an appropriate challenge performance statement for introduction into General practice. Experimental practice is associated with the introduction of less frequently executed shots that are confronted regularly on an any-day basis, and is the mechanism for the golfer to introduce new areas of growth. Golfers confront these less common shots regularly during play, but lack confidence to execute them successfully because of limited exposure to these situations or circumstances.

The first area of focus in Experimental Practice should be the shots that have never been benchmarked and are most frequently encountered during play. This ensures skill development in areas having the greatest positive effect on scoring and improvement. The determination of the shot competencies that are introduced as experimental practice priorities must be based on the frequency of its occurrence because this methodology validly and soundly determines the next most effective skill to introduce for monitoring and improvement. After all, it is going to be concerns on the course you experience most frequently that have the strongest influence on your performance.

For example, a golfer that has only benchmarked full swing shots, the competencies identified could include the benchmarking of the 7:30, 9:00 and 10:30 swings for a sixty-degree wedge. The golfer bases the decision to address these competencies on playing data showing weakness or declines in saves percentages.

Knowing these distinctive wedge shots are frequently called upon during a round of play, the golfer feels and knows the skills or competencies acquired will directly enhance the ability to get it up and down. The choice of introducing these particular benchmarking activities for the wedge is based on these shots being consistently encountered in save situations during play, therefore having a greater overall effect on improvement or performance enhancement. These are the shot types that should be benchmarked first, because of their greater influence on performance increases. There is great value and reward experimenting with new shots that are confronted on an occasional basis. The time set aside for Experimental practice is the way new performance statements are created, by first benchmarking the competency, and then identifying a challenge performance statement, and bringing this new skill or competency into the area of General Practice. Over time the golfer achieves numerous newly benchmarked skills or competencies that are monitored and developed on a regular basis, increasing the golfer's skill base.

As the golfer benchmarks and introduces new shots for improvement and monitors progression of these skills, there is a strong positive effect on consistency and performance levels. Executing shots from fried-egg lies, ball striking from the opposite side of the ball, shots from extremely deep rough, and extremely long putts are examples of where at least limited experience could prove to be extremely beneficial to scoring. Experimentation with slight fades to dramatic slices, or slight draws to strong hooks are examples of specific shot types that could also be explored in this area.

With Experimental Practice being a component of every practice, ample opportunities are created to experience or rehearse a wide range of shots. With the passing of time, the repertoire of shots types explored through experimentation will become quite extensive. As a result, on any given day, being called upon to confidently execute any of these previously experienced shot types greatly improves the likelihood of being successful, and will avoid putting some big numbers on the scorecard. This is due to confidence in your ability to effectively execute these shots, as a result of the experiences accommodated through experimentation. Having opportunities to experiment with less commonly confronted shot types, provides valued experience essential for building confidence. This will be especially true after a period of time and the number of shot types you have experienced is widely varied. Remember your overall confidence is a culmination of your experiences, and that your experiences with greater numbers of shot types will have a dramatic influence on your confidence growth.

Practice Time Allocation			
Available Practice Time	**General Practice**	**Remedial Practice**	**Experimental Practice**
1 hr	30 min	18 min	12 min
1.5 hrs	45 min	27 min	18 min
2 hrs	1 hr.	36 min	24 min
2.5 hrs	1 hr 15 min	45 min	30 min
3 hrs	1 hr 30 min	54 min	36 min
3.5 hrs	1 hr 45 min	1 hr	45 min
4 hrs	2 hrs	1 hr 12 min	48 min
4.5 hrs	2 hrs 15 min	1 hr 20 min	55 min
5 hrs	2 hrs 30 min	1 hr 30 min	1 hr
100%	50%	30%	20%

Section 4 - Make Time For Quality Practice

It is extremely important to establish practice as the time for the acquisition of newly established skills, or when remedial issues are to be rectified and corrected. Never partake in any type of remedial improvement activity, while playing on the course, unless that is the specific reason for being there. Your practice time should be devoted to improvement and performance enhancement, or benchmarking activities to better perform in competition. Consider competitive play to be any round of golf played with the intention of the score being used in handicap calculation. This would apply to the majority of rounds played by most golfers. Your on-course play should be the testing ground for all that you accomplish during practice. The round following a practice session should be eagerly met as an opportunity to use newly acquired competencies to take on the course with added confidence and skill.

The most common error made regarding practice is the limited portion of time the average golfer devotes to it. This obviously has a huge impact on play, but golfers also entrench numerous bad habits with practice methodologies that detrimentally affect growth. Specific blocks of time must be set aside for the planned acquisition of skills outside of playing time. Blocks of time set aside for practice provide opportunity, without fear of failure, for skills to be honed and improved, justifying the move to the next level of performance to be demonstrated. This certainly is not the way most golfers approach practice time. The scenario to be described below is based on experiences of witnessing the actions of hundreds of golfers for almost fifty years. Granted many golfers are reluctant to spend allocated practice time devoted to specific skill development, however the methods adopted by most golfers regarding practice is primarily where the problem begins.

The primary issue or concern is far too many golfers adopting the time immediately before a round of play as their designated time for practice. It is understandable why golfers that never schedule regular practice sessions are caught in the trap of viewing the time before a competitive round of play as the only time available for this purpose. Despite the golfer's admirable intentions to set aside some time for practice, their efforts are futile and without purpose because of the poor methods they employ. Trying to create a practice session during the time when a golfer should be getting mentally prepared to play is the primary issue. It is a common occurrence to see golfers adopting this poor approach to hit a number of shots, evaluate their concerns, and then proceed to address these issues as they see them emerge during the pre-round session. It is not uncommon to see golfers employing the sound practice of hitting a number of wedges, then short irons, progressing to long irons, then the fairway metals, and finally the driver. The good intentions of the golfer are admirable, but this approach to practice is inconsistent with maximizing efforts to excel. This routine of warming up with a shorter club and progressing to clubs of greater length is a commonly accepted and valued approach taken by thousands of golfers as a basic methodology of practice, but its application during a warm-up session is inappropriate

The logic and justification of this approach is not the concern, the issue is how golfers use this warm-up time, first for assessment, then improvement and practice. For golfers that never set aside time specific to practice, there is a tendency for the warm-up before their regular rounds of golf to become their normal or regular practice session. Trying to assess and remedy concerns is not a wise way of getting prepared to play, This is especially the case given the limited time available in a warm-up session and the need for proper planning of a practice session. The time before playing a competitive round of golf should be devoted to feeling confident in your abilities, and reaffirming the sensations of a rhythmic swing having good tempo and rhythm. The time before a competitive round should be devoted to activities enhancing confidence in your abilities, and focusing on factors providing a mentally stabilizing effect.

For golfers that do not devote specific time to practice, it is a common occurrence before playing to witness them hitting a number of wedges shots, and if there are no identifiable concerns, then moving onto a longer club. Assessment of another number of shots is made for this club. The golfer addresses any concerns or issues for this particular club before moving onto the next club to be evaluated. As a result of this process, practice sessions become focused on random issues that are based on a very limited number of shots, rather than tackling major problems or concerns based on true on-course play and real issues. In addition, never lose sight of the fact that virtually every golfer hits many more superior shots on the range, as compared to the golf course. This means golfers employing this poor approach to practice create an incapacity to address weaknesses, and waste time on activities having little direction or benefit. As a result, practice time is without purpose or benefit. This extremely unproductive approach to practice has been adopted by far too many golfers, and must change to give practice time the priority it deserves, and avoid time wasted on worthless activities.

With the enhanced opportunities for positive reinforcement offered through practice sessions, confidence is heightened and a success breeds motivation, motivation breeds success cycle is experienced by the golfer. This experience is usually all that is needed to discover the true value of establishing performance achievement targets and maintaining them. Knowing you are improving based on real evidence causes the very powerful realization that guaranteed improvement is truly within grasp, as long as the effort and fortitude to persevere with the re-creation of new performance target statements is carried out as challenges are achieved.

Section 5 - Creating Progressive Practices

The conventional nature of target statement achievement is based on the required demonstration of a skill meeting a measurable criterion or standard of performance. Effective practices are maintained by defining a criterion for a level of performance that must be attained for every practice activity. This methodology promotes target achievement and success as a regular part of practice sessions. Golfers can control the size of the incremental steps defining the rigour associated with a target, by simply modifying the criterion portion of the objective or challenge performance statement. By maintaining practice sessions that are based on attainable criteria, improvement is assured for as long as the golfer is receptive to establishing new challenges to be attained. Golfers simply redefine new standards of performance in new challenge statements, as other target statements are achieved. This is the conventional methodology for the identification and achievement of performance criteria as outlined in the previous chapter on Goal Setting and Planning.

In this chapter golfers are introduced to methods providing added flexibility when identifying target performance criterion. Having the ability to readily adjust a number of variables defining the criterion of challenge performance statements:

- Improves practice time efficiency,
- Better accommodates the quantifying of mind state skill development performance statements,
- Provides ability to customize areas of emphasis
- Enhances the enjoyment of practice sessions by engaging the golfer in fun, personally tailored self-competitions reflecting or simulating conditions during competitive play.

It is essential that the identification of performance statements and management of practice sessions be attainable, practical and easily managed. This ensures golfers can easily maintain the planning of practices to reap the benefits of continuous and immediate positive reinforcement for achievement of all the challenges guiding practice sessions. The measured improvement the golfer realizes, as the result of achieving the challenges set for a practice is a constant and reliable source for confidence building. Be reminded that it is through achievement of the challenges guiding practice sessions and on-course performance that represent the limited means available for a golfers to enhance confidence through positive reinforcement.

All aspects of practice are implemented in a progressive manner based on variables like time, accuracy, consistency, shot shape, frequency, distance, repetitive requirements, predefined success rates and other standards of performance, depending on what is to be achieved.

Utilizing Timed Activities

The criteria for a challenge statement could include time as a parameter for the achievement of a standard of performance. When timed activities are used, immediate progression to subsequent practice activities, greatly improves the efficiency of your practice time. This approach keeps the golfer working on those aspects of their game posing more of an issue and being rewarded for targets they achieve in less time. In cases where a criterion is easily met, the golfer is free to redefine the rigour of the criterion of the target statement or challenge and quickly add a new practice activity, or move on to the next practice activity. If a criterion for a challenge is too rigorous to be achieved and an allotted time was insufficient for the golfer to meet the defined criterion, then the golfer is free to lessen the rigour of the criterion to a level that is achievable. You can make your practices progressively more responsive, by simply modifying challenge performance statements to keep practices progressing and productive. These slight modifications in methodology heighten the effectiveness and enjoyment of practice, expediting improvement, and providing an ongoing progressive facet to skill development, amplifying their competitive realism. The approach of setting performance criteria based on time adds new interest and challenge to practice activities, which will invigorate motivation and your competitive interest as a golfer. In addition, the tagging of practice activities with specific time allocations can be beneficial when practice sessions do not have free time at the end of their scheduled time.

You will become so intimately familiar with characteristics or aspects of your own game that the adjustment of challenge statement criteria to maintain achievement and progression will become automatic and efficient. By carrying out practice activities in this manner, success and goal achievement become a standard and repeated feature of practice, with fun and enjoyment being derived from achieving progressively changing success criteria.

Practice - Mind State Development

The ability to adjust the criteria of performance challenge statements through different variables like time, rate, frequency, tolerances and even variable combinations, like time and rate in the same performance challenge statement, easily permits the creation and maintenance of mindset skill development challenge statements. Variable combinations create unique rigour into performance challenge statements, which easily permits the creation of pressure-like situations into practice, allowing for performance achievement developing mindset skills.

Through the use of multiple variables like time and accuracy it is easy to identifying Challenge statement creating varying levels of pressure for completion. This creates practice opportunities more reflective of true on-course circumstances. It will be easy to establish Challenges to be met for practice having varying levels of pressure to complete, which closely simulates the anxieties experienced in real on-course pressure situations. The ability to freely add and define practice session challenge statements, specifically directed at mind state skills, permits enhanced development of the Positive Competitive Mindset, by providing opportunity to specifically take steps controlling negative influences. The establishment of Positive Competitive Mindset is much easier to foster, when the golfer sees measured improvement in mind state skills, and has experienced real benefits of their demonstration. Just as the accuracy of your tee shots can be improved with practice, likewise, the health of the mind state can be improved with practice. Integration of mind state and psychomotor skill development into the challenges identified for practice promotes a much more comprehensive approach to golfer development.

Through the introduction of mind state development activities, flexibility defining areas of emphasis, and the strong link of achievement to progression, practices should be viewed quite differently regarding a golfer's development. Enjoyable, challenging and productive practice sessions can be created causing more golfers to see the value of quality practice time and the resulting benefits.

CHAPTER 9

Stress And Anxiety

"Ability is what you're capable of doing. Motivation determines what you do. Attitude determines how well you do it."
Lou Holtz

Section 1 - Preliminary Considerations

This chapter examining Stress and Anxiety is representative of a strategy primarily supporting the Eliminating Negative Influences premise of the Positive Competitive Mindset Model.

Recognizing the symptoms and being able to proactively address the mental tension that is created by stress and anxiety gives the golfer the ability to proactively control circumstances leading to scoring inconsistency and periodic ballooned scores on a hole. This strategy also provides the golfer additional confidence in knowing there are ways of reducing negative distractions brought on by circumstances initiated by stress and anxiety. In this chapter, the golfer will also become aware that the tension brought on by stress and anxiety is not necessarily a bad thing.

The difficulty arising when compiling this chapter was the apparent difference of opinion regarding the defining of stress and anxiety. Through research, it was clearly apparent that psychologists, psychiatrists and other professionals do not agree on the definitions of each, with some experts expounding they are synonymous terms, and others going to great lengths to differentiate them. What is agreed upon, whether they are defined the same or not, the negative results or consequences brought on by stress or anxiety, are the same. The symptomatic problems triggered through anxiety and stress, have identical physiological effects on the body. What is important is to provide all relevant and pertinent information regarding the physiological changes caused by both, and providing a manner to manage them.

Most golfers can easily relate to personal experiences where stress or anxiety has had devastating effects on play, ruining many wonderful rounds of golf. Golfers are fully aware of the damaging effects of these sources of tension, but for the most part have been at a loss for how to effectively deal with them. This is particularly the case for millions of golfers having personal long-standing mind state issues preventing them from reaching their potential. Having an understanding of the origins of stress and anxiety, recognizing their onset, and knowing their psychological effects are topics of great value, because it is these interferences that spawn the nervous tension leading to the problems being experienced. To understand the origins of stress and anxiety, each will be studied as distinctively separate topics. Likewise, the ways stress and anxiety can be avoided will also be presented separately. This approach is taken so golfers can easily determine the source of their issues and facilitate ways of resolving them.

In <u>The Golfer Mindset</u> stress is associated with the negativity experienced as a result of external factors outside the control of the golfer, while anxiety starts as the result of psychological or cognitive factors originating in the mind of the golfer. This differentiation between stress and anxiety permits the golfer to identify the source of their ensuing physiological changes, and helps define practical ways of handling stress and anxiety based on tactics specifically designed to deal with either. On the other hand, since the effects of stress and anxiety are treated synonymously based on their common effects on the body, it is extremely important to realize the tension felt is the culmination or sum of the tension arising from both.

Differentiating Stress and Anxiety

Richard S. Lazarus is attributed with today's most regarded definition of stress. Lazarus defines stress as a condition or consequential feeling when an individual perceives that "demands exceed the personal and social resources the individual is able to mobilize." In other words, an individual manifests feelings of tenseness and inadequacy to control aspects of life's events and their impact on personal experiences. This interpretation of the definition of stress clearly points to factors immediately outside the control of the golfer. Life is constantly creating detrimental conditions that are manifested as stress based on events that are out of the control of the individual. Examples could include, financial insecurity, death of a loved one, troubling issues confronting a sibling, social ridicule and other uncontrollable events experienced in life.

On the other hand, anxiety is viewed as an internally self-induced state of apprehension, uncertainty, or fear resulting from the anticipation of a realistic or fictitious threatening event or situation, often impairing physical and psychological functioning. Contrastingly, the effects of anxiety can be viewed as the product or consequence of something conjured up in the mind of the golfer, whereas stress is viewed as originating from conditions triggered externally.

As previously discussed, stress and anxiety will be examined independently based on this simplified "external factors - internal factors" view of stress and anxiety, respectively. This differentiation of these two concepts based on internal and external factors provides opportunity to more effectively apply strategies dealing with either. By equipping the golfer with the ability to immediately identify stress or anxiety as the source of their agitation permits quick response to controlling the negative effects of either.

Section 2 - Optimizing Overall Tension Levels

It has already been ascertained a certain level of mental tension or pressure is needed for optimum performance. Without some pressure (stress plus anxiety) there would be a total lack of drive or initiative to attain anything. If a golfer is under too little mental tension, then there is little motivation or concentration to produce a good performance. The feelings of boredom and lack of excitement originates with not being challenged or not taking a risk. If this state persists for an extended time, then golfers may find the sport tedious, and even give it up. At an optimum level of stress you will gain the benefits of being mentally alert and engaged prompting a good performance.

The mental tension brought on by stress and anxiety is what initially motivates us to act, however when unmanaged mental tension takes hold of the golfer, motivation and performance suffer greatly. Permitting the pressures of stress and anxiety to become excessive damages performance and the golfer's enjoyment of the sport. Where stress is too high, performance suffers dramatically. Your flow can be disrupted, you can be distracted, and competition can become threatening and unpleasant. If you are under too much stress, then you will find that your results suffer, because you find it difficult to focus on technique and fail to flow with the performance. The key to maximizing performance is not to allow stress levels to move into the unmanageable range or above the optimum level.

When there is a balance at an appropriate level of mental tension performance is maximized. If golfers can keep their overall tension level, as a result of stress and anxiety at this optimum level, conditions for a "best performance" are greatly enhanced. If you can keep yourself within this zone, then you will be sufficiently aroused to give a high quality performance, rather than having overall tension levels too high or too low precipitating a poor performance.

This zone of optimum performance varies widely for different people. Some people may operate most effectively at a level of stress that would leave others, either bored, or completely stressed out. If you interpret a situation saying 'I'm in trouble', then you are much less likely to do well. Think positively, view a new situation as an opportunity to exhibit your skills at a higher level. It is possible that someone who functions superbly in a low level competition might experience difficulties in high level competition. Alternatively someone who performs only moderately at low levels of competition could give exceptional performances under extreme pressure.

The illustration below shows the concept of cumulative tension level and its relationship to maximized optimum performance.

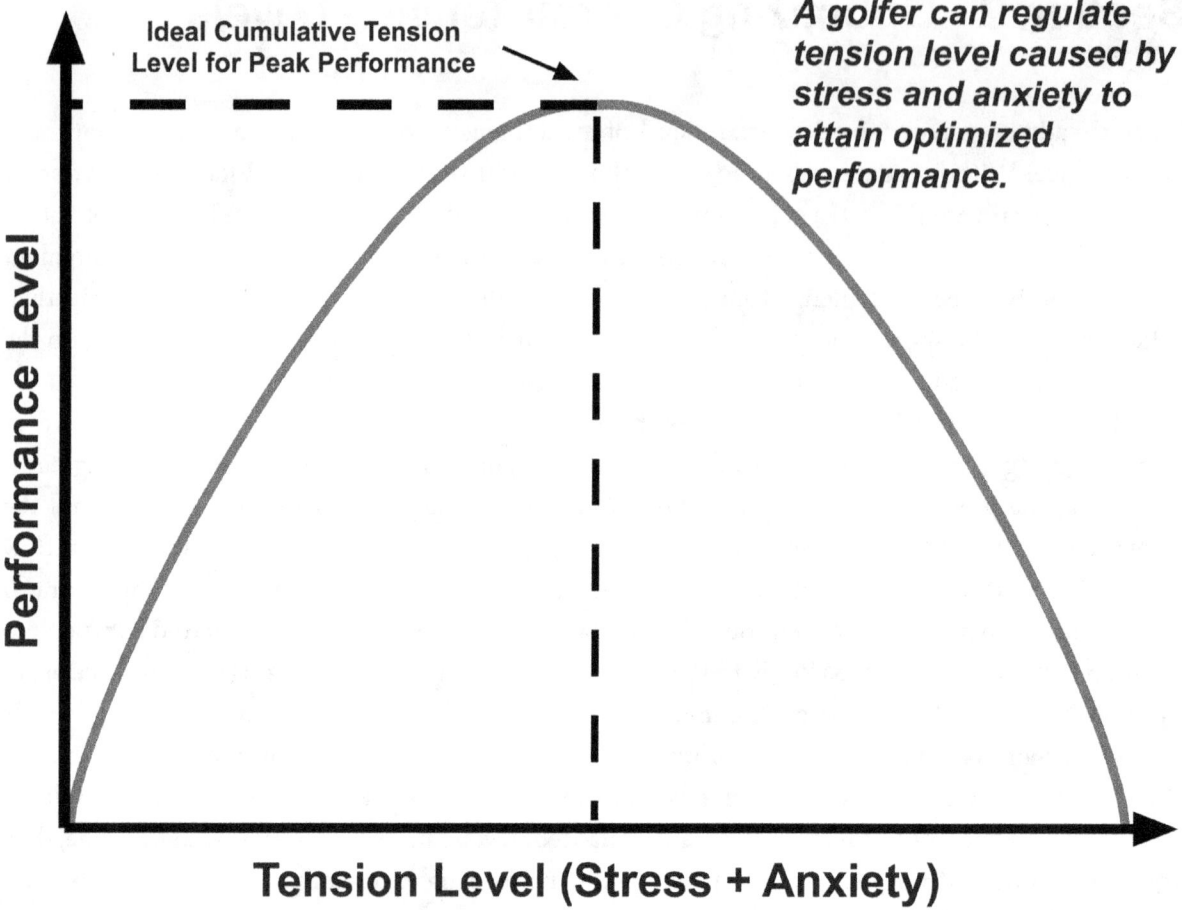

This concept is extremely important because the notion of maintaining a balance or a status quo state is what is trying to be achieved. This idea precludes that a golfer must actively monitor their circumstances in an attempt to maintain a familiar and comfortable overall tension level for maximized performance. This is an important idea to highlight, as this is a similar concept underlying the foundational premises of the Positive Competitive Mindset and the purpose of the strategies supporting the model.

If a golfer approaches practice and competitive play in a manner that is consistent with the prime intent of maintaining a stable supportive mind state, then this begs for the golfer to treat all competitive play the same. Treating different competitions with different emphasis or varying importance only creates new distractions and negative influences in these instances. If the golfer approaches the game in a consistent manner this creates the best conditions for maintaining mind state stability. The strategies falling under the model are specifically directed at controlling tension levels, giving the golfer the ability to bring tension levels back to a level for maximized performance.

Section 3 - Effects of Stress and Anxiety

When an individual is under stress, the adrenal gland releases corticosteroids that are converted into cortisol in the blood stream. Cortisol helps regulate cardiovascular function and blood pressure, as well as the body's use of fats, proteins, and carbohydrates. Cortisol is often called the stress hormone, as a result of increased secretion levels in response to physical and psychological stress during the fight or flight response. Cortisol also has an immune suppressive effect in your body.

Care must be taken to allow the body's functions to return to normal following a stressful event. Although elevated cortisol levels are an important response to stress, it's important that the body's relaxation response be made active to permit an opportunity for the body to return cortisol levels to normal. In today's high stress society, if the relaxation response is not permitted to occur, then repeated or constant stress will lead to a state of chronic stress. To keep cortisol levels healthy and under control, the body's relaxation response should be started after a high-tension response occurs. You can learn to relax your body with various stress management techniques, and you can make lifestyle changes to keep your body from reacting to stress in the first place.

Symptoms of Stress and Anxiety

The following is a list of the major symptoms of stress that you might feel:

Physical Symptoms - mainly in response to increased levels of adrenaline:
- Nervousness
- Fearfulness
- Apprehensiveness
- Impatience
- Tenseness - restlessness
- Increase in heart rate
- Increase in sweating, cooler skin due to reduction in the blood flow to the skin.
- Butterflies in your stomach
- Rapid breathing
- Tense muscles
- Dry mouth
- Desire to urinate
- Mental symptoms
- Worry
- Confusion, inability to concentrate or difficulty making decisions
- Feeling ill or odd
- Feeling out of control or overwhelmed

Regardless of how you define mental tension, almost every person understands how it feels. In today's fast-paced society, the tension caused by stress and anxiety is surprisingly common.

Adrenaline

When experiencing stress and anxiety, adrenaline may enters the bloodstream having the following positive and negative effects on the body:

Positive Effects:
- Adrenaline causes physiological arousal
- Causes alertness
- Prepares the body for explosive activity

Negative Effects:
- Inhibits judgment
- Interferes with fine motor control, and makes executing complex skills difficult.

The initial flow of adrenaline into the bloodstream typically culminates as the common sensation of feeling 'butterflies in the stomach'. In sports like golf where fine motor control is important, adrenaline can often have negative consequences. A common example of this is the typical case of the "yips" adversely affecting a golfer's putting. Excess adrenaline in the body has a dramatic negative effect on fine motor control of smaller muscles. Golfer's experiencing the "yips" indicated feelings of a total loss of control of muscle action. Others indicate feeling as if someone else executed the putt or being possessed.

In sports like sprinting, football, hockey, soccer, basketball or power lifting, where explosive activity is required of the larger muscles, adrenaline is useful in generating optimum performance. The sport of golf does not readily permit the tensions created by stress and anxiety to be regulated or dissipated through explosive physical activity. Without some sort of pressure relief valve to offload the tension brought on by competition, the golfer is left no alternative, but to proactively try to regulate tension levels to maintain performance.

Section 4 - Stress

Everyone has experienced different types of stress at one time or another. Stress could result from a death in the family, a lost job, desires of attaining a promotion at work, or fear of financial insecurity. Stress can originate at home, in the workplace or through other life events. It could be personal stress arising from the work place, strained family relationships, retirement, or an unhappy emotional event, like an automobile accident. All these various types of stress can be categorized into four main types of stress. They include Eustress (Good stress), Distress (Bad stress), Hyperstress and Hypostress.

1. Eustress

Eustress is defined in the model of Richard Lazarus (1974) as "stress that is healthy or gives one a feeling of fulfillment". Literally, "eu" is Greek for good, thus eustress means "good stress." Examples of events or situations creating positive stress include:

- Accomplishment of a challenge
- Thrill of winning a lottery
- Fulfillment of belonging
- Excitement of participating in a big event
- Excitement of winning a tournament

The stress experienced as the result of events or situations resulting in eustress have a healthy effect on the golfer. A feeling of achievement, fulfillment or contentment is precipitated making an individual excited about life and promoting a positive attitude. Eustress is sometimes referred to as curative stress because it gives a person the ability to generate the "best performance" or maximum productivity.

Eustress can be viewed as stress that is created as a result of personally initiated goals, aspirations or initiatives resulting in agitation and tension. The positive aspect of this type of stress is its positive effect on the individual experiencing it. For example, setting a goal of graduating with honours marks can add extra stress to a student's year of schooling, but the achievement of the goal results in feelings of accomplishment, or fulfillment, raising stress levels that are welcomed and favourable in nature. This is exactly what is accomplished through the Goal Setting and Planning strategy and the establishment of target performance challenges identified for practice sessions. A controlled stress level originates from the prospect of accomplishment, the eagerness to engage in the activities necessary to attain a goal and the prospect of success. Controlled levels of eustress have a positive effect on performance, but the issues arise when stress levels rise above controllable levels.

2. Distress

Many events in our lives bring on stress having a negative effect on our wellness. Just like Eustress having positive effects on our lives, there are also "bad" or "negative stresses" having a negative effect on our lives. These negative types of stress are the opposite of Eustress and are called Distress. Distress is a "negative stress". It is stress that is caused by negative or adverse events that occur in our lives and is strongly influenced by a person's ability to cope. Some events leading to distress include:

- Financial insecurity
- Chronic or prolonged illnesses
- Death of a loved one
- Heavy work responsibility and workload
- Divorce
- Loss of Employment

Ideally, the pressure driving us to achieve maximum performance would best be positive in nature, because of the fulfillment or excitement associated with this type of stress, but this is not the case, because physiological biochemical effects of stress are indiscriminate, whether the resulting feelings are viewed as positive or negative. In short, this means excess positive stress over a level required for maximum or optimum performance is as detrimental as the excess stress being negative in nature.

Distress can be classified further as acute stress or chronic stress. Acute stress is short-lived while chronic stress is usually prolonged in nature. Events or situations creating acute stress include deadlines, work pressure, over exertion in physical activities, minor incidents (car accident), or the inability to resolve a minor life issue, and other similar short-term issues.

Acute stress is common with people who take on too many responsibilities and are overburdened with work, disorganized to the point of feeling a lack of control, and always in a rush to be on time. Generally, acute stress is associated with individuals holding job positions of responsibility, which precipitates a lifestyle characterized by constant tension because of external demands.

Chronic stress is the more serious of the 2 types of distress. Chronic stress is a prolonged stress that extends over an extended period of time ranging from month to years. This stress is due to poverty, dysfunctional families and marriages, serious illness and successive failures in life. People suffering from this type of stress get used to it and may even not realize that they are suffering from chronic stress. Due to its prolonged effects on the body, chronic stress is very harmful to an individual's health.

3. Hyper-stress

When a person is pushed beyond what he or she can handle, they will experience what we called hyper-stress. Hyper-stress results from being overloaded or overworked. It's like being stressed out. When someone is hyper-stressed, even little things can trigger a strong emotional response. People who are most likely to suffer from hyper-stress are:

- Working parents who have to multitask, juggling between work and family commitments
- A broker who are constantly under immense tension
- People who are under constant financial strains.
- Generally people working in fast paced environments.

4. Hypo-stress

Hypo-stress stands in direct opposite to hyper-stress. That is because hypo-stress is one of those types of stress experienced by a person who is constantly bored. Someone in an unchallenging job, such as a factory worker performing the same task over and over, will often experience hypo-stress. The effect of hypo-stress is feelings of restlessness and a lack of inspiration or motivation. It is a state when there is no challenge or problem and the person gets bored for lack of stress. This point will be raised again later regarding how a degree of tension must be maintained to foster motivation, and an engaging attitude.

Knowing the types of stress will enable you to determine the kind of stress you are going through and how to deal with it.

Causes of Stress

If stress is viewed as the manifestation of feelings of inadequacy to control unpredictable life events and their affect our personal lives, then there are countless ways stress can creep into our lives. Stress can originate with family and home life, work, and other life events that are unpredictable and out of our personal control. Listed below are many of the stress causing events or situations affecting us all.

Causes of Stress at Home
- Money issues
- Injury or sickness affecting a family member.
- Marriage
- Death of family member or friend.
- Separation or divorce
- Relocation of home
- Family member behavioural issues.
- Children's educational performance.
- Criminal activity affecting family members or friends.
- Conflict with family members, friends or neighbours.
- Pregnancy of family member or friend.
- Investment losses

Causes of Stress at Work
- Promotion issues
- Meeting the demands of the job
- Lack of support from superiors
- Relationships with colleagues and co-workers
- Work related sexual misconduct
- Changes in work hours
- Control issues with subordinate staff
- Job performance reviews

- Work related harassment
- Change of job or addition of job role
- Excessive work pressure
- Deadlines
- Changes in work assignment
- Conflict with co-workers or boss
- Working overtime and on holidays
- Work against will
- Work role

Other Causes of Stress
- Income tax issues
- Jury duty
- Retirement issues
- Defamation of character
- Fear, intermittent or continuous
- Threats: criminal, physical, safety, social, financial
- Uncertainty
- Lack of sleep
- Somebody misunderstands you

Managing Stress

People feel little stress when they have the time, experience and resources to manage it. They feel great stress when they think they can't handle the demands placed upon them, which manifests as experiencing some degree of unmanaged stress. Clearly there will be wide variations in ability of individuals to deal with stress. A particular set of circumstances may be stressful for someone, but a similar set of circumstances may be viewed as a welcomed challenge and easily handled by someone else. Ultimately the degree of stress experienced depends primarily on the individual's perceptions of their own life's situation and their real ability to manage or deal with it. In short, people in control of the stress they experience keep their stress levels managed, while others that feel a loss of control over it are experiencing stress levels that are unmanageable.

CHAPTER 10

Proximity Acceptance

"Optimism means expecting the best. Realism means knowing that the best may not happen. Confidence means knowing that even if it doesn't, you will survive. Never make a move if you are merely optimistic."
Anonymous

Section 1 - Overview

PROXIMITY ACCEPTANCE – Overview

Proximity Acceptance is a unique strategy supporting all three premises of the Positive Competitive Mindset Model. The strategy is an excellent source of positive reinforcement provided through consistent goal attainment, resulting in a dependable source of confidence building. Additionally, the strategy also provides valuable on-course performance information, regarding the ongoing accuracy of all approach shots into the green. Finally, the strategy directly supports reducing negative influences or distractions by eliminating extreme and over zealous shot expectations.

Proximity Acceptance is a strategy incorporating the power of consistent positive reinforcement for the steady growth of confidence. The strategy is ultimately directed at improving the accuracy of shots, while at the same time, setting more reasonable shot expectations based on a methodology for enhanced confidence growth. In order to establish the accuracy or proximity of your shot making it is necessary to hit 40-50 shots with each of your clubs and determine a base line acceptable proximity distance for all the clubs in the bag, except for the putter. A proximity distance for each club is based on a radius measure of the distance from the hole that includes 60% of approach shots into a pin for a particular club. For example, to benchmark the acceptable proximity distance for a 4 iron, hit 40 approach shots, and then create an imaginary circle around the pin that includes 60 percent or 24 of the shots taken. The radius of this circle is the original or starting baseline proximity distance determined for the 4-iron.

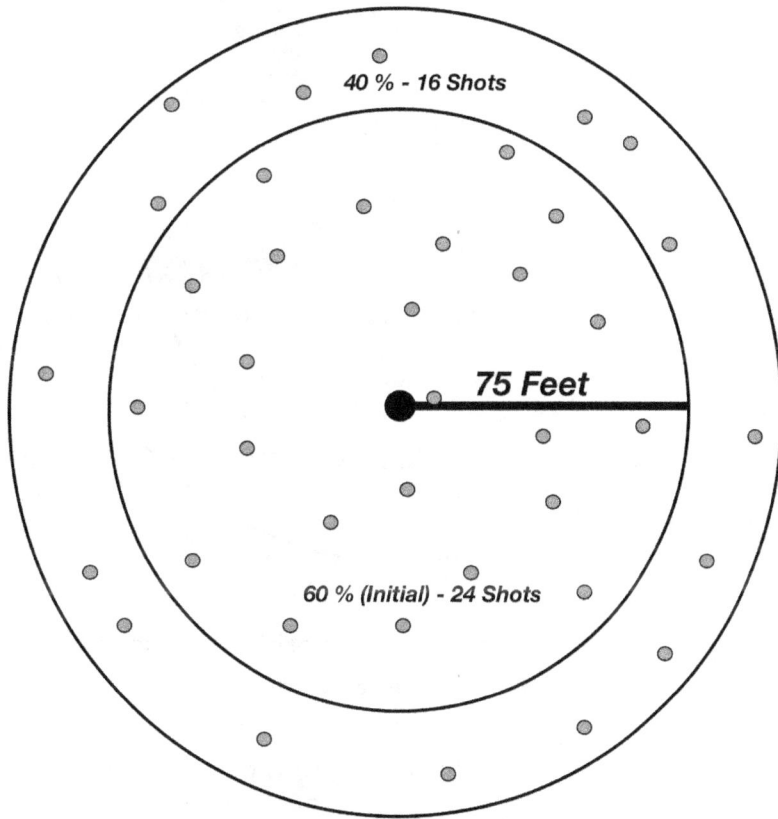

Establishment of an initial 60% accuracy level for determining the acceptable proximity distance is to have slightly more than the majority of shots representative of an acceptable positive result. This entails the golfer is experiencing positive reinforcement for at least 60% of approach shots into the green for any given club. Understandably, as a golfer's skills gradually escalate, and as improvement occurs over time, the percentage of shots meeting the original 60% proximity acceptance baseline level will increase. The dilemma arising as the percentage of shots meeting the original acceptable proximity radius increases is the determination of the percentage to be reached before re-establishing of a new proximity acceptance radius. This is an important question because the value of the originally determined proximity distance loses significance to the golfer as it becomes easier and easier to meet the standard. As a result, rigour for improvement may be lost and the motivation created through successes is diminished. At the same time it is important to maintain at least a 60% rate of success for effective positive reinforcement to occur.

With the previous example as a start point, when is the appropriate time to reestablish a new proximity acceptance distance to a 60% level. For example, the resetting of the proximity radius could occur when the percentage of successful shots reaches 80% or it could be postponed until it reaches 90%. The diagram below illustrates the percentage of successful shots falling within the original 75-foot acceptable proximity distance reaching 80%.

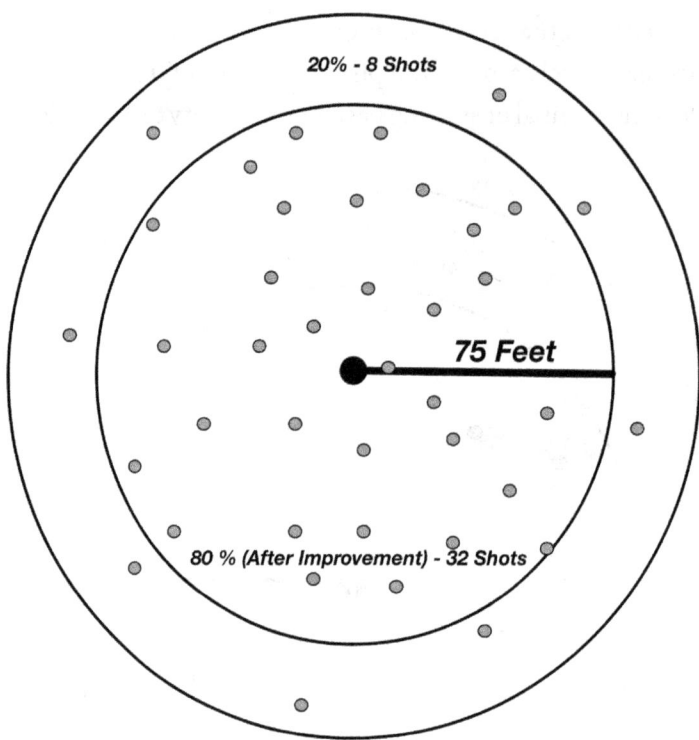

The percentage triggering the reestablishment of the proximity distance is a choice the golfer makes depending on the goal to be achieved. For example, a higher percentage of 90% triggering a change in the proximity distance emphasizes positive reinforcement because of experiencing more shots as being successful, however, the drawback of the 90% trigger is that much of the challenge in meeting a successful outcome is lost as this percentage climbs. Contrastingly, 70% accuracy triggering the reestablishment of a new proximity distance is probably premature because of the amount of room still left for improvement of accuracy for each club. When an 80% success rate for a specific club has been reached, this is an appropriate time to reestablish a new proximity distance for the particular club. An 80% threshold is ideal for maintaining reasonable levels of challenge, and maintaining good levels of positive reinforcement. When the 80% threshold has been met, it is at this time that the golfer readjusts the acceptable or successful percentage of shots back to 60%, which reduces the acceptable proximity radius, reducing the size of the target for the club being reset. Based on the previous illustration of a scatter diagram for a four iron reaching an 80% success rate, the following illustration shows the results when the 4-iron was reassessed to determine a new acceptable proximity distance.

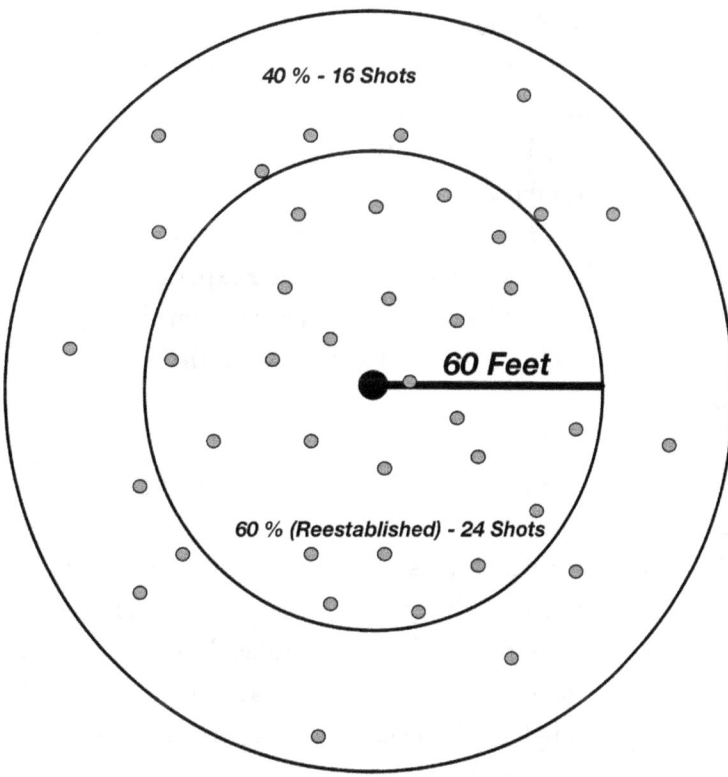

Improvements in accuracy from 60% to 80% and the reestablishment of a new proximity acceptance distances are true indicators of accuracy improvement that can be included in the goal-setting plan to quantify improvements in this area. As a result, the golfer has at their disposal a real and measurable way of monitoring on-course shot accuracy for all approach shots into the green. In the On-course Assessment Strategy, where your on-course performance is recorded for improvement purposes, provision for including accuracy records of all your shots is included in the recording tool. This will also permit determining when the success rate for a particular club's proximity distance has reached 80%.

The advantages a golfer gains through implementation of this strategy are specifically directed at enhanced improvement and overall superior performance. This is accommodated in a number of ways. Proximity Acceptance brings some fun back into the game, by providing a reasonable expectation of experiencing success for the majority of approach shots taken into the green. The frequency of meeting a more general predetermined objective for every approach shot taken, and regularly seeing evidence of quantified improvements in accuracy, provides repeated instances of positive reinforcement, and consequential confidence improvement. This has a strong positive effect on a golfer's demeanour.

Unreasonably demanding shot expectations can easily lead to the formation of negative influences or distractions compromising shot execution. It is important to understand the pressure or issues created by unrealistic shot expectations are unnecessary and unwarranted with implementation of the Proximity Acceptance strategy. You have probably experienced many golfers that overreact to a shot not meeting their strict standards and how this often leads to disastrous holes. The benefits gained by redefining more tolerable shot expectations far outweighs the concerns arising from the golfer's flawed perception that standards of performance are being compromised. The lowering of acceptable shot standards in no way deters a golfer from trying to achieve the ideal or perfect shot in every situation. The lowering of individual shot expectations has the benefit of greatly reducing the negative influences or distractions associated with a shot outcome not meeting a golfer's unrealistic standards and being exposed to positive reinforcement on a consistent basis.

This strategy can be integrated closely with the Goal Setting Plan by permitting challenge performance statements to be established directly related to on-course approach shot accuracy. This also provides the ability to readily assess or determine areas requiring improvement to modify practice sessions to address weaknesses. For example a golfer experiencing success with all proximity distances, except for 175 - 225 yards out from the green, knows immediately that a little extra practice is required with the long irons and fairway woods to keep pace with improvements being realized with the remainder of clubs.

Taking the time to assess all your clubs for their accuracy into the green could take the better portion of a day, but the immediate gains made in confidence and the extinguishing of negative influences related to unrealistic shot expectations will be the immediate benefit. When determining the average distance every club is stuck for the Benchmarking strategy, at the same time determine your initial acceptable proximity distances for each club. By performing both the distance benchmarking and the acceptable proximity distance determination at the same time, the golfer will cut the total assessment time in half. The confidence and valuable information these activities provide will result in immediate performance gains, primarily through the knowledge and experience golfers acquire regarding their ball striking abilities.

Monitoring Proximity Acceptance

With the recent release of GPS devices and applications available for SmartPhones fully capable of recording every shot taken on a specific golf course, access to data specific to on-course play is immediately at the fingertips of the golfer. Following the initial establishment of acceptable proximity distances for all clubs, it is possible to easily maintain these proximity distances based on actual on-course play. This will provide the added benefit of knowing these numbers represent on-course performance during actual play and are not skewed by the lower tension levels of the initial benchmarking carried out during a practice session. At the start of the season, going through the process of establishing the acceptable proximity distances during a practice session is a valuable experience, and is warranted after a winter layoff period, however, if you play the year round tracking these distances through on-course play is the better option, after the initial in-practice benchmarking has been completed.

CHAPTER 11

Distraction Management

"Failure seldom stops you. What stops you is fear of failure."
Jack Lemmon

Section 1 - Correcting Mind State Instability

The mindset of any golfer is extremely fragile and easily susceptible to changes in stability. It is not uncommon for the golfer's mindset to be in a state producing extremely high levels of play and at other times exhibiting shot-making of a player having a handicap 15 points higher. Why is performance so easily altered, in many cases, following seemingly trivial events and thoughts? Why can't some golfers get over longstanding issues and problems they have confronted for years? Most golfers have experienced the high of playing at euphoric levels, with heightened confidence, having numerous shots finding their targets, and suddenly find themselves recklessly striking shots with a sense of bewilderment, trying to determine what has gone wrong. What is even more disappointing is that these times of superior performance are infrequent, occurring a limited number of times in a season. What is the secret to preserving the experience of being in control and avoiding the chain of events responsible for a deterioration in performance? The golfer didn't't instantly lose their physical capabilities, but mentally something is certainly occurring, and the results are often catastrophic.

Surprisingly, the solution to the problem is simple, but the typical golfer requires access to implementable ways of dealing with this issue before it can be addressed. Distraction Management a critical strategy supporting the Eliminating Negative Influences of the Positive Competitive Mindset Model and is fundamental to providing tactics specifically directed at maintaining mind state stability during play. The ability of the golfer to maintain a stable and familiar playing environment keeps negative thoughts at bay, plus the capability to specifically address longstanding psychological issues builds additional confidence, further enhancing the ability to perform.

It is the Elimination of Negative Influences premise of the Positive Competitive Mindset Model providing the impetus for the development of the mind state tools golfers can use to avoid many of the additional strokes brought to the game, as a result of their own personal distractions and issues. The ability to circumvent the effects of uncomfortable and tension raising circumstances, or "pressure" comes from the ability to eliminate, mask or deal with those cognitive issues that heighten anxiety levels. Many of the implementable strategies supporting the Positive Competitive Mindset Model specifically reinforce the ability to eliminate or mask negative influences, but the golfer must always be searching for new ways and means of fostering a playing environment that separates negative distraction from play.

The Distraction Management Strategy provides golfers with a regimen of methods, activities and tactics to control or eliminate negative distractions arising from a wide range of sources. Golfers are well aware of the many sources of negative influences and their strong impact on performance, but must be proactive when dealing with these disruptions and controlling their outcome. By implementing a number of tactics golfers can garner some control of their psychological game to bring about positive results to performance. This unit also examines a number of tension relieving techniques, preparation for competitive play, relaxation techniques and a few other topics directly related to addressing distractions. Let's explore some of the benefits afforded through the acquisition of skills dealing with negative influences.

Supporting Evidence is Overwhelming

How is it possible to increase the frequency of your superior performances and avoid the factors causing the majority of rounds meeting with varying degrees of dissatisfaction? The answer to this question is based on an abundance of evidence that most golfers have experienced for themselves, but has not been formally conveyed in a manner to formulate solutions that would change their approach to the game. It would be an insult to the intelligence of any golfer to state "your performance is strongly influenced by your mental state," but having an understanding of the psychological mechanisms influencing play, could cause many golfers to reevaluated how they approach the game to maximize their playing success. Bringing to light a series of examples demonstrating how negative influences or distractions affect performance is to illustrate the volatility of mind state and how dramatic an impact the mindset of a golfer has on performance. The foundation for purporting the need to control the negative influences is not going to be by stressing how these influences negatively affect shot results, but rather to illustrate how their absence fosters improved performance.

Consider the following examples illustrating how the absence of negative influences promotes superior ball striking and enhanced performance. In each example, consider the negative influences that are absent or removed and the reason for their removal. Most importantly, notice that the elimination of negative influences or distractions normally results in immediate performance improvements in all the examples illustrated below.

- After completion of a portion of a round of golf where you have lost interest or given up because a targeted score is no longer achievable.
- When playing a round where the score will not be included as a recorded score toward your handicap.
- When playing a practice round or a round of golf where experimentation or practice is the primary objective
- When playing with a player that is new to the game or lesser ability.
- When practicing on the driving range or in a practice area.
- When playing alone.
- Playing when in an extremely good mood or sound state of mind.
- When playing in better-ball scramble format events.
- Playing when the pace of play is not delayed.
- When playing in a regular round with your friends, as opposed to a competitive round like a club championship
- When playing a familiar golf course, as opposed to playing a completely new course.

The variety of examples above illustrate different playing conditions where the formation of self created pressures or negative influences are minimized or eliminated based on the conditions or circumstances of each situation. The specific negative influences that have been suppressed vary not only in number but also in degree. In all cases, the suppression of a negative influences or distractions is the primary reason for the often radical improvements in performance that are witnessed.

In the first example, the realization that a score was unachievable removes the progressively increasing pressure to play at a higher level as the round progresses in order to achieve a targeted score. Following the realization a targeted score is unlikely, or is unattainable, the golfer starts approaching each individual shot free from the negative influences associated with having to perform super human feats to reach a goal. The golfer's performance immediately improves because of resigning to the fact the original objective they hoped to reach is a futile effort. The mental attitude regarding the remainder of the round is free from self-imposed pressure to perform well. The golfer is freed to execute shots without disruptive thoughts as the result of the elimination of self imposed pressure to attain a specific score or level of play.

In the second example, the golfer has lost the distraction of any pressure felt to perform as a result of the score not being recorded as a factor determining their handicap. In addition, the golfer tends to place less emphasis on the importance of each shot because of the downplayed importance of the final score. As a result, many of the detrimental thoughts that adversely influence shot execution are eliminated and superior play usually results.

In the third example, the experimental golfer playing a practice round is secure in the knowledge that if poor play results, then justifiable reasons for playing poorly are readily at hand. Statements like "I had a couple triple bogeys, but I was trying a few new things," are easily available as a defense mechanism protecting the golfer's pride, when disastrous or erroneous ball striking is encountered. The security in knowing that a poor score can be justified and the mere fact the golfer recognizes errant shots are possible, extinguishes many of the negative influences associated with placing high expectations on shot-making results. The result is an elimination of many of the negative influences affecting performance.

In the fourth case, when playing with a player that is new to the game, the golfer is secure knowing that no matter what his or her level of play may be, there is not going to be a critic in the novice player. In addition, the golfer finds comfort in knowing his or her ability will impress the greenhorn. Further, the golfer is free of all the negative influences associated with playing with golfers of similar or slightly higher capability, where similar skills create a more competitive environment.

In the fifth example, when striking shots on the driving range or in a practice area, all the negative influences associated with trying to attain a score or impressing the playing partners are nonexistent. In addition, the golfer's ability to immediately correct a mishit shot by simply re-teeing and striking another ball provides prompt reaffirmation of his or her ability. On the course, you have only one chance to hit any particular shot, but on the range the golfer is not limited to a single opportunity to prove themselves. Many of the pressures a golfer conjures up on the golf course are nonexistent on the range. The result is many more satisfying superior ball strikes on the range, as compared to actual playing situations.

These examples illustrate how the absence of destructive negative influences allows golfers to play the game in its purest form, without distraction. Golfers are well aware the management of the negative influences experienced during a round of play is critical to attaining top-level performance. Moreover, the mere prevalence and variety of negative influences requires the golfer to adopt strategies for controlling these distractions and avoiding the detrimental effects they bring. With the primary goal of this publication being to help golfers establish a highly effective competitive mindset, then controlling the negative influences during play must be a prerequisite to the attainment of this goal. If the golfer can successfully control the negative demons, then it follows the effects on ball striking will be similar to the results cited in the examples above.

A good example of eliminating negative influences before they can be created is having a clear understanding of the significance of the Handicap Index, and what it represents. Remember, having a true evaluation of your capabilities is critical to setting realistic shot making expectations and maintaining confidence levels, however, the common perception of what the "Handicap Index" represents is a source of many of the distractions confronting golfers today. Let's look at the significance of this number a little closer.

The Handicap Trap – Just Another Source of Distraction

Considering how the handicap index is determined, it's understandable the interpretation of what it represents leads to a consistent barrage of negative influences, damaging confidence and causing needless frustration, leading to big numbers on the scorecard. Understanding the handicap index calculation, and being cognizant of the potentially skewed or distorted information provided by this number will eliminate these frustrations. The misinterpretation of what a handicap index represents creates frustration for millions of golfers because it is assumed to be a valid and accurate assessment of a golfer's abilities. This assumption is completely false, creating nothing but problems for golfers making this error.

The common mistake made is an unawareness the primary motive for determining a handicap index is to permit golfers of different ability to play competitively against one other, not specifically represent a measure of a golfer's abilities. If a golfer has the perception the handicap index is a reflection of competency level, it is believed they should be able to play at an certain minimum level, after all, although in error, it is believed this number is a valid calculation of skill reflecting actual performance on the course.

When the handicap is closely examined, it is understandable why golfers are basing their capabilities on a misinterpretation of skill level. First, the index is based on the 10 "best" scores of the last 20 rounds played. In short, this means that 50% of the worst golf played is not even considered in the calculation. This means the handicap index is based on the "best 10 rounds", with no consideration given to the 10 highest scores of the last 20 rounds played. It is important to recognize only scores in the better half of the rounds played are used to calculate the handicap index. If it is viewed that the golfer's handicap index is a measure of performance level, then the golfer must be fully aware that their handicap is a distorted or inaccurate measure of their capabilities.

For example, a golfer with a handicap index of 10.7 commonly interprets this to mean scoring 10.7 strokes above par, for the courses played. With a Handicap Index of 10.7 and an approximate par of 72 for the courses played, millions of golfers would expect to score approximately eighty-three (72 + 10.7) = 82.7 (83) when playing these courses. This is faulty reasoning, but it is commonly interpreted in this way by far too many golfers. This certainly is not what the index number represents, but this is a common interpretation made by so many golfers. This erroneous understanding leads to immediate frustration, because golfers deceptively expect better results to be the norm, when they are the exception.

Handicap Index Calculation – 20 Rounds			
Round	Course Rating	Course Slope	Score
1	71.4	114	75
2	71.4	114	84
3	71.4	114	82
4	71.4	114	95
5	71.4	114	93
6	71.4	114	98
7	71.4	114	86
8	72.3	116	85
9	72.3	116	88
10	72.3	116	90
11	71.4	114	102
12	69	112	78
13	69	112	80
14	72.3	116	96
15	71.4	114	92
16	72.3	116	96
17	71.4	114	83
18	71.4	114	85
19	71.4	114	85
20	72.3	116	88
Calculated Handicap Index		10.7	
Average Score (10 worst rounds)		93.3	
Average Score (10 best rounds)		82.8	
Average Score (All rounds)		88.05	

Let's consider the example of the 10.7 handicap index in the illustration above and provide some notion as to how misleading this number can be to golfers and some issues it can raise. Many golfers would expect or believe their abilities to be to score at an 83 level on a regular basis, but clearly this is not the case. The average score of 93 for the ten worst rounds is 10 strokes worst than the golfer's anticipated 83 scoring level. In this particular case, the golfer fails to recognize that based on accurate calculations, over half the rounds they play will average 10 strokes higher (93 – 83 = 10) than they believe their capabilities to be. In short, golfers are expecting to shoot around 83, but will on average score 88 over the full 20 rounds played. This error of 5 full strokes on the part of many golfers creates issues regarding the negative influences that evolve because of misleading expectations, plus in the case of the worst rounds, the added devastating effects to confidence.

Ultimately, each individual golfer's definition of what they will accept as a personally satisfying level of play is a factor contributing to how well golfers play the game and the satisfaction they gain from it. Unfortunately, golfers demonstrate better performance levels with much less frequency than they expect, and this usually leads to frustration. In other words, if a golfer is more aware of their true capabilities, then expectations should be altered to reflect this assessment. This illustrates how an attitude or perception can be based on unfounded or inaccurate information and be a constant longstanding impediment to improved play.

The discrepancy between the capabilities being interpreted by golfers regarding their handicap and their actual play on the golf course must be eliminated. Golfers wishing to play more consistently with a confidence-level based on sound assessment, must be more realistic in their interpretation of what handicap measures and adjust their expectations to be more reflective of their actual play. This will immediately eliminate many of the negative influences or distractions being created by unrealistic expectations. In this example simply keeping an average of your scores over the last twenty rounds is going to give a much better idea of your capabilities than the common misinterpretation of the handicap index.

THE HIGH IMPACT BENEFITS OF MANAGING DISTRACTIONS

Improvement in Confidence Levels

A key benefit of access to skills combating distractions during play will be the shedding of numerous strokes by being tooled with the ability to deal with issues associated with mind state stability. The avoidance or control of negative influences will have a supplemental or additional positive impact on overall development and performance by eliminating many of the negative distractions that would have emerged had the original influences not been avoided. The effects on quality of play will certainly be enhanced by the initial shots gained, but there is an additional untapped source of confidence earned as the result of simply having the ability to address these issues. The ability to deal with negative influences during play also aids in eliminating or minimizing the effects of a golfer's most costly shortcomings. Many golfers will finally defeat demons that have haunted them for years, while others will perhaps put to rest the most devastating issues that have been plaguing their on-course play.

Enhanced Consistency of Play

If higher confidence levels, and a more positive state of mind improve chances of a "better performance", then their occurrence will become more prevalent for golfers. The ability of golfers to develop mind state skills will minimize the wide variability in the distribution of scores experienced, with an increase in the frequency of the scores being used in the calculation of the handicap index. Providing golfers with the tools to manage mind state issues will result in a narrowing of scoring distribution and a skewing of this distribution by eliminating the worst scores and increasing the likelihood of a "better performance".

There is the additional benefit of eliminating the source of extreme scores from on-course play providing a much more stable mind state for enhanced performance. Eliminating the distractions and negative consequences associated with extremely high scores avoids the crushing blows to confidence, causing golfers to question their abilities, and requiring extended periods of time to bring confidence back to previous levels. The avoidance of higher scores eliminates many anxieties and issues associated with widely varying confidence levels, which provides enhanced mind state stability and more consistent performance levels.

The Ultimate Benefit

Scoring a career best round is the hope of every golfer, but just to play at even "better performance" levels on a more consistent basis" is difficult to achieve. The milestone of attaining a new record score is an occasional event for golfers, but golfers want to more often experience the reaffirmed confidence and satisfaction that comes with playing at a higher level. Golfers would even be blessed to play at "better performance" levels, where the resultant score is included in the best 10 of the last twenty rounds played. After all, any score that has the potential of being used in the handicap index calculation is in the better half of scores recorded over the last twenty rounds played. The problem is that golfers still experience over half their rounds of play where the scores are not even included in the calculation. Golfers simply want to re-experience the satisfaction of having a sense of control the better rounds bring, which makes the game so much easier and fun to play.

Despite these "better performances" being representative of the better half of your scores, do not lose sight of the fact; you were the architect of these superior scores, with each representing a glimpse into past capabilities and confidence levels. Through implementation of mind state skills it is not unreasonable to expect these opportunities to be more prevalent and the number of "better performances" to increase in frequency.

The most advantageous means of making the greatest quantitative gains in improvement and performance come from those experiences placing yourself in circumstances that actually test your competitive abilities. If this notion is extrapolated, it is most beneficial to the golfer to experience as many rounds as possible where they are given opportunity to achieve something significant. Increasing the frequency of putting yourself in a position to attain a "better performance" every time you play provides the reward of becoming experienced and successful meeting this type of achievement. An increase in the number of better performance rounds experienced carries additional value due to the opportunities they provide to demonstrate the skills necessary to achieve milestone performances. You become confident in your ability to be successful, further enhancing performance.

The rounds having the greatest merit are those providing opportunity to achieve a desired goal or target. Their merit comes from the experiences gained in meeting or falling short of the goals. The positive effects of meeting targets, and the valued wisdom acquired when falling short of them, must both be experienced and assimilated to improve resiliency for reestablishing confidence. If it is possible to more consistently experience "better performance" levels, the benefits to the golfer are significant because of exposure to experiencing what is required to make these successes transferable to new and different situations. The experience of these pressure situations and having the opportunity to experience the failures and successes they bring, only reaffirms the importance of confidence being based on achievement of skills.

Purely based on traditional distribution of scores by most golfers, the likelihood of playing numerous rounds at "better performance" levels is an even split, but being armed mentally to offset inconsistencies due to mind state instability should help to reduce the wide variations in scoring, resulting in a greater number of rounds being included in the handicap index calculation. I believe the introduction of mindset development, as an integral component of improvement will permit golfers to play a greater percentage of rounds at "better performance levels", and have a higher portion of rounds played included in handicap index calculation. This is a significant step above the norm of having half the rounds played not being considered for a handicap index calculation. If "better" performance levels can be achieved on a more consistent basis confidence levels are stabilized and performance will be enhanced.

New Options For Complete Golfer Development

Having access to implementable means of effectively controlling or reducing the effects of negative influences through mind state development strategies and methods opens a whole new set of options for complete golfer development. The golfer has the novel ability to hone and improve mind state skills avoiding the strokes of their costliest longstanding issues, naturally accelerating occurrences of superior performance. No doubt the methods and strategies open to golfers related to mind state development will create many surprising benefits to their games. Establishment of a mind state enabling the golfer to address possible distractions and negative influences during competitive play is a position golfers will surely embrace. Having the ability to develop or shape mindset skills offers opportunity for the progressive benefits alluded to earlier, but also opens the door for new and innovative approaches or ways of addressing psychological or cognitive issues related to playing the sport.

Section 2 - Distraction Management - Tools and Tactics

Mental Energy

You need a minimum level of cognitive alertness or mental energy to be able to concentrate your attention, manage tension levels and maintain a good mental attitude. If we consider concentration to be the ability to focus our attention on the task at hand, while not being affected or influenced by internal or external distractions, then during the process our attention must alternate between assessing and choosing to attend to some stimuli, and ignoring other stimuli. The internal and external stimuli or distractions having an effect on our ability to concentrate can vary widely.

Some prime examples of internal distractions include the fear of poor performance, fear of making errors, dwelling on mistakes, and over thinking swing mechanics execution. Good examples of external distractions include poor weather conditions, competitor performance, aircraft flying overhead, and presence of family members in the gallery. Your on-course success ultimately depends on your ability to not be affected by these, and other similar internal and external distractions, which are the sole source for the woes being experienced by nearly every golfer. You must learn how to focus your attention in a manner that controls or avoids these distractions. You must always address situations in the present tense or the "here-and-now". Your performance success depends on your ability to concentrate on these situational cues, resulting in behaviours or reactions within your ability to deal with them. This means different distractions may require concentration entailing varying approaches to attention. When concentrating effectively, and managing mental energy levels, the golfer executes skills more proficiently, demonstrates greater ability to push or drive the body through pain and fatigue barriers, and is better able to deal with pressure situations.

A major concern common of all golfers is the waste of mental energy on worry, stress, fretting over distractions, and negative thinking. In competition, these not only seriously damage the enjoyment of the game, but drains valuable mental energy, adversely affecting performance. If you are a golfer that is consistently wrestling with these types of issues, this is like being the driver of a car for an extended period of time in adverse weather conditions, when there is heavy traffic. The need to be constantly attentive for the varying conditions being met causes the driver to be mentally fatigued. Similarly, the golfer constantly worrying about negative results or always being self-critical becomes susceptible to mental fatigue, resulting in the inability to be effectively reactive to the pressures or tension felt during play. Maintaining mental energy for when it is needed is important when dealing with numerous varying distractions. It is important to have the ability to be alert when necessary, but to emphasize relaxation or tranquility at other times. Knowing when to intervene for different distractions, and implementing different techniques for dealing with them, provides the golfer with the means of introducing new options for improvement. Other supplemental activities like a healthy diet, effectively resting between events, and ensuring adequate sleep are essential to being sharp mentally.

Tension Reduction Techniques

To effectively deal with distractions, first assess whether they are controllable. It is critical to distinguish between factors, which are controllable or uncontrollable. By this simple assessment you are in a position of identifying the distractions you will have to deal with, rather than ineffectual concentration focusing on uncontrollable variables.

In circumstances where play is adversely affected due to mental tension being high, this section examines some effective methods for reducing the physiological and psychological effects of stress or anxiety to levels conducive to more effective performance. The technique selected is dependent on the cause of the tension and the situation in which it occurs. The effectiveness of the method selected is dependent upon providing opportunity to become familiar with the process, and experimenting with the benefits. For example, if anxiety is based on the feeling of adrenaline in the body, then it may be best to relax the body and slow the flow of adrenaline. Relaxation techniques would be best in solving this issue.

It is important to experiment with the different techniques presented to gain experience in their use and to become familiar with tactics increasing your ability to resolve the issues being confronted.

Progressive Muscular Relaxation

Progressive Muscular Relaxation (PMR) is a purely physical technique for relaxing your body when muscles are tense. The idea behind PMR is that you tense up a group of muscles so that they are as tightly contracted as possible, and hold them in a state of extreme tension for a few seconds. Then relax the muscles to their previous state. Finally you consciously relax them again as much as you can. Although relaxation is the goal, tensing the muscle helps to initiate the exercise, and helps to gauge the initial level of tension in the muscle. You can apply PMR to any or all of the muscle groups in your body, depending on whether you want to relax just a single area or your whole body.

Experiment with PMR by forming a fist, and clenching your hand as tight as you can for a few seconds. Then relax your hand to its previous tension, and then consciously relax it again so that it is as loose as possible. You should feel deep relaxation in the muscles. PMR can be used in conjunction with breathing techniques and imagery (e.g. stress flowing out of the body) for maximum relaxation.

Breathing Control

Deep breathing is an effective method of achieving relaxation, which is a core component of everything from the 'take ten deep breaths' approach to calm someone down, right through to yoga relaxation and Zen meditation. It works well in conjunction with other relaxation techniques such as Progressive Muscular Relaxation, relaxation imagery and meditation to reduce stress and anxiety levels.

Imagery Relaxation Techniques

Imagery is an extremely powerful method of stress reduction when psychological factors are driving mental tension. The effectiveness of the technique is even further enhanced when combined with physical methods such as deep breathing. A common use of imagery in relaxation is to vividly imagine a calming and serene scene, place, or event that you remember as quiet, relaxing, peaceful, restful, beautiful and appealing. The place you create is a customized utopia for yourself personally. The more senses and reality you bring to the image the greater its value in achieving the effect being sought. Sounds of running water, rain hitting surfaces, chirping birds, the smell of fresh cut grass or fireplace, the taste of a superb wine, warmth of the sun, or the freshness of a slight breeze utilize numerous senses giving your utopia added realism, improving the results of the process. Create an imagined place completely free of stress and pressure, where relaxation or satisfying comfort is felt through all the senses. Use reference to this tranquil place as an effective way to combat times of excessive stress and anxiety. The more real the place created, the more effective the imagery will become combatting stress and anxiety, when using this technique.

Imagery as a relaxation technique can also include direct images or mental pictures of stress flowing out of the body; or that stress, distractions and everyday issues are being folded away and tossed in the garbage. Use of imagery is as flexible as the innovation you put into developing images meeting your specific needs. This use of imagery to drive relaxation is one of the main ways that Eastern mystics have achieved spectacular reductions in pulse rate.

Hypnosis and Autosuggestion

Normal hypnosis is not usually effective in sports, as it requires the presence of a hypnotist. Self-hypnosis, however, is just as easy, and has the additional benefit of the golfer being completely in control of inputs to the mind, when in a suggestible state.

Self-hypnosis is used to specifically program your unconscious with affirmations and suggestions that would otherwise have to run through critical thought processes in your mind. This programming can be used as an effective method to reduce stress and induce relaxation.

Self-hypnosis is not a magical state. It is merely a state of mind in which the golfer is:

- Extremely relaxed
- Paying close attention to the suggestions to be implanted
- Not being critical of the suggestions made, and accepting them at face value.

When first trying self-hypnosis, it is best to find a location where you can be undisturbed for a period of time. Sit or lie down, eliminating any distractions, and completely relax. You can experiment with music, lighting, or any other aspect of the situation to best achieve a completely comfortable and stress-free environment. This puts you in the best possible conditions for using the technique. As you get more practice using the method, you will find that you can use self-hypnosis almost anywhere.

The first step is to completely relax yourself, close your eyes, and imagine yourself in the ideal environment for being completely relaxed and in perfect comfort. A white beach against an aquamarine coloured ocean, a calm river valley, a mountain meadow, imagine yourself in your own ideal place where stress and anxiety are nonexistent. Let this place be where you can truly kickback and be totally content. As you enjoy the relaxation of the place you have created, begin feeling the waves of relaxation running down your body from your scalp downwards, washing away all the stress. Let the waves run in time with your breathing, first washing down over your head, then your neck, then your torso, then your arms, and finally your legs and feet. Feel the muscles in your body relaxing as the waves of relaxation wash over them.

Alternative methods can involve fixing your eyes on a spot on the wall, or riding down an elevator from the top of a tall building, slowly dropping down into relaxation and drowsiness. The method you choose to induce hypnosis is up to you. The examples cited are only suggested ways of bringing yourself into a self-hypnotic state. Experiment with the alternative ways to create the ideal state for introducing hypnotic suggestion.

The next step is to use suggestion to deepen the state. This can be accomplished by making descriptive suggestions to yourself like "Feel the sensation of becoming totally relaxed and comfortable in an utopian state." A suggestion like "With every breath I am becoming more relaxed and comfortable" can be used to trigger even deeper states of relaxation."

After becoming completely relaxed and totally focused on your own suggestions, a useful state of self-hypnosis is achieved. An additional step of great value is the introduction of a trigger word to immediately refer to, or associate with this relaxed state at times when relaxation is paramount in warding of higher degrees of mental stress. Self-hypnosis is similar to imagery relaxation with the addition of "suggestion making".

As indicated earlier, there is nothing magical about self-hypnosis, but if used effectively it can enhance confidence, remedy long-standing issues and deal with your games most costly shortcomings. The brain is a wondrous part of the human body capable of amazing things. Being able to let your logical side see the value in letting your brain envision reality, making hypnotic suggestions, rationalizing, and realizing the value of mind state related topics, opens doors to some aspects of improvement not previously at the disposal of most golfers.

Before you enter a hypnotic state it is useful to think about the suggestions that you want to apply in it. Suggestions can be simple affirmations that undo the damage done by negative thinking, or can be used to make psychological adjustments or reinforce confidence to help to achieve goals that you have set. After deciding on your suggestions, spend a little time determining appropriate words for each that are short, positive, and powerful. Repeat your carefully worded suggestions to yourself when you have reached a self-hypnotic state.

Effective use of suggestion can:

- Build confidence
- Reinforce goals by etching them into your mind
- Reduce stress
- Increase motivation and reenergize when you are feeling sluggish.
- Reduce uncertainty

Biofeedback

Biofeedback systems are tools to aid relaxation and assist in stress and anxiety management. Biofeedback systems use electronic sensors for measuring stress levels, which feed the results of this measurement back to the athlete, where they can experiment in real time with the lowering of stress. This feedback may take the form of ink lines on a graph plotter, or may be through the pitch of sound coming from a set of speakers or earphones. This feedback allows the golfer to experiment with stress management techniques, and actually see or hear them taking effect on the body. It also allows ways of using different relaxation techniques and immediately determining their effectiveness.

There are three main approaches to biofeedback:

- **Skin temperature indicators:** adrenaline forces blood from the body surface to the core of the body, in preparation for response to danger. As less warm blood is going to the surface, skin temperature drops. Changes in skin temperature are used to calibrate stress levels.
- **Skin electrical activity indicators:** when you are under stress more sweat is secreted. Skin that is moist conducts electricity more effectively than skin that is dry. These methods of biofeedback measure the amount of electricity conducted between electrodes on the skin. Changes in indicated current characteristics are used to calibrate stress levels.
- **Muscle electrical activity indicators:** these methods measure the electrical activity of muscles under the skin. This is useful in measuring the tension of these muscles. Changes in electrical activity are used to calibrate stress levels.

Biofeedback methods are useful ways of validating the value of any methodology of mental tension management by permitting different techniques to be evaluated for effectiveness. After all, biofeedback can add validation to somewhat nebulous practices such as imagery or rational thinking to determine their value in managing pressure levels. They convert vague feelings into hard, observable information, helping the golfer fine-tune the use of stress and anxiety management techniques.

Combating Negative Thinking

There are three useful tools or tactics to specifically combat negative thinking. Negative thoughts occur when you tear yourself down, criticize yourself for mistakes, question your abilities, expect failure, or feeling you will only botch it again. Confidence is the victim in these cases because of the questioning of your abilities. Just as making positive statements of yourself builds confidence and improves performance, negative feeling that are reinforced have a progressively crushing effect on confidence, often leading to thoughts of questioning your motives or lowering your aspirations. Negative thinking is the negative side of suggestion, which is not a place you wish to frequent if you hope to maintain confidence levels.

You want to have the feeling of suggesting to yourself exactly what you would like to do, and simply executing a reasonable facsimile of your intentions in as many situations as possible. There are methods of combating negative thinking that do aid in eliminating or masking these distractions so this can happen.

Thought Awareness

Thought awareness is the process of monitoring your thoughts for a period of time, and being consciously aware of the thoughts going through your head. There must be no attempt to suppress any thoughts, letting them pass through your consciousness while you observe them. Consciously note the negative thoughts and their nature as you continue experiencing your thought process. During the assessment, promote your regular demeanour on the course, and do not attempt to assess what it is that is being identified. The value of the information learned must wait until after the round is concluded to maintain an unimpeded stream of thoughts during play.

Noting the nature of your negative thoughts while you experience your 'stream of consciousness' will help lead to identifying the source of the most costly distraction issues. When performing this activity the first few times, be extra sensitive to grasping those fleeting negative thoughts because they tend to appear and disappear very quickly. Often, you may not even notice them. Examples of common negative thoughts are:

- Worries about performance
- A preoccupation with the symptoms of stress or anxiety
- Dwelling on consequences of poor performance
- Feelings of inadequacy

Thought awareness is the first step in the process of eliminating negative thoughts. You must be observant and alert to note the negative thoughts you have. You will learn a lot about yourself by periodically monitoring your thought process when playing.

Rational Thinking

Following identification of the sources of your negative thinking, make note of them and review them rationally. Determine the origin of the thoughts and whether they have any basis in reality. When you analyze unfounded negative thoughts, they disappear as soon as it is realized they are wrong and unjustified. Golfers often create negative thoughts that are not justified and without foundation. Rational thinking is a means of taking time to bring back into proper perspective the misguided thoughts and perceptions causing your negativity. The technique has additional value because the resolving of issues and concerns is golfer driven. The added benefit comes from the golfer being armed with the ability to overcome personal issues or problems brought on by negative thinking, which in the past went unchecked having devastating effects to confidence and scoring.

Positive Thinking and Affirmation

Just as negative thoughts can be harmful, using positive thinking to bring about positive changes is the most powerful means of countering negative thoughts and building confidence levels. Countering negative thoughts with repeated positive affirmations is a powerful means of maintaining confidence. Positive thinking is a tool that should be habitually and consistently used by all golfers to introduce positive affirmations to build confidence, and change negative behaviour patterns into positive ones. Golfers must base their affirmations on clear rational assessments of facts, using them to undo the damage negative thinking has had on confidence. A golfer's awareness there is little validity or reason for their negativity quickly extinguishes these concerns. The worth of this tool is determined by how convincing the golfer can be to rally confidence levels to where they should be. The positive affirmations derived in this process can be used in combination with self-hypnosis and rational thinking to create some valuable tools for improving confidence levels.

Examples of affirmations are:

- I can do this.
- I can achieve my goals.
- I am completely myself and people will like me for myself.
- I am completely in control of my life.
- I have the capabilities to perform
- I learn from my mistakes. They increase the basis of experience on which I can draw.
- I am a good valued person in my own right.
- I am prepared and ready

An interesting point is that the best timing for demonstrating the highest confidence level for good shot execution is just before and during shot execution. This means it is critical to stringently follow routines preparing for every shot, because their implementation garners an improvement in the frequency of better shot results. The continual use of a routine fosters improved consistency, reinforced through repeatability, and having an immediate positive impact on the overall success rate of shots.

Positive thinking has value when used wisely. It can provide immediate confidence gains for the golfer viewing their capabilities negatively, or when rationally deciding on the targets you have realistically set for yourself, then using positive thinking to reinforce these attainable outcomes.

DEMOTIVATION

Demotivation occurs when a person who has previously been committed to a sport, loses interest and the zeal to participate. Typically it will occur in industrious hard working, and highly driven people, who become emotionally, psychologically or physically exhausted. Causes of demotivation and apathy can include:

- Being under a state of stress or anxiety for an extended period of time such as could be the case if you drive yourself too hard to excel.
- Experiencing an extended period of poor play
- Having a domineering coach that does not recognize your stress and continues to push for improvement.
- Difficulty in minimizing your commitments as the result of an inability to say "no" and minimize outside responsibilities.
- Trying to achieve too much to the point of starting to have a disdain for the game you love.

A key to eliminating negativity is keeping practices fun and challenging, to the point of being competitive. It is very easy to have practice sessions, which are enjoyable and entertaining, generating an excitement to participate. If a level of training is adopted having a great deal of rigour and commitment, then it is essential to introduce fun and enjoyable activities, serving as a reprieve from a grueling schedule, and offering rewards for the commitment and effort you have demonstrated. Training sessions should have fun, challenging and enjoyable activities incorporated to create practice time that is exciting to participate in. Anticipating practice as an enjoyable time involving new and interesting activities certainly stalls disinterest in its tracks.

If you feel like a victim, feeling apathetic, or things are getting a little out of control, there are numerous ways to rebuild your love for the game. If you feel and wish to reset your bearings, here are a few things that can help avoid a meltdown, and provide a refocus. By exploring the following, feelings of defeat could be corrected.

- Ensure adequate sleep daily
- Investigate areas other than golf that may be bringing tension into your life.
- Implement stress management techniques and relaxation methods
- Reexamine your Goal Setting Plan to reevaluate the appropriateness of the targets set and put a plan in place that is reflective of all your actual and intended commitments
- Congenially be less accessible to outside demands and reduce overall commitments.
- Seeking assistance in areas where assistance is readily available can reduce stresses contributing to demotivation. Do not be afraid to get the assistance of others.
- Gain the support of significant people in your life. The support of people aware of your efforts can provide inspiration and a desire to excel.
- Maintain a healthy lifestyle. Ensuring a consistent healthy diet, coupled with appropriate levels of aerobic and anaerobic exercise, and provisions for the emotional and spiritual aspects of well-being
- Eliminate self-criticism. The game of golf creates enough anguish without having to be concerned with issues created as a result of your own actions and behaviour. More importantly, the immediacy or necessity for purging self-criticism from your demeanour is to reduce the progressive negative impact it has.
- Adopt a system of rewards for your efforts that give pleasures for your accomplishments and efforts.

BURNOUT

Burnout is often characterized by a reduction in motivation, and is often associated with trying to do too much. The symptoms can become so strong as to even have the golfer considering exiting from the sport. Golfers believing they are able to devote a substantial amount of time to improvement must be wary of the slow progression of burnout. It usually comes on slowly making it hard to detect. Being aware of some of the early symptoms of burnout will help in ensuring it never occurs. These symptoms include:

- Feeling of a lack of control over commitments.
- Felling of being excessively tired and lethargic.
- Increased negativity.
- The loss of a sense of direction or purpose to normal interests and concerns.
- Isolation from outside sources like family, friends and associates
- Strengthening of the belief you have to make more commitments to see improvement

CHAPTER 12

Routine

"I think we have opportunities all around us – sometimes we just don't recognize them."
Lou Holtz

Section 1 - Preliminary Considerations

Routine is an easily implemented strategy supporting all three premises of the Positive Competitive Mindset Model. The Knowledge Application premise is supported through the processes employed ensuring shot decisions are made following the consideration of pertinent variables and information for all shots taken. The Building Positive Influences element of the model is supported through a Pre-Shot Assessment Routine providing confidence all considerations have been made supporting a well founded shot-making decision. It is in the area of Eliminating Negative Influences where implementation of activities associated with Routine are of special value. The positive outcomes and improvements to performance as the result of the concepts presented in this chapter will arm the golfer with one of the most powerful tools at their disposal to eliminate distractions and improve performance. The progressive benefit of this strategy being consistently applied or used comes from the supplemental confidence gained as a result of the golfer knowing they are able to deal with concerns, which previously went unchecked.

Golfers will enjoy the benefits of activities and strategies, where routine is introduced as a systematic procedure or process, supporting conditions for more consistent play. Routine brings with it some inherently advantageous mechanisms and characteristics supporting the development of a golfer's mind state, resulting in efficiencies and enhanced effectiveness in shot making. The appropriate implementation of routine will also be a powerful means of extinguishing negative distractions emerging just before and during shot execution, but can also serve a number of other valuable functions enhancing performance. In this unit, you are introduced to a number of ways of utilizing the concept of routine to greatly improve your performance, through the elimination of negative influences, and efficiency it brings to other supporting activities and processes. Instilling aspects of routine into different facets of your game is a powerful and under-utilized way of getting over many long-standing issues, while providing conditions for experiencing more positive shot outcomes. Routine and how well you engrain it into your everyday golf game will have a dramatic impact on your consistency of play, rate of improvement, on-course performance, peace of mind, and appreciation for the game of golf.

Considering the many actions a golfer could take to improve their games, instilling routine is one of the most efficient means of showing immediate performance gains and improved consistency in shot making. Considering the minimal effort required to take advantage of the huge benefits gained through diligent utilization of routine makes its implementation an essential activity at the outset of any improvement plan. Not establishing a well-engrained pre-shot assessment and an execution routine shortchanges golfers of the most effective and simple means of improving their golf game. If golfers were aware of the many benefits awarded by taking the time to implement routine into a number of on-course activities, there would be far more golfers diligently utilizing it as a part of their game.

This unit introduces golfers to the concept of "routine" as being extended into a number of aspects of the game, and serves a highlighted role in support of building a healthy Positive Competitive Mindset. Of all the strategies included in the Positive Competitive Mindset Model, the implementation of routine into aspects of the game has profound effects on a player's consistency of play and performance. Aspects of routine include the golfer physically providing short periods of time for shot assessment and shot execution, which is faithfully carried out in the same manner for every shot taken. Due to the obvious differences in assessment and execution requirements for a putt and a regular golf shot, two different procedures are required, both including an assessment segment and an execution segment.

Aspects of routine are supported and integrated with other strategies for the strong positive influences this brings to the resiliency and effectiveness of the mental demeanour to be established. There are huge dividends paid to the golfer that effectively incorporates routine into their game. The golfer implementing aspects of routine introduces the creation of a familiar and comfortable playing environment, with resiliency and effectiveness of a mindset based on the strengthening of the interrelationships and linkages of the routines and strategies utilized. Considering the relative minimal effort required for a golfer to incorporate routine into their game, and the value of its benefits should place this strategy at the top of every golfers improvement plan.

Section 2 - What's Trying To Be Achieved

When most golfers think of routine, they immediately associate the term with shot preparation. Routine is generally viewed in the narrow context of the shot execution routine, which is only a single aspect of the principles to be presented in this unit. With routine in mind, think of all the golfers you have ever played with and estimate the percentage that diligently follow a regularly repeated shot execution routine. From my own research, it is less than 15% of golfers faithfully using a planned repeatable routine, prior to every shot. Granted there are golfers that perform a routine before most shots, but the routines vary, depending on the situation, having limited elements of similarity or repeatability. There are an extremely small group of golfers that follow a repeated procedural routine, performed identically every time a shot is made. This low percentage is surprising, considering the benefits extended through effective implementation of routine into on-course demeanour, and its effect on consistency of performance. It is not surprising it's the better players in the world that diligently follow a routine. Learning how to achieve a mind state setting up the ideal conditions for the successful execution of a shot is well within the capability of any golfer. Learn how simple engagement in routine greatly aids in making confident shot decisions, and improves consistency in completing successful shots.

Most golfers consider routine as a casual sequence of actions regularly followed before a shot, but are unaware of the specific reasons why it is employed, or more specifically, how it can be effective in warding off negative influences or distractions during shot execution. Through the utilization of regular shot and putt routines, the golfer immediately introduces actions directed at improved shot success and consistency, but more importantly, golfers must become aware of the characteristics of what it is they are trying to achieve during shot execution. If golfers are aware of specific strategies for developing a mind state free of outside influences, there will be progressively larger steps in improvement simply based on golfers eliminating costly performance issues and improved confidence.

Implementing a number of routines has its greatest affect on golfer development by providing a tool that will improve consistency of superior performance. This is the primary reason for the assertion that routine implementation is the single most influential strategy of the Positive Competitive Mindset Model enhancing overall performance. Golfers will be introduced to a methodology greatly reducing or eliminating outside distractions before and during shot execution.

If golfers are aware of the many benefits of routine, then why are there such a low percentage of them embracing its usage? Perhaps providing an understanding of what can be achieved through routine, and being aware of its benefits, will result in greater motivation to take advantages of its implementation and use. Golfers are aware the top players in the world have firmly established routines that are consistently used, but despite this, most golfers still haven't embraced its use as being of great enough value to warrant its implementation. Golfers may not be embracing the concept of routine, and its relationship to their day-to-day performance, because the topic has never been presented in a manner that generated an understanding of what can be achieved through a diligently followed routine.

It was primarily through the principles of routine implementation that I was able to achieve a scratch handicap and enjoy a period of playing sub-par golf on a consistent basis. Any golfer aspiring to excel, or see dramatic improvement, or more specifically aspiring to be mentally tougher, has no choice but to fully implement aspects of routine into their game. Routine implementation and its diligent use may be the simplest and most effective way of seeing improvements in performance and improved consistency of play. Golfers only have to diligently implement routine to soon realize the many benefits it brings to their games. Golfers will be capable of achieving a state of mind free of negative distractions during shot execution, resulting in greater frequency of better quality shots.

Routine implementation provides the benefits of bringing normalcy to every shot. On the days when you have played your best golf, everything just seemed to fall into place, void of the disruptions causing issues and problems affecting performance. Your play seemed completely natural without anything occurring out of the ordinary. There were no major disruptions or incidents breaking the round's continuity. Everything just happened naturally and uneventfully, with you simply witnessing things going well. The result is an extremely gratifying round of golf.

I had the privilege of caddying for my son, when qualifying for his card, and clearly remember him stating " Dad, it's really strange, but it seems like I am just playing another regular round of golf today, not qualifying for my card." It was on the eighteenth tee, just before his final tee shot, my son uttered these words, solidifying my resolve to bring this book to completion, It is a unique feeling to experience a record or rewarding performance associated to being a regular round of play that seemed uneventful without any disruptions or distractions detracting from what was to occur. Similarly, I had felt the same feelings and had the same impressions as my son when I was playing extremely well. My son's feelings and thoughts only strengthened my hope and wish to bring this publication to fruition, by sharing sound practices promoting a playing environment, that is familiar, consistent, comfortable, simple, uneventful, tranquil, inviting, and purposeful.

The mindset is characterized as steady and unchanging, or regular and ordinary, without any mental interference causing negative influences or distractions to diminish confidence. On the days when playing well, your shots are enthusiastically confronted and confidently executed in an eager and purposeful manner. Routine brings with it more consistent play at a higher level of performance, simply based on the improved likelihood of successfully executing every shot. The details and intricacies of routine development and implementation will be discussed in greater detail later, however, awareness of the huge benefits it affords should cause a commitment to instilling a number of aspects of routine into your game. Utilization of routine and its resulting benefits inherently supports a mindset conducive to superior and more consistent play, due to the enhanced confidence it brings, and the comfortable familiarity of the playing environment created for the golfer.

A golfer's ability to maintain normalcy while under the pressure of competition is an absolute necessity for optimum performance. Effective management of distractions enables the golfer to selectively use the appropriate information and discard the irrelevant junk. Golfers may not always be able to control distractions, but to be successful; they must learn to take control of their performances, by reducing unnecessary distractions and appropriately responding to important cues. Even under the most adverse conditions, a mentally prepared golfer can achieve amazing results. Golfers lacking this mental toughness crumble under pressure, falling victim to disastrous results. The ability to ward off both internal and external distractions and keep your focus on the task at hand is representative of your ability to concentrate or focus on the execution of a task to meet an objective or outcome you wish or hope to achieve.

When the average golfer thinks of the performance of top professionals, they are amazed with their ability to perform precise and accurate shots, despite the pressure they perform under. What is it that permits these superior players to perform at such a high level, despite the pressure and distractions? A close examination of "routine" as a generalized concept will provide an understanding of the reasons for the strong positive impact its implementation will have on your improvement and performance, and arm you with a powerful tool having a tremendous positive affect on mind state. You will understand the mechanism for how the professionals on tour are able to accomplish great feats, while under seemingly intense pressure.

The professional player on tour earns a living playing golf, which inherently immerses them in the professional game and the tour lifestyle, providing development time and experience, which becomes standard, regular, typical, and having a comforting familiarity. In short, playing in tournaments, meeting qualifications requirements, being on the leader board and having top ten finishes, start to become typical or familiar occurrences in their lives, and the lives of their friends and acquaintances. Professional players become experienced and comfortably familiar with the day-to-day activities associated with being on tour. The familiarity with their typical daily activities greatly improves their comfort level for performing on tour, all the while improving confidence to perform well. The experiences of these professionals accumulate over time, gradually increasing their comfort levels to perform well in more different and demanding situations. As comfort levels increase, so to does confidence, leading to superior performance.

What is important to realize and use in your own game is instilling any tactics creating a perception or impression of familiarity, normalcy or consistency during practice and play. The ability to enhance or support the feeling of a regular, typical or common day at the golf course will provide the advantages of eliminating or reducing negative influences and distractions, augmenting consistency, resulting in better play and enhanced performance. Routine must be given a prominent position in the strategies and activities devoted to minimizing negative influences, but the importance it serves is also acting as a binder or glue that strengthens all the other foundational premises of the Positive Competitive Mindset. Be cognizant that routine's emphasis in this book has aspects directed at specifically building positive influences for the purpose of precipitating improved confidence. The advantages of incorporating the notion of "routine" into a number of activities and strategies is to improve their efficiency, simplify supporting tasks, and ensure consistency in their application and use. In addition, routine brings with it the reliability of repeatability and adaptability, which through the use of mnemonic tools creates efficiencies in performing tasks like shot and putt assessment.

If golfers expand the term "routine" to be inclusive of actions promoting the notion of normalcy, comfort, and complete familiarity into their approach to the game, the benefits will be far-reaching and dramatic. The ability to expand the connotation of routine to mean anything typical, common, or regular into many aspects of your on-course demeanour will vastly improve your preparedness for controlling pressure and negating damaging distractions. Routine becomes a fully integrated strategy through its application to other strategies falling under each component of the Positive Competitive Mindset. In this chapter you will be introduced to some very powerful applications of routine, not only the traditional pre-shot routine, but included in other activities that will change the way you approach the game. Lets examine routine in much closer detail.

Section 3 - Principles and Primary Activities

Routines have been utilized for a number of strategies identified under each of the foundational premises of the Positive Competitive Mindset. In this section, application of routine will be addressed by providing a means of understanding what is to be achieved through the different tactics used and sharing ways the golfer can advantageously incorporate routine into many aspects of their golf game. We will first examine the area of the game most often associate with routine, the execution of a shot. However, you will be introduced to a methodology for shot execution that will help to assure getting the greatest benefit when applied to your own shot making. Due to the approach taken, and to gain the greatest advantage of using routine when associated with shot execution, there are four distinct routines to be explored, two associated with shot assessment, and the other two addressing shot execution.

The routines include:

- Shot Assessment Routine – (mnemonic)
- Shot Execution Routine – (choreographed)
- Putt Assessment Routine – (mnemonic)
- Putt Execution Routine – (choreographed)

Preparation for any shot or putt is composed of two routines, one addressing assessment and the other execution. Assessment and Execution routines have completely different objectives regarding the overall preparation for any shot. These are the routines most golfers associate with when the discussion of routine arises.

Preparation for the execution of any shot is divided into two activities - first, consistently and effectively assess in a repeatable manner the appropriate shot to execute and committing to an expected outcome, and second, the establishment of a detailed choreographed physical routine for execution of a shot or putt. This is repeatedly duplicated every time a stroke is executed. The assessment routines presented are mnemonic in nature, due to the memory tools that are utilized to memorize a list of factors that must be considered for a shot or putt.

The execution routines specifically outline the chronology of repeatable choreographed actions carried out for the execution of every shot. The choreographed routines are religiously used once a decision and commitment to a shot or putt has been made during the Assessment Routine. In short, every shot requires two separate routines – an assessment, which is mnemonic in nature, and a choreographed routine, which is physically identical every time.

The importance of making these routines an identical recurrence every time they are performed cannot be overemphasized. The routines you implement into your game must have the characteristics of being the same all the time, and used every time you strike the ball. These shot-preparation routines serve as cues to focus your shot execution attention in the appropriate manner, at precisely the right time, whereby the actual execution of the shot becomes an inclusive component of the habitual and mundane shot execution routine, carried out for every shot you execute. The process of religiously going through a choreographed routine so deeply engrains the procedure of the entire process it becomes automatic, with the actual execution of the shot simply a part of an encompassing process where the mind is idle when the shot is executed. Religiously following your assessment routines and execution routines begins to create a comfortably familiar place for the golfer, which is insulated from distractive and negative thought, as the result of the robotic and repetitive nature of the process.

You will become consistent in performing the same familiar and comfortable steps every time you execute a shot or a putt. There may be slight alterations to setup, but the process or procedure remains the same for all putts or shots to be made. The monotonous tedium or boredom of your routine is the catalyst to creating a shot execution environment without mental interference, permitting the shot to be executed as previewed at the conclusion of a Shot Assessment Routine. Performing the shot execution routine takes the golfer to a comfortably familiar environment. What is more important, it is the routines familiarity and the mundane nature of the procedure causing the mind to become preoccupied with the monotony of the habitual process, causing internal or externally created distractions to be masked or blocked by the routine itself.

The longer a routine has been instilled, the greater the positive effects offered during shot execution. Another benefit of the familiarity and repetitive nature of the shot execution process is the positive effect this has on the rhythm or tempo of your shots. An area that many golfers have difficulty getting a feel for on a consistent basis is rhythm or tempo in their swing, which greatly improves when aspects of routine are implemented in an effective manner. These routines will serve to keep you relaxed during shot execution, by creating a comfortable familiarity for the procedures engrained, as a result of their repeated execution over time.

In addition, the constant utilization of routine will create recognizable feeling and sensations that can be associated with good and poor execution of shots. At the conclusion of a shot there is great benefit in evaluating the resultant shot in comparison to feelings felt during execution. Seeking to repeat sensations and feelings from positive shots permits the golfer some controlling presence at the moment of shot execution, while avoiding the conjuring of negative thoughts. The greatest benefit of adopting these routines is comfort in a commitment to perform a specific shot at hand, plus having the ability to thwart or repelling distractions that could arise during the shot. The routine serves as a mask to possible negative distractions because these negative influences are not normally a component of your regular routine, resulting in the mind simply carrying out an habitual process and eliminating or avoiding distractions from becoming conscious during shot execution. These routines will also keep you in the present for every shot, while eliminating possible oversights through the repetitive checklist nature of the assessment process.

Golfers will find the use of these procedural routines to be effective tools improving their ability to focus on the task at hand, which is totally familiar, and comfortable in nature. Comfort and confidence in taking a shot comes from the shot execution routine's familiarity, plus the added confidence of an Assessment Routine providing the best chances of arriving at the results hoped to be achieved. Consistency in shot making is the result of the habitual process that precedes every swing. Shot execution being void of any conscious thought is the result of the repetitive nature of the routine being "so boringly familiar"; it is simply executed in the same manner without any thought.

A powerfully effective way of increasing your focus and concentration, raising confidence, and controlling distractions is through the use of shot execution routines. Routines are commonplace among successful athletes and serve the purpose of attaining conditions for enhance performance, improvement, and consistency. Accomplished athletes use routines consistently, regardless of whether things are going well or not. Shot execution routines help golfers block out irrelevant internal and external distractions by providing them with a different focus, other than the negative thoughts that often lead to negative consequences. Ultimately, routines assist in avoiding anxiety by providing a sense of familiarity and comfort with shot execution, producing a mind state supportive of superior performance.

Assessment Routines (mnemonic)

For the assessment of any stroke, whether a putt or an iron shot, the number of variables to be considered in both instances is significant enough to warrant the creation of a mnemonic routine that aids in arriving at a shot commitment in either case. Routine is an excellent tool to use when an often used and repeated series of steps or a checklist of activities must be accurately recalled. Mnemonic routines are extremely valuable where an extensive list of factors must repeatedly be considered. As a result, two mnemonic routines will be introduced to provide the means of insuring all necessary factors or variables are consistently evaluated prior the execution of a putt or a shot. A Shot Assessment Routine and Putt Assessment Routine are presented, which may be modified or changed, permitting the golfer to supplement or personalized a routine meeting their requirements. A formal Shot Assessment Routine is presented for general shot execution and does not claim to be exhaustive, but will provide a sound start to implementing an effective mnemonic routine for regular shot assessment. Feel free to include any other factors in your own assessment routines to customize them to your needs.

Mnemonic Routines provide the advantage of consistently assessing the major factors or variables having a bearing on the outcome of a shot or a putt. After all, consider the number of shots that are unsuccessful because a factor affecting a shot's outcome is overlooked. In the case of assessment routines, this begs for a methodology of simplicity for easy recall and efficiency of use. The easy recall of a list of variables to consider during the assessment process is a prime example of where routine can be used to ensure consideration of all factors affecting a shot or a putt are assessed before committing to a shot-making decision. Assessment routines provide a reliable and consistent way of never overlooking a shot or putt variable that could have substantial affect a shot's successful result.

In addition, Assessment Routines positively affect the confidence level of golfers. Before putt or shot execution, preparation provides the golfer with the assurance everything that could possibly affect a shot has been considered, raising the golfers confidence in the likelihood the shot will be successful. Additionally, the routine helps to extinguish the emergence of negative influences because of a preoccupation with a positive mental activity, which isolates a golfer's thought processes, helping to prevent negative distractions from consciously surfacing. This has a huge impact on the success rate of shots taken.

How often have golfers witnessed the execution of a shot or putt, only to be upset that they failed to allow for a variable, resulting in an unsatisfactory outcome? Not accounting for an elevation difference, the firmness of greens, the grain of the green, wind direction and speed, or other variables affecting regular shots and putts, invariably results in a shot falling short of expectations. There are numerous variables the golfer has to consider before every shot, but without a mechanism to insure all factors have been taken into account, opens the door to omissions causing mistakes or errors, leading to additional strokes.

All golfers experience these disheartening confidence-robbing shots, resulting from failing to consider some factor affecting a shot, or a putt. Golfers are constantly adding strokes to the scorecard, where a variable or factor is overlooked, resulting in shots never having a chance of being successful. Instilling a consistent routine for shot assessment leads to wise shot making decisions, supporting the ensuing commitment necessary to perform a shot successfully. A golfer is going to be more committed to a shot-making decision knowing all possible factors or variables have been considered. There is a dramatic positive effect on confidence level, when all shot variables have been given consideration, culminating in the best possible chance of a predicted result.

In summary, Putt and Shot Assessment Routines beg for a methodology of simplicity, flexibility and clarity to ensure the benefit of their consistent and calming effects. A routine's calming effect and ability to mask or eliminate distractions comes from its repetition, familiarity, and tedium, and why diligently following them is critical. Assessment Routines easily allow the golfer to efficiently carry out extensive checklist type activities repeatedly, without forgetting or missing any factors or variables to be considered prior to a shot or a putt. Moreover, assessment routines provide the golfer with added confidence a shot to be executed has the greatest chance of being successful.

Section 4 - The Shot Assessment Routine

Let's explore the Shot Assessment Routine by first examining a list of potential variables to be considered for any given shot. The list provided certainly is not exhaustive, but will provide an excellent starting point to add, delete, or modify factors considered to make a sound and valid shot making decision. The variables to be considered are classified under the following headings:

- Club Selection Factors
- Shot Type Factors
- Strategy Factors

SHOT ASSESSMENT ROUTINE – Factors Considered

Club Selection Factors

Shot Distance – D

The distance from ball to the targeted area must be accurately determined because this is the primary factor determining club selection. Pocket caddies, GPS devices, rangefinders, or on-course yardage markers can be used to accurately determine these distances. The electronic devices provide vital information like yardages to the front, center and back of the green, bunkers, water hazards, topographical features, typical yardage locations, and features like fairway, rough and trees or forest. With todays GPS devices it is possible to have this information at your fingertips. Some GPS devices are capable of having additional information programmed into memory, making it possible to input yardages for any location you wish. The value of the information provided by a GPS device more than warrants their cost. With GPS applications available for digital devices like smart phones providing overhead fly-by video clips, it is only a guess as to the types of information that will be available to the average golfer in the future. As presented earlier, Benchmarking is an activity golfers must completed to identify ball striking capabilities and tendencies, to effectively utilize the Course Management strategies presented in the next chapter.

When establishing a Course Management Plan access to personal capabilities and inclinations is essential to strategically assess options, effectively manage risk and reward, resulting in the wisest shot making decisions. Following Benchmarking, utilization of an on-course assessment tool or GPS device makes it very easy to maintain information for the distances of all shots taken during play. This will be explored later in the On-Course Assessment strategy.

Wind – W

Determination of wind velocity and its direction is essential to predict the effect of wind on the flight of the ball. The direction of the wind may influence the shape of the shot as a means of reducing risk or increasing the likelihood of reward. To accurately assess wind speed and direction, it is best to get this information from the reaction of branches and leaves on the top of nearby trees. Many trees give off a light cotton type material that is carried with the wind and provides an excellent idea of the winds direction and speed. Having the ability to gather information from indicators at greater height in close proximity to the shot location is the best indicator of the direction of the wind in the vicinity. Simply throwing some grass into the air is unreliable, because air movement in the shielded ground level portions of a hole is often influenced by nearby trees and landforms. Since wind has such a strong influence on a golf ball's flight, it is always advantageous to know the speed and direction of the wind at all times. Inaccurately determining wind speed and direction will likely result in a negative result adding strokes to the scorecard.

For shots with or against the wind, the ball will travel 10 yards further or less for every 10 mph increment in wind speed. This equates to compensating by approximately 1 club for every 10 mph of wind speed. This is of course the case where a golfer has approximately 10 yards difference in carry distance for each club increment. This is a general guide, but benchmarking will clarify your mean or median shot distance for every club.

For crosswind shots, greater effects will be evident for high shots as opposed to low shots. High shots are more greatly influenced due to the extended time the ball is exposed to the wind's influence. In the case of crosswind shots, the ball is influenced by 10 - 15 feet for every 10 mph increment in wind speed. The variance of 10 – 15 feet is dependent on the height of a shot.

Elevation Change – E

Determining the difference in elevation of a shot's execution location and the landing area is required to compensate for how shot distance is affected by elevation change. Every 10 feet in elevation change results in approximately 10 yards difference in a shot's carry distance.

For example, hitting into a green with a 10-foot higher elevation would require a club having an additional carry distance of 10 yards more than the distance to the hole. Hitting a short iron into a par 3 with a tee 30 feet above the green's surface would result in using a club having a mean carry distance 30 yards shorter than the distance normally required for the shot. Elevation differences are not immediately apparent, so always checking this variable can make the difference between a superb shot, or one landing just short or long of the mark.

Be aware that the elevation of the course you are playing has a substantial influence on the carry distance of shots. This is due to variations in air density at different elevations. At higher elevations where the density of the air is less, there is less drag on the ball as it passes through the air, permitting it to travel a greater distance.

Below are two basic guidelines that can be applied when making shot making decisions related to elevation compensations.

For courses 3000 – 4500 feet above sea level subtract 15% off the yardage to be hit then choose the appropriate club to use and you will hit the ball the intended yardage.

Example: Playing a 168-yard shot on a course with an elevation of 3500 feet above sea level would result in selecting a club that would be used for a shot

168 - (168 x 0.15) = 168 – 25.2 = 143 yards

For courses greater than 4500 feet above sea level, subtract 20% off the yardage to be hit, and then choose the appropriate club to use and you will hit the ball this yardage.

Example: Playing a 215-yard shot into a par 3 on a course with an elevation of 5200 feet above sea level would result in selecting a club that would be used for a shot

215 - (215 x 0.20) = 215 – 43 = 172 yards

Temperature – T

The air's ambient temperature has a large influence on the distance a ball will carry. It is not uncommon for as much as 30 yards of distance to be lost due to cool temperatures. The resiliency of the ball is greatly affected by temperature. In addition, in cooler temperatures there is an increase in density of the air, also reducing the distance the ball travels. Every 10 degree Fahrenheit drop in temperature will cause a 5-yard reduction in the distance the ball will travel. This equates to approximately a half club difference for every change of 10 degrees.

To provide a better perspective on the impact this has on a shot, consider two drives hit by the same individual almost identically. One drive hit at 40 degree Fahrenheit and the other at 100 degree Fahrenheit. The individual usually hits his or her drive approximately 270 yards on their home course on a 70 degree Fahrenheit day. Based on this information it is quite easy to determine there would be approximately in slight excess of 30 yards difference between the two shots.

When benchmarking the distance the ball travels for different clubs, it is wise to note the temperature to permit calculating any compensation for different temperatures. If you have an accurate knowledge of the distance you hit your clubs when playing at 70F, then you know club selection will change by a full club length for a change of 20 degrees. This would mean shots would travel one club further at 90F, and one club less at 50F, as compared to a shot taken at 70F.

Firmness of Greens – G

The firmness of the greens will have a strong influence on where the golfer chooses to land an approach shot. Extremely soft greens, for example due to recent a rainfall, results in shots traveling very little after the ball strikes the green. On the contrary, a ball hitting a firm green will bounce higher and roll a much greater distance. During the warm-up for a round and while playing the first few holes, the golfer should assess how the ball is reacting to the green and the speed of the green to permit compensations for this variable later in the round. The ability to quickly assess the reaction of greens to shots early in a round certainly provides the information needed to enhance the ability to get the ball close to the hole on subsequent approach shots. After two to three holes you should have a good idea of the firmness and speed of the greens to better assess the best landing location for approach shots, providing the best available opportunity for one-putt greens and avoiding three-putts.

Approach Into The Green – A

The area 40 - 50 feet in front on the green is often clear of obstacles, providing the option of landing a shot short and running the ball onto the green. This could be an excellent option when there is little green to work with, or when greens are not holding shots due to being extremely firm or dry. When the approach into the green is free from obstructions or hazards a whole new set of options opens up regarding where the ball could be landed for a particular shot. Landing short off the green could be the best option to get the ball close to the hole. Always look at different shot types for delivering the ball to the hole, because this opens up all the options to assess the risks and advantages of each, resulting in your best shot making decision.

Shot Type Factors

Lie – L

Lie refers to the immediate environment where the ball rests. (hardpan, fluffy, 1st cut rough, heavy rough, sand, fairway, fringe, green) The lie of the ball affects club selection, because of varying spin affecting the ball's flight, and the varying reactions of shots when hitting the green or fairway.

The lie of the ball is a major consideration when executing a shot. Any situation where you could possibly get grass or other material between the club and the ball, there is going to be the effect of ball spin reduction. This has substantial effect on the flight of the ball and the amount of spin imparted to get the ball to stop at the target. Shots where there are spin reductions due to imperfect contact of the ball with the club can result in what is termed a "flyer". Since the ball has a reduced rate of spin, it tends to have a more boring and flatter flight. Also, the ball hits the green on a flatter angle with less backspin, bouncing further and releasing for an extended roll, rather than stopping quickly.

Being aware of proven tactics aimed at improved scoring better prepares the golfer to make wise shot making decisions. Learning the effect of different types of lies and how this affects ball flight, and the ball's varying reaction to the green, permits better visualization of intended shots, and greater chance of shot success.

Hardpan

Clean contact with the ball is essential for shots off hardpan lies. Using a less lofted club and a slightly shortened swing can greatly aid in assuring solid contact with the ball is made. One of the most dangerous concerns with hitting off a hardpan lie is the possibility of the club contacting the ground before the ball, being deflected upward, and contacting the ball near or above the horizontal equator of the ball, resulting in a skulled or topped shot. A less lofted club has a flatter horizontal approach to the ball lessening the chance of a deflection off the ground before contact with the ball. As a rule, a less lofted club will improve the chances of a successful shot off a hardpan lie. If a greater lofted club is chosen, then the golfer must take great care to deliver the clubface to the ball with the leading edge of the club reaching the ball in the desired manner. The steeper approach of a more lofted club increases the risk of the shot being unsuccessful. The decision of using a high-risk club will often be based on how well you are playing, and the reward versus risk felt at the time of assessment.

Rough

Any shot initiated from the rough will usually result in some grass between the clubface and the ball at impact, resulting in less spin being imparted to the ball. The lack of backspin will cause this shot to bounce higher off the green and roll further. It is always an option to land a shot from the rough short and let it bounce and roll up to the hole. Factors like the size of the green and the placement of the pin will have a bearing on where a shot taken from the rough should be landed.

Shot Shape - SS

Different types of shots will prove to be advantageous in different situations. For example, shots having a slight fade, draw or having a high or low trajectory can greatly enhance the likelihood of a positive shot result. Depending on the circumstances being confronted, the golfer should consider these shot alternatives to enhance shot results. Considerations for different shot shapes should be made to provide the greatest likelihood of a successful shot, by choosing the highest percentage shot, providing the best reward to risk ratio.

Let's consider an example where shot shape could be advantageous to the golfer, and why there may be a decision to fade a shot into the green. Consider an approach into a green with a right to left and front to back slope in the area around the pin. With the slope of the green away from the approach shot there will be a tendency for the ball to run a little extra after landing. In addition, a shot coming from the golfers left to right will land more into the face of the slope to the left, helping to settle the ball quickly. Finally, a ball with a fade spin tends to settle quicker than a shot with draw spin because a fade has a slight backward spin and a draw has a slight forward spin. In this particular case, executing a shot with fade would be an excellent shot choice to improve the ability to get the ball closer to the hole.

Low Trajectory

There will be obvious times when a low trajectory shot is required to negotiate low branches, but there may be time a low flying shot is preferred. Choosing to hit a shot with a less lofted club to hit a flatter shaped shot or hitting knock down shots with irons and wedges for a lower trajectory is generally desired for shots into the wind, by reducing the winds ballooning effect on the ball, and avoiding many of the distance and accuracy issues caused by the wind. Hitting a low trajectory shot into the wind provides greater control, because the wind does not have as great an influence on the ball, due to the reduced time in the air, and its more piercing trajectory. Lower trajectory shots into the wind travel greater distances than higher trajectory shots. This is another example of shot shape considerations providing options for more successful shot execution.

Fade

A shot with a slight fade for a right-handed golfer will tend to land softly on the green and have a tendency to fly higher than a ball hit straight or with a draw. Being aware of this gives the golfer additional shot options, which improve opportunities for getting the ball closer to the hole.

Draw

A shot with a slight draw generally has a lower ball flight than a fade, tending to want to kick ahead and roll, due to its slightly forward spin. When greens become exceedingly firm, there could be difficulty in having a ball with draw spin staying on the green. On the other hand, an approach into a green having a left-to-right slope may best be tackled with a shot having a right-to-left draw spin, taking advantage of the shot settling quickly, as a result of the landing into the slope of the green.

High Trajectory

There will also be times when an obvious high trajectory shot is required to go over trees, but there may be times when you require this type of shot when wanting the ball to travel very little after hitting the green. High trajectory shots tend to have more backspin than shots with a lower flight, plus the slightly more vertical drop of these shots tends to keep them in closer proximity to their landing area.

Stance Topography – ST

The topographical position of the feet relative to the ball has an immediate impact on shot shape. During a round of play, the golfer will experience a variety of ball positions relative to the feet for various shots, which have a strong influence on the ensuing shot's behaviour and characteristics. Uphill lies will promote high trajectory shots, while downhill lies will produce low trajectory shots. Shots executed by a right-handed golfer with the ball above the feet will inherently cause shots to have a draw to the right, and shots with the ball below the feet will tend to fade to the right. The golfer must consider how stance topography or placement of the feet relative to the ball will affect spin, ball flight and distance. Being aware of the characteristics of a shot to be executed allows for the appropriate compensations to arrive at a desired positive shot decision and outcome.

Special care must be taken to set-up for proper club face alignment when using high lofted irons and wedges when the ball is well above or below the feet. For example, a right-hander on a side hill lie with the ball well above the feet must take care to align the stance to the right until the face of the lofted club is aimed at the target. For a right-hander with the ball well below the feet, the face of more lofted clubs aim to the right of where the feet are aligned. It is extremely important to make slight alterations of the stance to the left until the imaginary perpendicular line off the face of the club is aimed at the target. There will be a tendency to feel you are aiming right of the target, but the results will be a shot straight at the pin. Similarly, a right-handed golfer addressing a ball well below the feet with a highly lofted club, must make stance alignment adjustments to the left of the target, compensating for the greater tendency of these shots travelling to be right, due to face alignment with the ball.

Landing Area Topography – LA

The landing area of a shot can have a large impact on the direction and distance a ball is affected upon landing on the green or fairway. Paying close attention to the directional influences of the topography of the landing area permits the golfer to decide on an appropriate combination of shot shape and landing area, resulting in more shots finishing closer to the hole.

For example it may be more appropriate to hit a low trajectory chip shot that will land on a large flat area of the green and run down to the pin, as opposed to hitting a more lofted pitch shot requiring a much larger swing having a smaller margin for error and greater risk of an unsuccessful result.

In another example, on an approach into the green it is noted the left side of the green is skirted for its entire length by a 20-foot high hill or ridge having a steep slope toward the green. With the hills highest point 15 feet to the left of the green's left edge, and little likelihood of the ball holding up on the hill, then any shot into the right side of the hill will likely result in the ball finishing on the green. This factor has a strong influence on the shot making decision, due to the attractive bail out area to the left of the green, and the ridge minimizing the margin for error of the shot.

Finally, consider the case of a pin located in an area of the green sloping away from the golfer with little green to work with, utilizing a shot with a higher trajectory will promote the ball being less affected by this slope upon hitting the green, resulting in less roll and improved chances of getting the ball close to the hole.

Golfers have a variety of shot shape options available to enhance the outcomes of approach shots into the green, with the shot's landing area topography often overlooked during a shot's assessment. Many golfers fail to account for what will happen to the ball after making contact with the green's surface or the landing area short of the green. The results of many shots can be greatly improved by anticipating what the ball will do after landing. Paying attention to the effects of green and landing area topography must become a part of a regular shot assessment routine to insure consideration is given to this important factor for getting the ball closer to the hole. Golfers are aware of the importance of landing area topography as a factor for attaining satisfactory shot results, but fail to make it as a consistent part of a Shot Assessment Routine. Getting into the habit of considering green and landing area topography for every shot will result in a far greater number of initial putts having realistic chances of being successful, and three-putting a less frequent event.

Obstacles Between Ball and Pin – O

There will be times when extreme loft, low loft, hook spin or slice spin may be required to negotiate obstacles on the course. The golfer may be required to fade or slice a shot around a tree to hit the green or hit a low trajectory shot to avoid low hanging branches. There may be occasions where draw on a shot is desired to negotiate a corner in the fairway, or a fade-slice is the best option to get around an outcropping of trees and land softly on the green. Inevitably, the golfer must increase their repertoire of shots types to avoid obstacles and achieve the best possible shot results.

Strategy Factors

Management Considerations – MA

The golfer must always consider the strategies they hope to employ to negotiate a hole. This entails determination of the highest percentage shots creating the greatest likelihood of a planned successful outcome for the hole. The golfer should always follow high percentage tee shots with approach-shot combinations selected based on a green to tee assessment as outlined in the Course and Game Management Strategy. This gives the golfer the opportunity to put together the best combination of successful shots to meet the golfer's goals, while providing a constructive focus for what is trying to be achieved.

Hazards-Trouble - T

Any Hazards or other types of concern thwarting a successful outcome to the hole must be considered to ensure the highest percentage shots are employed when taking on a hole. Sand Bunkers, water hazards, out-of-bounds, heavy rough, trees and other unfavourable locations must all be considered to avoid being put into situations adversely affecting scoring.

Bailout Area(s) – BO

A key component of successfully addressing a hole is an awareness of the bailout areas surrounding a green. Choosing a high percentage approach shot is preparing for a shot result having the least chance of resulting in trouble if the shot goes array. For example, if the area to the right of a green is positively more favourable than the left, the execution of a fading shot for a right-handed golfer will aid in avoiding the more dangerous area to the left of the green. For all approach shots into the green, the bailout side of the green should always be determined as a component of the shot making decision to improve the chances of success, and avoid higher numbers being indicated on the scorecard, if a shot does go array.

Pin and Preferred Putt Location – P

A very important component of any decisions for an approach shot is determining the preferred 10 foot putting location on the green as outlined in the Course and Game Management chapter. Identifying the preferred or best position of a 10-foot putt on the green helps ensure the appropriate landing area has been considered for the shot to finish in this preferred location. Pin positions will strongly influence the type of shot options open to the golfer, affecting the shot's shape and the ideal spot to land the intended shot to arrive at the ideal 10-foot putt location on the green.

Not only is pin position and landing area considered to arrive at a favourable shot, but also to be aware if a short side pin condition exists. A short side pin condition exists if you have a shot to the pin with little or no green between the ball and the hole. A short side condition makes it more difficult to get a chip or pitch shot close to the hole, due to the limited green available to work with. In cases where the slope of the green is away from the golfer, it is virtually impossible to get the ball close to the hole. It seems reasonable that avoidance of this area be considered before shot execution, simply based on the premise that if the green is missed elsewhere, there is a much better opportunity or chance of saving a par and avoiding a bogey. Be wary of compromising a high percentage shot to avoid a catastrophe by hitting a lower percentage shot to get to the ideal spot on the green. It is wise to base shot decisions on assessment of all possible shot making scenarios to avoiding potential disaster on a hole. In the above example, it is wise to play the safer shot forsaking getting closer to the hole, when the alternative shot is a lower percentage shot, potentially resulting in a much higher score.

For most high handicappers, rather than shooting at tight pin placements that bring hazards and other negative conditions into play, good advice is to execute approach shots to the generous portions of the greens in closer proximity to bail out areas and away from short side positions. Leaving yourself options and opportunities on every shot into the green is an excellent indicator good game management tactics are being employed.

Margins For Error – E

There may be aspects of the hole, which serve as a means of reducing or eliminating errors made and having an influence on your shot-making decisions. For example, the pin location is on a front lower tier of a green with an extensive upward slope leading to a higher second tier. The decision to play a slightly longer iron could be based on the minimized risk of using this iron shot due to the upslope behind the pin helping to keep the ball from traveling to far.

In another example, you face a short 30-yard pitch shot over a bunker to a tight pin. As a means of reducing the risk of dropping the shot into the bunker, you elect to purposely hit the shot slightly long, increasing the margin for error to avoid dropping short and ending in the bunker. Always choose the shot you feel confident executing, providing the greatest chance of being successful, while at the same time minimizing the risk of subsequent shots. This is the position you want to place yourself in to ensure consideration of the "best" shot alternatives.

Personal Performance Factors – P

Always make your shot choices based on evaluation of pertinent factors affecting a shot's outcome, but shot making decisions should not be changed unless there are very good reasons for an alternative plan of attack. If you feel you are hitting the ball exceptionally well, the decision to use a 5 iron over a 4 iron could be based on simply feeling "confidently aggressive". Always be aware of your physical and mental state, and base decisions on good information, using the knowledge gained from shots taken previously in the round.

This factor or variable in the Shot Assessment Routine is specifically included to accommodate any new variables to be considered affecting a shot's outcome, or to raise personal cues the golfer wishes to include, prior to shot execution. For example, as a final component of the shot assessment routine the golfer may desire to include two stress relieving swings to attain a feeling for what is to be achieved before moving into the actual execution of the shot. This factor in the shot assessment routine is where the golfer is free to add anything that is deemed important enough to be actioned for improved results.

Final Decision of Shot to be Executed – D

At this point, consideration of your pre-shot assessment should be completed based on consideration of variables in the checklist and a final shot-making decision made or concluded. The golfer must have a clear understanding of the shot to be achieved and be committed to its execution. Do not make a move from the assessment position to take the shot until you are fully committed to what it is you are trying to attain.

Imagery of Shot to be Performed and Shot Execution – I

While still in your assessment position, envision the shot you decided on. Do not proceed to address the ball for shot execution until you have envisioned the shot exactly as decided. When you get a good image of the desired shot, move to the shot execution position and carry out your shot execution routine exactly as you have choreographed hundreds of times before.

All the items assessed in the Shot Assessment Routine have been presented, but it is now time to create a mnemonic tool that can be used to ensure the above shot considerations are assessed for every shot taken. Each of the factors or variables has been assigned a single letter, which is listed in a manner permitting the easily recall of variables to be considered for a shot. The letters representing each factor or variable can been combined to provide easily remembered acronyms, words or phrases permitting easy recall of the factors. The mnemonic words or phrase created for the above variables considered are listed below:

TRADE WIND TOOLS MAST – SAMPLE ACRONYM

Temperature	T
Greens Receptiveness	R
Approach Into The Green	A
Shot Distance	D
Elevation Change	E
Wind	WIND
Landing Area Topography	T
Stance Topography-Orientation	O
Obstacles Between Ball and Pin	O
Lie	L
Shot Shape	S
Management Considerations	M
Bail-Out Area(s)	A
Short-Sided Location	S
Trouble-Hazards	T

As you can see the memory aid included is not difficult to implement and the golfer is free to use whatever letters, order or other factors to ensure the tool serves its purpose. The golfer must memorize the factors or variables associated with the appropriate letters to establish their Shot Assessment Routine. With consistent use it will become an engrained habit, forever avoiding the distractions arising from a shot because something was not considered. Once this simple process is put in place, the golfer will never overlook or forget a shot variable before executing a shot. By using a mnemonic tool for simple recall of all these variables, the golfer knows and is confident all factors have been considered for every shot to have the greatest opportunity for successful execution.

Certainly more time can be spent constructing your acronym to give greater significance to the words making it up or to customize the assessment to include other items you wish to add. Having a Shot Assessment tool in place is a simple means of insuring all variables have been considered for every shot, but it also provides a strong confidence boost just before executing the shot. The Shot Assessment Routine is an activity directed at eliminating negative influences by avoiding many possible distractions, building confidence through preparation, and providing the golfer the confidence and assurance all personal skill factors and options have been considered to achieve the best shot result possible.

Section 5 - The Putt Assessment Routine

Lets us now explore some factors and variables included in the Putt Assessment Routine. The variables and considerations for successful execution of a putt will obviously differ from those for a regular shot, but a similar habitual process taken for all putts must be instilled. Putting is a completely different aspect of the game requiring different considerations to predetermine a feel or notion for the force and direction of a putt, based on an envisioned stroke moving the ball across the green and into the hole. Your Putt Assessment Routine may include movement around the green to assess different slopes from different locations. Be sure these specific movements around the green are included in the Putt Assessment Routine to preserve the habitual and calming effect of the entire process. Just like the Shot Assessment Routine, the factors considered will be assigned a letter to create a similar mnemonic acronym, permitting and simplifying the recall of factors included in the Putt Assessment Routine.

1. Putt Length – L

With reasonable accuracy determine the length of putts because the primary factor determining the distance a putt travels on the green is the force of the stroke imparted by the putter on the ball. Consistently and accurately determining the length of putts is a key step of the Putt Assessment Routine, coupled with consistent and repetitive references to comparing intended putt outcomes with actual results creates and enhances real experienced based ability to appropriately judge or determine the force of a stroke to successfully achieve an envisioned putt. Through the adoption of a consistent assessment routine for all putts, the golfer is constantly exposed to comparing expected putts with real results, providing ongoing feedback that improves the golfer's ability to determine the force of a stroke for any putt.

Determination of the distance of an initial putt can occur while repairing ball pitch marks and marking of the ball. Determination of distance can be made by pacing-off the putt during this time. With the implementation of On-Course Assessment strategy and the recording of its associated data, determine an appropriate time to record the putting data being gathered.

2. Speed – S

The speed of a putt could be described as the distance a ball will travel when started at a specific speed. With all other conditions held constant, the ball will roll less distance on a slow green and a further distance on a faster green. There are numerous reasons for the differences between the speeds of greens. Type of grass, grass length, grass thickness, moisture content, ground firmness and other factors creates speed differences of greens, not only for different courses, but for different holes on the same course.

The golfer must make a point of always assessing the speed of each green, always ensuring to include an examination of the intended path of the putt. When walking near the intended line get a feel for the ground conditions through your feet regarding the sponginess of the ground and the flexibility of the grass. The ground becoming crusty would indicate the green drying out and an increase in the speed of the green. Rich deep green coloured grass will generally be slower than dried out grey looking grass or brownish dry grass.

3. Grain – G

The direction the grass is pointed or lying has an influence on the lateral direction a putt moves to the right or left and the speed of the putt. A putt will move left or right due to the influence the grass collectively imparts on the ball as a result of the ball rolling across the blades of grass rather than inline with them.

A ball rolling across blades pointed toward the left of the line will cause the putt to move left. A ball rolling across blades pointed toward the right of the line will cause the putt to move right. A ball rolling in the same direction as the grass is lying will tend to be faster or having greater tendency to roll. A ball rolling opposite the direction the grass is laying will tend to be slower because the blade ends of the grass restrict or impede the ball's roll, resulting in a slower putt travelling less distance.

The colour or appearance of the grass as viewed down the line of the putt is often used as a barometer helping determine the way in which the grass is laying. If the grass appears shinier and lighter, the grass is reflecting light as the result of the grass being sloped in the direction of the putt. The grass appears darker with no reflection when the grass is sloped in the opposing direction to the path of the putt. In this later case, the golfer would make compensation to strike the putt with greater speed to allow for the slowing effect of the grain on the ball.

4. Break (Lateral Slope) – B

Break can be defined as the effect gravitation force has on the ball to cause it to move to the left or right. As long as a green was perfectly flat or consistently perpendicular to vertical, any putt hit would travel in a straight line. When the travel line of the ball starts to roll on a surface that is sloped or tilted laterally to the left or right, the forces imparted on the ball as the result of gravity will cause the ball to be moved left or right, respectively. As the degree of the slope increases, the resulting effect causes the ball to move a greater distance to the left or right. This will cause the putt to change direction quicker resulting in the putt having more break.

The golfer must predict the effects of break to start the ball in the right direction and strike the ball with the appropriate speed for the shot to finish at the hole. Without an accurate assessment of the lateral slope conditions existing for a putt's path, it is impossible to determine or predicted changes in direction of the putt due to break. This is why a putt making decision cannot be soundly made without fully assessing this variable to arrive at an initial putt line having the appropriate speed to be deflected the assessed amount to terminate in the hole.

5. Elevation Change (Inline Slope) – E

In-line Slope can be defined as the effect of gravitation force on the ball, when the elevation of the ball is different from the hole. When a slope indicating the hole is above the ball, gravitational force will tend to reduce the distance the ball will roll, decreasing the speed of the putt (Uphill). For a slope indicating the hole is lower than the ball, gravitational force will tend to increase the distance the ball will roll, increasing the speed of the putt. (Downhill)

As long as a green is perfectly flat or consistently perpendicular to vertical the speed of a putt will not be affected by the inline slope of the putt, because there are no additional forces acting to cause the ball to roll further or inhibiting it to roll less. When the ball is to be putt uphill, there is the force of gravity restricting the roll of the ball, requiring a putt to be struck with slightly more initial speed to arrive at the hole. When a putt is to be struck downhill, the force of gravity aids the putt, requiring a putt to be struck with less force to make it to the hole.

An important concept assisting predict the path of a putt is to consider two putts having the same lateral slope or break; one putt being downhill and the other uphill. A downhill putt will be influenced to a greater extent by lateral forces acting on it due to its lower initial speed and the greater amount of time lateral forces influence the ball before reaching the hole. In contrast, an uphill putt must be hit with greater initial speed and has a shorter travel time, causing it to be less influenced by the lateral slope or break. As a result, uphill putts tend to break less than downhill putts, despite both putts having the same lateral tilt or slope.

There are fewer variables or factors required for consideration when making a decision to commit to a putt, as opposed to a fully executed shot. There may be fewer factors considered affecting a putts outcome, but the procedure followed during the Putt Assessment Routine to ascertain this information could entail a fair amount of movement on the green. The assessment of regular shots can be completed while standing in close proximity to the ball because all variables can usually be considered from a single location. This difference makes the assessment process for putts quite different. Even the initial location of a putt on green and its relationship to the hole makes it difficult to isolate the times in the procedure certain factors are noted and assessed to insure their inclusion in the process.

Since it is required to move around the green to evaluate the factors affecting a putt, it is advisable to provide some provisions in your assessment routine outlining the general movements on the green for a putt. Allowing for putt differences, and the movement differences for varying putt lengths, it is a good idea to establish choreographed movements around the green for long, medium, and short putts. After all, it is natural to assume closer proximity to the hole requires far less movement to arrive at a putt decision. This provides easy access to the assessment routine required based on the length of putt encountered. For example, when a putt is shorter, there may be no need to take a side view, prompting the use of your short putt assessment routine. A routine for long putts may be followed when putts are over 20 feet in length, or whatever length suits comfort levels. The golfer would merely access the putt assessment movement profile established for a set length of putt, and follow these routine movements on the green every time. This is easy to do when the variables and factors considered for a putt are few enough to let your mnemonic tool be repeatedly accessed during the movement routines established. This will readily provide the cues to accommodate the necessary assessments. The Putt Execution Routine presented later in this chapter is a listing of the choreographed steps taken immediately following the Putt Assessment Routine.

Let's now create a mnemonic tool that can be used to ensure the above putt considerations are assessed for every putt taken. Again, each of the factors or variables has been assigned a single letter, which is listed in a manner creating an acronym permitting the easily recall of the factors considered for every putt. The mnemonic words or phrase created for the above variables considered are shown below.

SAMPLE ACRONYM
Break – L – E – G - S

Break	Break
Putt Length	L
Elevation Change	E
Grain	G
Speed	S

The variables or factors considered in this sample Assessment tool are only examples of possible variables, which can be modified to suit any golfer. No matter the experience or skill of the golfer, their adoption will at minimum provide confidence-building preparation for any putt. Performance improves because a more confident golfer is executing a stroke that is more likely to be successful, because factors influencing the ball have been duly considered.

The evaluation of putts becomes more time consuming, requiring greater time to assess as their length increases. On the other hand, putts of less than 4 feet in length take much less time to assess before arriving at a putt decision. For this reason, a golfer could have 3 different procedural movements on the green for putts of 3 different lengths. All the variables presented above would be assessed at various locations in the repeated movements set for 3 putt lengths. For example, putts of over 20 feet will require a different movement on the green than those from less than 20 feet, with those putts under 5 to 6 feet using a third simplified movement around the green. The distances a golfer uses to establish different movement on the green may vary based on personal preferences. The value of the benefits gained establishing comfortable and familiar ways of assessing the roll of putts, plus knowing all relevant factors and variables have been considered leads to a more confident and decisive commitment to the putt you intend to make. Once commitment to an expected outcome is achieved, this triggers the start of the Putt Execution Routine.

Section 6 - The Shot Execution Routine

We have established Assessment routines for both regularly executed shots and putts, but still must develop the Shot Execution Routine and the Putt Execution Routines. These are the choreographed actions a golfer follows after coming to a shot-making decision following an assessment. These separate routines include a very specific list of actions or steps that are repeatedly carried out every time a putt is stroked or a shot is made. The specificity of the actions included in the routines is such that, if a video camera recorded a golfer's actions every time the golfer moved to the golf ball to execute a shot, viewing the videos would result in seeing the same actions occurring repeatedly. The likeness or similarity of what occurs from when the golfer moves in to make the shot, to when the shot is completed, is critical to the overall effectiveness of an execution routine. A good indicator of an effective execution routine is the similarity of the elapsed times for numerous shots from the start of the routine to the completion of the shot. Due to the repetitive nature of a routine, there is constant reinforcement of a regular sequence of events greatly aiding the fostering of a good sense of timing and tempo during shot execution. After all, the consistent and repeated use of the same procedure should precipitate similarities in execution time, providing a constant for timing and tempo.

The length of time a routine has been in place is likewise critical to a routine's effectiveness. This is why it is extremely important to establish routines early, because their effectiveness is dependent on extended usage. The care you take to insure even the most minor actions in your choreographed routine are repeated for every shot better entrenches the dependability and effectiveness of the routine, to better eliminate negative thoughts and distractions, greatly improving successful stroke execution. The diligent use of these choreographed routines is critical in controlling negative influences just prior to and during shot execution. The assessment routines evaluate critical factors and variables to aid in envisioning the best possible shot making decision, which immediately initiates the appropriate choreographed execution routine.

Routine triggers a recurring activity for every shot, adding an element of consistency by providing a commonality to all shots taken. Routine also has the effect of establishing a mind state where decisive action like a golf shot can be automatically executed without conscious thought, which ultimately should be the goal to be achieved for every shot. The repeated association of the physical actions of the golf swing, coupled with the physical actions of a shot execution routine, causes a blending of all physical actions into a cohesive single event. The ongoing and repeated association of the physical actions of the swing to the repetitive actions associated with the mundane nature of a near robotic routine, causes the physical act of the swinging the club to become consolidated into the boring repetitiveness of the process. This bending of both the swing and the routine sequence into a single act, performed repeatedly over and over, creates a shot-making environment greatly improving ability to ward off distractions, improving shot consistency.

The essence or nature of what it is trying to be achieved, is not only supported by the routines presented, but should be reflected in many aspects of your game. There have been references made to adjectives describing the nature of the playing environment being created through the establishment of a Positive Competitive Mindset to provide some idea of the type of playing environment trying to be created. More precisely stated, the following adjectives in part describe the nature, feelings, and impressions to achieve for top performance to be experienced. The psyche is dominated by an awareness of the present only and is characterized as being customary, precise, usual, expected, typical, common, conventional, habitual, familiar, routine, comfortable, natural, regular, steady, dependable, focused, attentive, able, and realistic. Considering the above adjectives describing the essence of the mind state to be achieved, the routines must be repetitively practiced and performed the same way every time, without variation, to achieve this goal. Consistently using these routines is critical for them to be effective. The more mundane and boring the routines, the more effective they will be at preserving an ideal mind state during the execution of the shot.

KEY CHARACTERISTICS OF EXECUTION ROUTINES

The process of building your own Execution Routine is quite personal, but should display the following characteristics to ensure their effectiveness and permanence. Execution Routines will:

- follow the same procedure every time it is executed.
- be followed for every shot executed.
- be initiated by a trigger at the conclusion of an Assessment Routine.
- be repeated when anything breaks or interrupts the process.
- be simple enough to be easily remembered and repeated, but inclusive enough to serve its purpose.
- have a post shot assessment comparing swing sensations or feelings with the shot result; making every shot a learning experience.
- instilling consistent timing into the swing to establish a swing having good rhythm or tempo.

Execution Routines have repetitive physical actions associated with them, thus requiring a form of choreography to insure the same actions are initiated and carried out for every shot. Videotaping your routine can help insure you always perform the same steps or actions, and permits assessing if the routine meets your needs. Remember your routine can be something that is evolving, so a few changes here and there are fine, but try to establish routines you can use over extended periods of time. The value of an execution routine increases with the time it is used. Over time the repetitive nature of the routine conditions the golfer to carry out the sequence in an almost robotic manner, without thought. Unnecessary or excessive changes to routines should be avoided to allow them to become spontaneous and engrained, rather than constantly having to re-establish an updated routine.

Through the familiarity of endless repeated occurrences, the actions associated with the routine become repetitive, mundane and automatic to the point of being so chronically boring and monotonous that the mind is conditioned to execute the shot free from any thought process. The golfer feels the act as simply "going through the motions". The initiation of the execution routine acts like a switch shutting out any outside interference or conscious thought, leaving only the process of the routine itself, resulting in a shot being executed free of negative influences.

An analogy of what is achieved through the use of an identical repeatable routine and a how it spontaneously occurs can be illustrated through a comparison of performing some simple actions in your own car as opposed to a friend's or neighbour''s car. In your own car it is almost automatic for you to insert the key in the ignition, turn on the headlights, switch on the windshield wipers or to adjust the seat, without having to look or fumble around to perform any of these activities. You seem to just simply execute each task when desired. What is so amazing is you can perform these tasks with great precision, even in the dark.

On the other hand, if the same tasks were performed in the neighbour's or friend's car, you would have to look or fumble around trying to locate items in order to perform these tasks. It is the unconscious familiarity of repetitively performing these actions in your own vehicle making these precise actions thoughtless and automatic. Likewise, the shot execution routine causes a blending of the actions of a boring thoughtless procedure with those of the swing, causing the swing action to become automatic like the routine itself. Swing execution simply becomes a component of the routine itself. It is performed without distraction due to the preoccupation with the routine itself. Your swing becomes automatic, much like the actions performed in your own vehicle. Your golf swing should be performed automatically, without thought. You may wish to allude to appropriate feelings or sensations when making a shot, but avoid cues requiring mental thought once the shot execution routine has started.

SAMPLE SHOT EXECUTION ROUTINE

Below is a sample checklist to jump-start putting together a procedure for a shot execution routine. Be descriptive enough with each step of the procedure to identify the actions to be taken every time you address the ball to take a shot. Once a procedures or sequence of steps is established for a routine, it is important to engrain the routine by using it faithfully. Entrench the routine during both practice and competitive time. Making your routine an integrated part of your shot making improves the effectiveness of focusing on the task at hand and avoiding negative distractions. The more mundane and habitual your routine becomes through conditioning, the more effective it becomes for masking distractions and having a strong positive affect on improved shot consistency.

Below is a listing of the choreographed steps of a sample shot execution routine

Sample Procedure

Choreographed Action Steps

1. In the assessment area, position the body approximately 8 - 10 feet behind the ball directly facing the hole. Have the feet at shoulders width facing the hole with the club properly gripped by a freely hanging left hand, with the shaft of the club grounded and pointing down the intended line.
2. While still in the assessment position, commit to the execution of a specific shot based on relevant factors and variables determined in Shot Assessment Routine
3. While still in the assessment position behind the ball and viewing down the intended shot line, identify an intermediary reference point on the ground for club and stance alignment at the time of addressing the ball.

4. Still in the assessment position 8 - 10 feet directly behind the ball, and while facing the target, take an address setup position while still facing down the target line, ensuring having a proper grip with reference to the club head.
5. Still in the address position 8 - 10 feet directly behind the ball facing the target, take the necessary number of half swings until the correct swing feeling is achieved. Take the necessary number of partial swings to ascertain a feeling for the swing you intend to execute. It is at the moment a satisfactory swing sensation is felt when movement to address the ball will commence.
6. Still in the address position, visualize the intended shot. Visualization is inclusive of an image of the ball from club contact to the concluding bounces and roll of the ball. When there is unforced and more realistic visualization of the intended shot, there is a marked improvement in achieving the desired result.
7. At the moment a satisfactory swing sensation is perceived and visualization of the intended shot has occurred, move to face the ball with the feet together. With comfortable extension of the arms and bending at the hips, place the center of the club behind the ball; ensuring it is aligned with the spot noted earlier in step 3 for proper shot and address alignment. This ensures the ball is started on the intended target line.
8. Keeping the clubface properly aligned at the target, first move the left foot to the appropriate position for the initial setting of the stance. Next, move the right foot to the right to the appropriate position to initiate calibrating small changes in foot placement to arrive at the desired alignment and set-up. While establishing the final placement of feet and readiness for shot execution, periodically waggle the club, and the turn the head to view the target to remain loose and comfortable until triggering of the swing.
9. Ensure the amount of bend at the waist and the flex in the legs are in check through a feeling of tall stature in your stance, and check the appropriate distance between the hands and body ensuring a commonly felt reach for the ball is felt prior to commencement of the shot. This helps to maintain a swing that is more consistently on-plane arriving at the ball in the position for a well-executed shot. Periodic waggling the club and turns of the head to view the target may occur during this time until a sense of feel for the shot is ascertained, or to ease tension levels.
10. When the desired addressing of the ball has been achieved and final checks have been made, perform a final waggle and a last turn of the head to envision the intended shot, returning to the club head back to a address position.
11. With steady wrists, arms and shoulders, and through torsion of the spine only, initiate movement of the club head to a position approximately 16 - 20 inches (40 - 50 cm) from the ball. Return the club head slowly back to the ball, only feeling the turning of the spine controlling the club head back to the address position. This short swing movement is to provide a pre-feeling of how the swing must be initiated at time of execution. Emphasis on the spine turn helps ensure all swings are started on the same plane. Avoiding head movement, body sway, leaning, lower body movement, or wrist action during the initiation of the swing helps ensure shots start on the same plane, greatly improving shot consistency. The importance of getting the club on the correct plane coupled with an opportunity to engrain this feeling into the Shot Execution Routine as a common and regular part of your game immediately adds consistency to all shot making due to its universal application.

12. Reset the head of the club behind the ball to initiate your shot execution trigger. For myself, it is a minuscule movement of the right knee toward the ball. Some players use the slightest movement of the wrists toward the target as a trigger. This is a common trigger utilized in putting as well. Your trigger can be anything that will definitively initiate the shot execution process.
13. Start the swing by taking the club head away from the ball long and low using spine turn only, to attain the sensation of a "big swing arc". A consistent takeaway minimizes or eliminates the effects of irregularities created by unnecessary movements of the body and prevents small muscles in the wrists and arms from being over dominant, with both causing variations in club face alignment at impact and reducing shot consistency.
14. Execute the shot
15. Observe the shot until reaching its final location
16. Perform a Shot Assessment comparing the feelings and sensations of the shot with the shot result to reinforce the feelings associated with those that are successful, and to learn from those falling short of expectations.

NOTE:

In step 8, for **partial shots** in closer proximity to the green there is a slight variation in the shot execution procedure. Due to the feel associated with partial shots, rather than immediately addressing the ball following the Shot Assessment procedure, movement to the ball includes practice swings adjacent to the ball, to better ascertain the length of swing for a desired shot outcome. Based on a number of practice swings, when the appropriate swing length for the desired partial shot is determined, continue with step 9 of the procedure above.

The Shot Execution Routine will prove to be one of the most valued tools the golfer has at their disposal supporting distraction management, bringing improved consistency to general shot execution. The Putt Execution Routine is much different from the Shot Execution Routine due to wide variations in movement around the green to appropriately assess putts of widely varying length. In the next section we will take a closer examination of the Putt Execution Routine.

Section 7 - The Putt Execution Routine

Sample Putt Execution Routine

Below is a sample checklist of actions to be followed for every putt, following the Putt Assessment Routine. Remember to be descriptive enough with each step to identify the actions to be taken every time. Once a procedure or sequence of steps is established for a routine, it is important to engrain it through repetitive use. Be sure to use and entrench the routine during both practice and competitive time. Making your routine an integrated part of your putting improves the effectiveness of focusing on the task at hand and avoiding negative distractions. The more regular and typical your routine becomes through repetitive use, the more effective it becomes for masking distractions and improving putting consistency.

Below is a listing of the choreographed steps of a sample Putt Execution Routine.

Sample Procedure

Choreographed Action Steps

1. While in the final putt assessment position four to five feet behind the ball assume a crouching position viewing the ball inline with the hole and make a final commitment to a putt making decision based on the Putt Assessment Routine.
2. While in the final putt assessment position four to five feet behind the ball, visualize the intended putt rolling into the hole. Make note of the location of an identifiable spot a short distance from the ball on the putt's line that will become the target referenced during stance setup. Visualization of the putt must be from putter contact with the ball to the ball dropping into the hole to be most effective. At the conclusion of this step introduce a trigger that is always used to initiate stepping to the ball for putt execution.
3. While holding the putter with the left hand, move the couple steps necessary to turn and face the ball so it is bisecting a very narrow stance. Gently settle the putter on the green approximately three inches inside the stroke's intended line to accommodate for practice strokes. Check for the proper alignment of the club when placed on the green.
4. Release the grip from the left hand to just the fingers supporting the club to relax the arm and re-establish a firm but relaxed grip of the putter. Freeing the grip of the left hand permits relaxing and free movement of the fingers on the underside of the grip to aid with tension reduction.
5. Grip the putter with both hands (Left 1st, Right 2nd) and adjust the placement of the feet to arrive at a comfortably familiar position with the imaginary ball 1 - 2 inches left of center of the stance. This slightly forward position of the ball in the stance encourages a slight upswing contact with the ball promoting a good roll free from skidding and hopping. Ensure the left eye is directly over the imaginary ball for consistency of alignment..

6. Due to the care in assuring correct set-up and alignment for the putt to start on the right line, it is only the force with which the ball must be struck that is the primary focus of the practice swings taken. Since there is going to be a re-setting of the stance requiring realignment, getting a feel for the stroke required to successfully deliver the ball to the hole is the sole goal of this step. Emphasis must always be placed on the determining the force imparted on a putt for the ball to finish 16 inches past the cup. Always having an initial judgment of speed based on these 16 inches of additional roll past the cup provides a frame of reference leading to more successful putts. This speed is ideal because the ball carries slightly more energy or inertia resulting in less effect of small imperfections in the green knocking the ball offline. Let the care of your set-up ensure the ball is imparted on the correct line. The use of practice swings prior to set-up in the final putt stance are specifically directed at determining the swing length required to roll the ball on an envisioned line to the hole, plus an additional 16 inches.
7. Perform the necessary number of practice strokes to get a feel for a stroke having the ball stop 2-3 feet short of the hole. Now perform the necessary number of practice strokes having the force to roll the ball 4 feet past the hole. Noting the difference of the force and swing feel for these two putt lengths provides an excellent gauge to help pinpoint and determine the feel for a stroke having the intermediary force to strike the ball with the initial speed keeping the ball on the intended line.
8. Perform a 1-2 final strokes focusing on the decided swing of the putter being an average of the short and long putt strokes determined in the previous step. Note the feeling of the swing and the distance the putter is taken back as references for when the actual stroke is executed.
9. Upon performing a stroke with the ideal force, move the putter head to behind the ball and adjust the feet accordingly, ensuring proper body and putter head alignment with the spot on the intended line to the hole identified in step 2. This step is important to check because it permits the sole focus on the force the putt must be struck, without the distraction of concern for the putt being on the intended line.
10. With the proper alignment, slowly turn the head to the left to imagine the path of the ball to the hole and turn the head back toward the ball retracing the ball back to the putter face. Let the last image of the distance the ball will travel be the gauge for how firmly the ball is struck.
11. When the eyes reset directly over the ball following your scan of the intended line initiate the stroke with a rotation of the upper torso carrying out the stroke with a slightly pronounced follow-through promoting completion of the stroke.
12. Hold your finish position and observe the putt until reaching its final location
13. Perform a Putt Assessment comparing the feelings and sensations of the stroke with the putt's result to reinforce the feelings associated with those that are successful and learn from those falling short of expectations.

The Putt Execution Routine will prove to be another strongly valued tool the golfer has at their disposal greatly supporting distraction management and bringing much improved consistency to putting.

The advantages of implementing these four basic shot routines are only realized if care is taken to follow a carefully assembled series of steps that are consistently followed in all circumstances. The routines keep the golfer occupied and in the present moment, providing the confidence all necessary factors and variables have been considered, based on a sound shot decision, permitting an unimpeded confident stroke.

Routine serves as a shield deterring outside distractions and influences, by eliminating your consciousness of them. Routine creates efficiencies maintaining a sound knowledge of shot making capabilities and tendencies, through the On-Course Assessment strategy. Golfers can explore countless activities and methods for taking advantages of the benefits offered through various applications of routine. The value or benefit of routine could also come from the confidence gained through the "routine" achievement of performance targets within a well defined efficiently managed Goal Setting Plan. Even methodologies presented to manage Goal Setting, and Practice, are specifically structured by routine driven structured occurrences of positive reinforcement, promoting ongoing confidence building.

Making it routine maintaining your goal setting plan and on-course assessment records allows progress to be monitored and provides maximum benefit for your improvement efforts on and off the course. The maintenance of a Goal Setting Plan and the effective management of practice depend on sound information regarding your capabilities and tendencies as a golfer. Routinely addressing your Goal Setting Plan, and actively following the processes and procedures outlined for practice sessions, will eliminate the drudgery of record keeping, re-introducing challenge, fun, and interest back into play and practice.

Routine will have its greatest affect on the development of the golfer by providing a tool that will improve consistency of enhanced performance. This is the primary reason for my assertion that routine implementation is the single most influential strategy of the Positive Competitive Mindset Model enhancing overall performance. The huge dividends paid, plus the relatively minimal effort involved to incorporate routine into the game should put this strategy at the top of every golfers "to do" list.

CHAPTER 13

Game And Course Management

"Placing the ball in the right position for the next shot is eighty percent of winning golf."
Ben Hogan

Section 1 - Game and Course Management Defined

The effectiveness of Game and Course Management and their influence on performance is proportional to the effort the golfer puts into acquiring an accurate knowledge of their ball-striking abilities and prevalent shot tendencies, and effectively applying these to best play a shot, hole or entire golf course. Successful game and course management is based on satisfactorily utilizing a series of proven stroke saving tactics, applying them, and committing to executing shots enhancing the opportunities to score effectively. These tactics are applied when individual shot decisions and course management plans are based on a sound knowledge of shot-making abilities and inclinations. These tactics demand the golfer be aware of their tendencies and capabilities, then applying them in a sound and consistent manner, to consistently arrive at an informed and committed shot making decision.

Game & Course Management - Overview

The terms Course Management and Game Management are on many occasions used synonymously within some publications. Other publications make a clear distinction between the two, with each having a distinctive definition, clearly differentiating one from the other. In this publication, Game and Course Management are viewed as two different processes, each with a specific purpose, activities, and methodologies. Both are specifically directed at avoiding shots from unfavourable areas of the course, increasing shots from favourable areas, reducing risk, maximizing reward, and provides confidence in knowing you have given full consideration to a spectrum of strategies and tactics specifically directed at reducing the strokes taken.

The similarity of Game and Course Management is the need for a sound knowledge of your ball striking capabilities and tendencies. Clearly, possessing a confidence in your capabilities and a knowledge of your inclinations is essential because this information validates the decisions you make for individual shots, how to approach a hole, or how you intend to play a particular golf course. The decisions you make should be based on the best possible way of making this happen. Determining your shot-making skills and tendencies is essential to establishing strategies best suited to allow you to capitalize on your strengths, and minimize the negative effects of your weaknesses.

Despite the similarities of both, there is a clear distinction between the two. Clearly defining the difference between Game and Course Management makes it easy for the golfer to differentiate between the two processes and understand their relationship.

Game Management Defined

Game Management is inclusive of all activities and considerations specific to preparation for a shot. Game Management is equivalent or congruent to the Shot Assessment Routine presented in the Routines chapter, whereby the golfer considers all shot factors and variables, respective of sound shot saving strategies, before making a decision for a particular shot. Game Management entails preparing to play each individual shot following an assessment enhancing the greatest chance for a successful shot outcome. This unit explores one aspect of Game Management not closely examined in the Routine unit.

This unit will specifically look at tactics easily used and incorporated into your routines when executing shots during play. If any of the tactics presented are viewed as having value or there is benefit seen in utilizing any of these tactics, they can be implemented right into the Routine. This will supplement your routine with consideration for tactics further enhancing scoring and confidence.

Course Management Defined

Course Management can be defined as the application of Game Management considerations to formulate a pre-planned approach for playing a specific hole or golf course. Course Management examines strategies and actions the golfer can take to put them in favourable playing positions throughout a round, to maximize performance and achieve the lowest score possible. The golfer plans the negotiating of each hole according to a plan based on the characteristics of the course, relative to their own shot making capabilities and tendencies. Effective Course Management is essentially the strategic melding of Game Management, applying and comparing it to the appropriate course information to create a hole by hole Course Management Plan, based on utilizing strengths to gain advantages and minimizing weaknesses to manage risk, while reducing the number of shots from trouble or unfavourable positions on the course.

Section 2 - Course Management Considerations

Considering effective and up-to-date assessment of current and accurate shot capabilities and tendencies, the ability to maximize performance on a particular golf course is well within every golfer's grasp. Course Management is based on the ability to strategize the most effective way of using the knowledge you have of your game, employing proven stroke saving tactics, and comparatively analyzing pertinent course information to create a hole by hole shot execution plan. A key step in formulating how a golf course is confronted is the analysis of a hole's features affecting shot making decisions. Every golf course has its unique challenges in the form of strengths and weaknesses evident on every hole. The strengths of a hole can be viewed as factors making it more difficult, raising the likelihood of a higher score, and its weaknesses as factors increasing opportunities to score well. A hole could show strength with an extremely narrow fairway, a very small green, long rough, numerous bunkers, or strategically placed hazards. On the other hand, a hole could show weakness through short length, few hazards, a generous bale-out area, a large receptive green or a substantial elevation drop. Every hole is unique, presenting different sets of challenges to overcome, with each requiring a different means to successfully negotiate. The strengths and weaknesses characterized by a golf course strongly affect the tactics employed when formulating a Course Management Plan.

Through a number of strategies presented as key components of the Positive Competitive Mindset, valid and accurate knowledge of your shot execution capabilities and tendencies can be determined providing your Course Management Plans the greatest chance of being predictable and effective. The Benchmarking, On-Course Assessment, Proximity Acceptance and Goal-Setting and Planning strategies will provide the best possible information regarding shot execution abilities and biases. These connections are examples of the integrating effect of the strategies, which collectively foster the formation of a Positive Competitive Mindset. Implementing these strategies will strengthen the validity of your Course Management Plans simply based on having a more thorough knowledge of capabilities. These supporting strategies are also ongoing; therefore the information regarding shot execution will always be current, which is essential for planning to be reflective of your current game. This information is critical to achieving further improvement gains, by maximizing the benefits of your strengths, and minimizing the negative effects your weaknesses could expose you to.

There are effective management tactics to be presented that will help guide and support decisions made when formulating a Course Management Plan. These tactics are included to enhance performance on the course and provide the golfer with sound guidelines effectively supporting formulation of a hole-by-hole strategy plan having the greatest likelihood of reducing the number of strokes taken. Effective Course Management is dependent on sound application of these course management strategies, in relation to adequate and accurate information regarding the course you are playing. The application of Course Management tactics relative to the characteristics of the course being played is incorporated based on the ball striking characteristics of the golfer. Using the tactics presented, and appropriately juggling strengths, weaknesses, and tendencies, sets the conditions for better scoring, by effectively utilizing sound plans established to play a course in the least number of strokes.

COMMITMENT TO A COURSE MANAGEMENT PLAN

If you take the time to analyze specific information related to a golf course and strategize the way you would like to play each hole, consider any factor having the potential to negotiate the course in fewer strokes. Consideration of risk-reward, hole topography, margins for error, conservative play, course strengths and weaknesses, and other important factors must be assessed to arrive at a Course Management Plan having the greatest likelihood of improved scoring and growth in confidence.

There is comfort in knowing proactive consideration has been given to maximize performance, minimize the emergence of negative influences due to uncertainty, and boost confidence levels based on a plan enhancing the potential for success. Of course, like any plan, commitment to the decisions made, and carrying out your plan for 18 holes is crucial. The time, effort and value of your plan are only realized, if it is allowed to unfold as anticipated, with your full commitment. If the first couple holes do not go as planned, don't get caught making the error of scrapping the plan. Remember, the plan is based on information a lot more reliable than the outcome of a couple bad holes or errant shots. If you have gone to the effort to gather and manage pertinent information regarding your game, and strategically formulated a course management plan, never forsake a soundly based plan because it is not immediately successful. Besides, why change a plan that has used valid and accurate information specifically directed at attaining and enhancing success and improving scoring. Carry out the plan for the entire round. Your plan still represents the best opportunity of being successful for the remaining holes.

There will be the odd occasion where the plan could be modified on the fly, due to a drastic change of competitive status. There may be times where you are called upon to be more aggressive than normal, due to a possibility of winning a tournament with only a couple holes to play. It is not uncommon for a Course Management Plan to also be altered due to drastic changes in playing conditions. Wind, rain, temperature, or any other factors that greatly changes playing conditions may also result in completely justified reasons to alter a Course Management Plan. Unless you have a real good reason for altering a plan, it is wise to carry your plan through to its conclusion.

PLAN FLEXIBILITY

The formulation of a Course Management Plan should include some flexibility for variables like wind, rain, temperature or other environmental factors. The strategies you decide upon should have an element of flexibility, as in the case of an extremely windy day requiring you to adjust accordingly for the wind direction and intensity. Your intended Course Management Plan could result in slight changes on a number of holes because of very windy conditions. Plans could change causing you to take more club into the wind on some holes, or altering your plan to hit a 3 wood rather than a driver to stay short of a nasty bunker now easily within range, as the result of strong helping winds. Whenever formulating a Course Management Plan ensure there is flexibility in the plan for changing conditions. When making the plan be sure to note any planned shot execution changes, as the result of changing conditions within the plan. This will help to insure you do not make any hasty bad decisions when having to modify your plan.

Section 3 - Game Management Tactics

As alluded to previously in this chapter, Game Management is viewed as the tactics the golfer accesses while playing the game, with the Shot Assessment Routine seen as consideration of the factors and tactics affecting Game Management. These are the tactics that are employed while on the course as you confront each new shot-making situation. The chapter specific to the implementation of routine and what this entails is primarily focused on ensuring all variables for a shot to be executed have been considered, and a sound shot-making decision is made, and the actual shot-making process is executed as a part of an unaltered or choreographed sequence of events. Shot Execution Routines can be thought of as the activities and tasks performed just before and during the execution of a shot. Game Management tactics are the proven stroke saving methods that should be considered and will aid the golfer in arriving at sound and quality shot-making decisions on a consistent basis.

There are some Course Management tactics presented which can be easily adopted into Game Management or the Shot Assessment Routine, because of their easy interchangeability. It is clear there are going to be tactics applying to both Game and Course Management that apply equally to both, but for organizational purposes Game Management tactics have been included in the Routine strategy in the previous chapter. The factors considered previously will not be restated here, but a summary of these Game Management factors is provided first, then second, the tactics associated with Course Management are examined. Due to the interchangeability of the tactics and factors for managing these two aspects of the game, the golfer is free to adopt any of these tactics as a component to the Shot Assessment Routine.

Together, the Game and Course Management factors and tactics to be covered are proven factors adding to the golfer's arsenal to score more effectively by avoiding trouble, utilizing strengths, minimizing weaknesses and improving confidence both during play, or when strategizing a plan on how to tackle a particular golf course.

GAME MANAGEMENT TACTICS & FACTORS – Routine

Immediately below is a summarization of the Game Management factors introduced in the Routines Strategy. Please refer to this chapter for specific information regarding each of the following factors and tactics.

Club Selection Factors

- Shot Distance
- Elevation Change
- Green Speed and Firmness
- Wind
- Temperature
- Approach Into Green

Shot Type Factors

- Lie
- Stance Topography
- Obstacles - Ball to Pin
- Shot Shape
- Landing Area Topography

Strategy Type Factors

- Management Considerations
- Bail-Out Areas
- Pin & Preferred Putt Location
- Shot Making Decision
- Hazards – Trouble
- Margins For Error
- Personal Factors
- Imagery & Shot Execution

COURSE MANAGEMENT TACTICS & FACTORS

View A Round As A Series Of 18 Opportunities

Rather than look at a day as simply including "another round of golf", view the time on the golf course as 18 opportunities to strategically negotiate each hole according to a planned approach aimed at stroke reduction. View each hole individually as a challenge to be negotiated according to a plan you have formulated, based on the best possible way of reducing the strokes taken. Do not lose sight of your Course Management Plan being the best means of improving your score and providing positive reinforcement and building confidence. The plan is a hole-by-hole assessment of the best way to approach a course, with a specifically planned approach or set of anticipated outcomes for every hole.

Nothing can be done about the last hole or any subsequent hole anyway, therefore all focus and energy is best directed at the hole being played. The majority of bad shots are hit as a result of focusing on shots already played, which only results in negative influences and distractions degrading current shots. Play "in the moment" at all times. On each tee review your plan of how you will negotiate the hole before teeing the ball. Block out what has happened previously, what you could or should do in the future, or any other aspect of your play that is judgmental or predictive in any way. As examples, judgmental or predictive thoughts could include how you are playing, or considering what must be done to score on par for nine holes. Adhering to this advice will make a significant difference in performance because it keeps you in the present and prevents or eliminates wandering thoughts leading to compromising distractions seriously affecting spontaneous shot execution.

Analyze Each Hole Starting at the Green

When strategizing the way to approach a hole, always start at the green and work backwards to the tee. Begin this process by determining two important pieces of information to help determine the location of the ideal approach into the hole. First, if given the opportunity to place a ball on the green at a location 10 feet from the hole with the best chance of a one putt, this is the location to shoot for on the approach shot. For a Par 4, determine the best combined high-percentage tee shot - approach shot combination providing the greatest chance of achieving this ideal ball location on the green. This is the two shot combination that should be included in the Course Management Plan. For a Par 5, plan for a high percentage tee shot-2nd shot combination setting up the best chance of achieving an approach shot location permitting a high percentage shot into the specific portion of the green resulting in putting from the ideal 10 foot putt location on the green. Planning from the green to tee focuses on improved scoring, by using high percentage shots better matching a golfer's shot making abilities and inclinations. In addition, this reverse viewpoint enhances opportunities for the highest percentage shots to meet the objective of getting the ball in the ideal 10-foot putt location.

Your Course Management Plan should always be based on working in reverse from the hole to tee for every hole on the course. This permits you to select the most appropriate shots in your repertoire to end up in the most advantageous landing areas on the fairway, setting yourself up for the highest percentage approach shot to arrive at the ideal 10-foot putt location. With the vast majority of shots in golf coming from under 100 yards, it is understandable that the greatest opportunity for stroke savings comes as the result of significantly reducing unnecessary shots around the green. After all, it is within 100 yards of the green where the vast majority of golf shots are taken. Always attempting to be setup for high percentage shots into the green will naturally reduce the number of shots taken in close proximity to them. This tactic will further reduce the number of shots executed from within 100 yards, due to a reduction in the number of putts taken on the green, as a result of being in closer proximity to the hole. Furthermore, there will be an additional reduction in strokes around the green, with fewer recovery shots being required, due to higher percentage shots lowering the incidence of bad misses. Instilling this reverse viewpoint as a routine aspect of your Course and Game Management Planning provides the greatest likelihood or chance of effectively capitalizing on your capabilities, tendencies and strengths to attain the lowest scores possible for every hole played.

Determine The Preferred Side Of The Fairway

For every tee shot determine the "Preferred" side of the fairway. Most holes usually have a safe or preferred side that is less hazardous, avoiding potential strokes, or more conducive for entry into the green. Remember to plan your strategy from the green to tee. Most holes will give you a 'bail out area' to one side of the green. When assessing approach shots into the green, note the hole's placement on the green, and location of the short side pin, to aid assessing the best location on the preferred side of the fairway to place the tee shot, to provide the best opportunity of reaching the ideal 10 foot putt location.

Approach Shot Aggressiveness

Shooting at well-protected pins is disaster in the making. Even the tour professionals are very selective with the pins they eagerly attack, and others where the rewards are not worth the risks. A reasonably safe par on a hole is a better option than the higher risk of walking away from the hole with a double or even triple bogey. Golfer's must learn to be patient, graciously accepting opportunities the course presents, as they occur. Trying to force scoring on an extremely long par 4 will commonly result in the tee shot being compromised due to the preoccupation to make it down the fairway as far as possible. Falling victim to playing into a hole's strengths is a source of many negative influences affecting shot making and ruining many wonderful days on the course. Be more aggressive with approach shots having lower risk, greater rewards or calls upon a skill or capability you are more confident of achieving. Be less aggressive with approach shots having higher risk, little reward, or demand a skill or capability, you are less confident of delivering.

Determine a Style of Play for Each Hole (Conservative, Strategic, Aggressive)

Before the identification of club selection or specific shot planning in a Course Management Plan, it's important to determine the approach to be taken for each hole based on the strengths and weaknesses of each hole, as compared and evaluated with your capabilities and inclinations. A golfer can play a hole using a conservative, strategic or an aggressive approach, depending on the assessment of a hole's characteristics as compared to a golfer's shot execution weaknesses and strengths.

In cases where higher risk is evident when comparing a hole's characteristics with a golfer's abilities and inclinations, a conservative style of play should be chosen to avoid the possible additional strokes associated with higher risk. Golfers should take a Conservative Approach when the strengths of the course are relatively stronger, countering many of the golfer's strengths, or where the strengths of the course call upon a golfer's weaknesses to negotiate a hole.

A Strategic Approach would be taken in cases where there is relative equality or balance between strengths of the golfer and a hole, with the golfer having to be tactical to successfully negotiate a hole.

An Aggressive Approach would be taken in cases where the strengths of the golfer can readily take advantage of the weaknesses of a hole or the strengths of the golfer are dominant over the strengths of a hole.

This is an important concept to foster and use because it readily allows the golfer to understand being patient and not forcing things to happen. Letting things come as they are encountered allows the golfer to understand why there is a more aggressive attitude on some shots and a more conservative approach on others. To effectively score at the level of your skill capabilities, the golfer must learn to use their strengths and take advantage of the courses weaknesses to created scoring opportunities. In addition, but equally important, to avoid high scores on holes the golfer must learn to avoid their weaknesses and try to nullify or avoid a courses strengths.

High Percentage Shots

It is important to play a high percentage shot whenever possible to enhance the chances of success. For example, on a par 5, your tee shot is still a long distance from the green requiring a career 3 wood shot to reach the green in two shots for a possible eagle. Trying to pull off a miracle low percentage shot with high risk usually results in a big score on a hole. A golfer's plans should emphasize placement of higher percentage shots to a favourable fairway location for the set-up of a third high percentage approach shot into the green, providing opportunity for a birdie. Golfers could also be tempted to hitting an "ironman shot", as a result of a challenge from the buddies, or to impress someone in the group. Shots taken attempting a shot seldom or never hit will most likely end in disaster.

Sometimes golfers mistakenly make poor shot making decisions based on assumptions that are false or inaccurate. In some cases the assumptions may cause golfers to develop attitudes detrimental to scoring, which must be altered or corrected. For example, golfers are often witness to a professional playing what is mistakenly considered to be a low percentage shot and successfully pulling it off, leaving many golfers with the impression that great scores are achieved through aggressive play. If these golfer's goals or objectives are to shoot the lowest scores possible, then their attitudes must change to being less aggressive. What these golfers considered to be low percentage shots of professionals are indeed quite the opposite. Professionals spend countless hours acquiring abilities and perfecting skills on a long road of improvement that spans years. The reality is that to the professional these shots are higher percentage shots well, within their personal capabilities to achieve. The clarification of the issues arising because of misinterpretation of handicap index is another example of an assumption leading to unnecessary negative influences and consequences negatively affecting performance.

Setup for Your Best Shots

When playing unfamiliar courses or a difficult course, take the confident building approach, by getting in the position of using favorite short irons for approach shots into the green, from the preferred side of the fairway. The combination of being on the preferred side of the fairway, and using a club you have confidence in, makes for a much greater chance of successfully executing your shot as planned. As a precaution, remember the design options of the golf course architect regarding risk-reward. As an example, the fairway on a short par 4 could sharply narrow starting at 240 yards from the tee, with the fairway narrowing for the next 80 yards, from 60 yards to 30 yards. In this particular case, you may elect to hit your 3 wood 245 yards, avoiding the risk associated with trying to get closer to the green with a driver. What could be worse on a short par 4 than not having a shot at the green on your approach shot, because of being too aggressive, and ending in trouble or penalized position. It seems more appropriate and advantageous, to have a 6 - 9 iron approach shot from a safe part of the fairway, than to later realize that trying to advance the ball into wedge range, results in having less than half the fairway's width as a target. You must always remember to make strategy decisions looking for the best-shot alternatives having the most effective result. It's extremely frustrating and unproductive to face a short par four and then have no approach shot to the green at all. Being too aggressive on a short par 4 can be costly, depending on the risk-reward aspects of the hole

Emphasize Accuracy

Avoid the common mistake of trying to hit the ball as far as you can off the tee on par fours and fives at the expense of accuracy. The benefit of having a shorter approach shot to a green is more often than not lost once the ball rolls out of bounds or into a hazard because you have tried to hit the ball as far as physically possible. Novices will typically struggle to hit their driver with some degree of accuracy, and until the club is mastered, the lower-numbered woods should be used off the tee to be on the fairway, and have a realistic shot at hitting the green.

Have A Specific Target For Every Shot

Try to have a specific target for every shot taken on the golf course. Rather than simply hitting the ball in the general direction of the target, pick a landmark or spot on the envisioned starting line of the shot. Once you have become acquainted with a course and have a good idea of where it is advantageous to be on each of its holes, pick out specific targets in the background to aim for. Know where the hazards are, especially the "blind" ones that cannot be seen from the fairway, and have targets chosen keeping you clear of them.

A key aspect of golf course management is hitting shots that make your next shot less difficult. Rather than trying to hit at a flagstick on a green, it is sometimes advisable to hit to a spot that gives you an uphill putt at the hole, or keeps the ball away from a bunker. Having a specific target in mind during a shot defines the objective you are trying to achieve, which is often associated with imagery of the shot occurring just before shot execution. This imagery is extremely important to achieve because the process greatly enhances superior shot execution. The top players in the world consistently refer to how top performances reflect their ability to be imaginative, predicting the actions of the ball to arrive at good shot making decisions. There are many intriguing aspects of the brain and many of its surprising capabilities that have not been fully explained. Evidence overwhelmingly supports the value of visualizing every shot before execution as an activity greatly improving shot outcomes. Visualization provides the golfer with a rehearsal session for the shot to be executed. The ability of the brain to perform the physical actions required of the body to attain a specific visualized task is uncanny. Let go and let the brain perform its magic.

Increase Margins For Error

The golfer can keep it in the fairway, get it on the green in regulation, sink more putts, and greatly reduce the number of trouble shots by increasing the margin for error of shots. Increasing the margin for error of a shot provides a greater likelihood of a successful outcome. This has the added positive impact of increasing the number of strokes taken from lies or positions that help and support being successful with the next shot. Just the mere awareness of always trying to increase your margin for error will have a positive effect on your performance by increasing the number of shots from favourable conditions, and reducing the number of trouble shots or shots from unfavourable positions on the course.

Utilizing Increased Margin for Error can change a weakness into a strength.

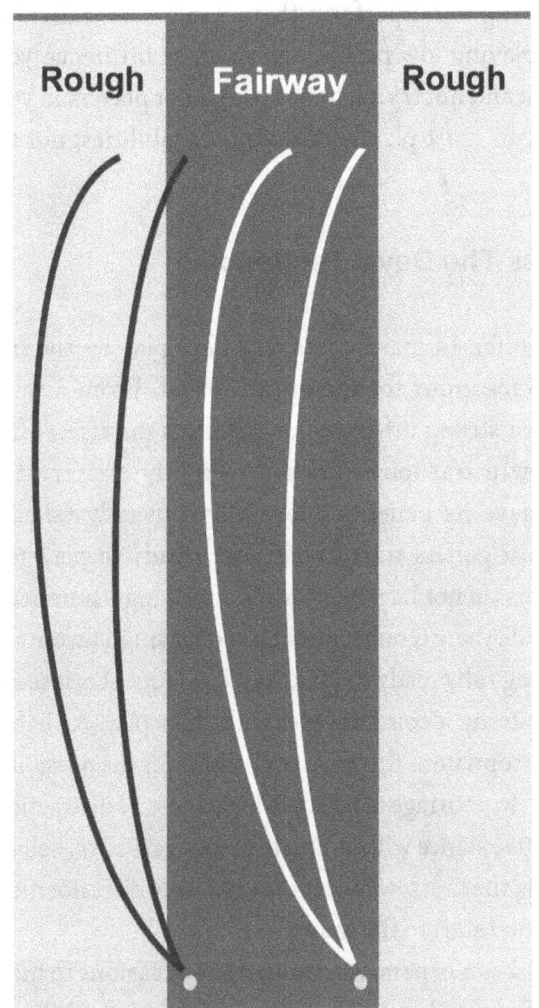

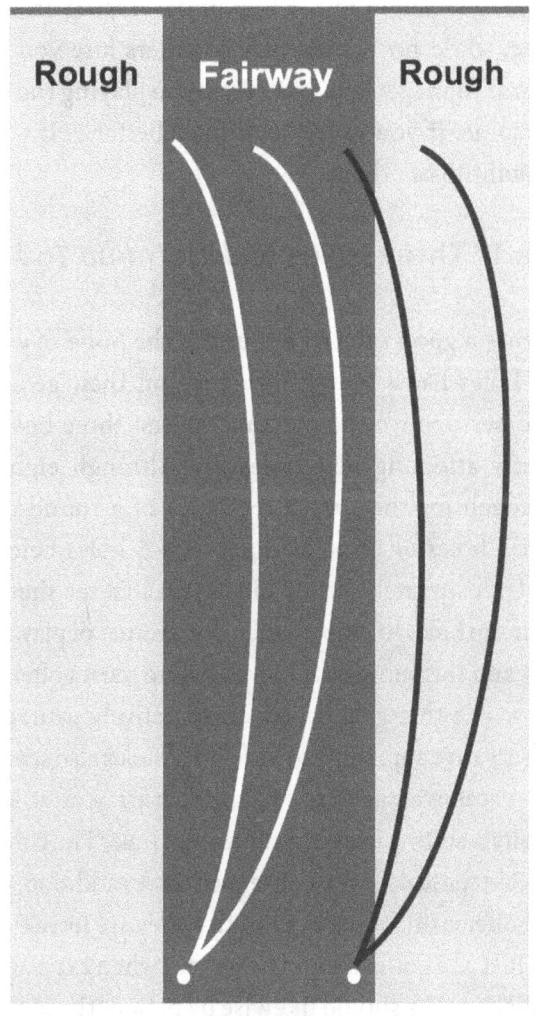

A **right-handed golfer** with a tendency to **slice or fade** the majority of tee shots will immediately notice improved success of shots finishing in the fairway by teeing the ball on the favourable side of tee.

A **right-handed golfer** with a tendency to **hook or draw** the majority of tee shots will immediately notice improved success of shots finishing in the fairway by tee the ball from the favourable side of tee.

Note the improvement of tee shots finding fairway by simply taking advantage of increasing the margin for allowable error to achieve this desired result by teeing on the appropriate side of the tee.

Play The Course - Not The Playing Partners

If you happen to be partnered with players having a lower handicap, or able to hit the ball a little further, do not get caught in the trap of developing an ego trying to outperform them. Golf is an individual game, so do not let the play of others lure you into playing low percentage shots or influence your Course Management Plan. Focus on playing the course and not trying to beat the other players in your foursome. If you want to produce better golf scores you must play within your capabilities, not the capabilities of others.

Use 1st Three Holes and Warm-up To Assess The Day's Tendencies

Having a good start to a round is the hope of every golfer. In many cases, a golfer's play on the first few holes has a strong influence on their general demeanour for the entire round. From a mind state perspective the outcome of first three holes has a strong influence on a golfers mindset, often greatly affecting how holes four through eighteen will transpire. Taking a slightly conservative approach for the first three holes of a round does have its benefits. Normally it usually takes at least 3 holes or up to as many as 4-5 holes before most golfers start to feel truly ready to play golf.

Unfortunately, before hitting the first tee shot, golfers do not have the luxury of playing a number of warm-up holes to prepare them for a round of play. After all, there is only one chance of having a favourable start and this must be achieved before most golfers feeling fully ready to play. As a consequence, it seems reasonable that golfers play conservatively while still gaining a comfort level with their play. A slightly conservative approach to the first few holes also seems appropriate as this style of play reduces the possibility of an excessively aggressive shot going array, often leading to a barrage of negative influences or distractions usually resulting in a big number for a hole. The conservative stance will eliminate being aggressive, helping to avoid these negative consequences. In addition, playing the first few holes conservatively does not mean the golfer is unable to score or that they are forsaking a good start to the round.

Just as a golfer should be patient when experiencing a run of pars, with numerous occasions to make birdie, a golfer should likewise be patient through the first few holes to not detract from their ability to score, despite taking a conservative approach to play. For example, on a par 4, a golfer may elect to hit a 3 wood instead of the driver, resulting in a longer iron into the green, but this does not preclude being forced to execute a low percentage second shot, nor negate a birdie opportunity. As a result, taking a less aggressive approach will improve confidence that a positive outcome for the first number of holes is more likely to occur. Consciously taking a conservative approach inherently provides additional initial confidence of being successful before play. Further, taking a less aggressive approach aids in avoiding a large number being scored early in the round, which could have disastrous effects.

Of course there will be occasions requiring a more aggressive approach to the first few holes, as in the case of requiring a score to make the cut, or to win a tournament as a contender. In the majority of cases playing the first number of holes conservatively will provide the most consistently satisfactory results. Despite taking a slightly more conservative approach to the start of a round, always execute planned shots aggressively. Don't get caught in the trap of electing to play more conservatively, resulting in the notion that more a conservative shot equates to executing the shot less aggressively. Remember a conservative approach refers to more conservative shot selection, not conservative shot execution.

Section 4 - Game Management, Preparing For Play

Before a round of golf it is extremely important to include a short warm-up session, including aerobic exercise to raise the heart rate, and a stretching period to loosen up, before hitting balls on the range or in a practice area. Aerobic exercise could include a simple 5 to 10 minute jog or period of active calisthenics. During the stretching period pay attention to stretching the legs, back, shoulders and abdominal muscles to prepare them for the numerous swings of the day.

When initiating hitting balls, initially choose a favourite short iron and hit 10 - 15 shots, not paying too much attention to the results of the shots, but instead reestablishing recognizable familiar feelings associated with your swing. Emphasize arriving at familiar sensations, intuitions, and perceptions to achieve a repetitive swing having your regular timing, tempo, and rhythm. Continue to hit the required number of balls until feeling confident the swing's usual sensations and feelings have been found. Continue the preparation by executing a number of shots using a variety of clubs in the bag. Do not judge or assess any shots during the warm up session. If you really want to prevent a nightmare experience on the golf course avoid any corrective or remedial type activities on the range during warm-up. The primary concern is to attain a feeling for the familiar tempo and rhythm in your swing, not to assess shot outcomes. The time on the range and the practice area before a round of play should be solely devoted to gaining a familiar feel for shots, not correcting issues or concerns. Don't get caught in the trap of trying to remedy issues for some errant shots made in the warm-up session. This creates problems because golfers are lured into making unnecessary-compensations that are unfounded, resulting in confidence losses just before play. Rather than heading to the first tee confidently anticipating the day's play, the golfer is left bewildered questioning expectations for the upcoming round of play. Do not fall victim to assessing shots during warm-up and remediating a non-issue. This scenario is repeated over and over by thousands of golfers on a regular basis.

After attaining the sensations and feel of your familiar swing, continue the warm-up session by hitting a number of shots starting with shorter clubs and progressing to the driver. Since the establishment of confidence and shot consistency are the primary objectives of your preparation, striking a number of shots with shorter clubs will provide the best and quickest means of meeting this objective. Experiencing successful ball strikes will be realized much sooner with shorter clubs. It is also advisable to first hit partial shots with these clubs as this further minimizes the margin for error, enhancing the likelihood of sound initial ball striking even further. Moving from your wedges, to short irons, followed by subsequent shots with longer irons, and progressing up to the driver, will provide the most efficient means of establishing confidence and consistency before a round of play.

During the warm-up it is extremely important to try to simulate real playing situations as much as possible, to further enhance your preparedness to play. There are a number of ways this can be achieved. It is advantageous to hit to different targets as you prepare. After all, every shot you face on the course is at a different location having a different target. Try to simulate some of the shots you expect to face as set out in your Course Management Plan. Pretend you are in some of the situations you have predicted in your plan and provide opportunities for executing these shots. Simulating the lower percentage shots or the shots perceived to be the most difficult provides the golfer the opportunity of enhancing confidence levels of being successful in these situations. Be sure to include any anticipated shots that may require shaping in your plan. Some of the shots you will face may require slight fades or draws to arrive at a planned outcome. Providing opportunity to execute these anticipated shots adds realism to what you are trying to accomplish and enhances confidence these shots will be successful when called upon.

It is extremely important to avoid any remedial practice activities for issues that have arisen during previous rounds of play. Correction of issues or swing faults must be addressed in regular practice sessions specifically devoted to correcting these concerns. A portion of the chapter devoted to the Practice strategy shares the biggest mistakes golfers make regarding preparation or practice methods. Avoid causing a warm-up session becoming a detriment, rather than an experience positively preparing for competitive play. It is unfortunate golfers all to often fall victim to this trap before a round of play, but it is repeated over and over by millions of golfers on a regular basis. The warm-up period is a time to get both physically and mentally prepared to play through confidence building and success driven activities.

Following the completion of a warm-up session on the range, move to the practice green to get a feel for varying lengths of putts, with emphasis on assessing the speed of the greens. Strike a number of level, uphill and downhill putts of varying length, with emphasis on getting a feel for rolling putts the appropriate distance. By randomly stroking level, uphill and downhill putts of different lengths will more quickly and effectively ascertain a feel for the speed of greens, by isolating green speed without a concern for line. Do not be concerned with putt line accuracy at this time. Remember, your warm-up is targeted at instilling confidence, which is more easily attained when confronting only the single variable of length. After all, the objective at this time is the determination of the speed of the green and distance control, which has nothing to do with putt direction.

After getting a feel for the speed of the green, move to being confident you are hitting putts accurately on line. To achieve this objective, first strike numerous 3-4 foot putts having no break, trying to ensure every ball enters the hole at the center of the cup. This isolated target will aid in narrowing the margin for error in your stroke and enhance the objective you wish to achieve. It should be noted that putts of this length essentially eliminates distance control as a concern. The golfer may wish to establish a specific number of putts holed from this distance as being indicative the objective of hitting putts on line has been achieved. Following being confident of holing putts of 3-4 feet, strike a number of non-breaking putts from 6-8 feet until you are satisfied with the results. Next, execute a number of 3 to 4 foot putts surrounding a hole on a slope to provide a feel for the combination of break and speed of sloping putts. When satisfied with the results from this distance, increase the length of these breaking putts to 6 to 8 feet, as done for the level putts. This type of progression regarding putting is specific to building confidence during warm-up. Finally, take a number of basic chip shots and pitches primarily stressing the sensitivity and feel you have for these shots. Hit a number of consecutive chip shots and pitches to different holes, at varying distances, to help establish sensitivity and feel for these types of shots, which are essential to enhanced scoring.

Utilize the same activities in the same manner before every competitive round and ensure the elimination of any judgmental or evaluative thoughts altering your approach. This time before competition is strictly to awaken your abilities and reaffirm your regular demeanour, not remediate a concern having no foundation.

CHAPTER 14

On-Course Assessment

"Wisdom denotes the pursuing of the best ends by the best means."
Francis Hutcheson

Section 1 - Overview

On-Course Assessment is a strategy supporting the Eliminating Negative Influences and Knowledge Application components of the Positive Competitive Mindset Model. The strategy has a unifying influence on the establishment of a healthy mind state by occupying the golfer with an extremely valuable activity or task having a strong impact on establishing an on-course demeanour favouring elevated play levels. A golfer having a sound knowledge of their on-course performance has a strong awareness of their abilities and inclinations, which inherently establishes a degree of confidence based on the skills knowledge acquired through actual playing experiences.

Golfers believe they have a good knowledge of their weaknesses and strengths, despite not having a reliable source of accurate information from which to draw their conclusions. Making the effort to collect playing data and manage this information leads to accurate determination of strengths and weaknesses, and learning a great deal about your tendencies during play. Most golfers have never taken the time to do any analysis of their on-course capabilities, but despite this, believe they are knowledgeable of their games. This causes misdirected initiatives spearheaded by misinformation, which results in the omission of opportunities for putting into place corrective actions having a more significant positive impact on progress.

Adopting the diligent recording of your on-course play and the valued analysis this provides, the golfer is rewarded with numerous benefits having a strong influence on the establishment of a healthy Positive Competitive Mindset. Information like club distance control, fade and draw tendency, pull and push tendency, scrambling ability, and other aspects of play can be monitored, providing the golfer reassurance of maximizing performance, through the ability to make better shot making decisions. Other more conventional data like fairways hit, greens in regulation, par saves, sand saves and number of putts are also aspects of play that should also be recorded with an on-course assessment tool. The golfer is free to be as extensive or detailed as they wish regarding assessment, at first recording common statistics and adding supplemental data as required.

Having a thorough and accurate knowledge of your shot making abilities and inclinations is essential to being able to provide the greatest opportunity of executing a successful shot. The distance you hit all your clubs, the percentage of shots left or right, knowledge of various ball flights for specific types of shots and other valuable on-course performance information results in raised confidence, further supporting the likelihood of successful shot outcomes. This is why it is so important to keep a finger on the pulse of your shot making tendencies. The gathering of information must be a continual and ongoing process, keeping you in tune with adjustments to improve the success of shots. The process of adjusting for variations in shot making, to enhance the likelihood of the favoured or most likely result, could be referred to as "compensation". The better knowledge golfers have for the variations and inclinations in their shot making, then the better equipped they are to make the appropriate compensations to give the best chance for a shot to be successful. Knowing the compensations to make when setting up for a specific shot, provides reassured confidence in a successful result.

The mindset of the golfer is strongly affected by the increased confidence of knowing the information regarding their abilities is based on actual on-course play. Much of the guesswork regarding ball striking is avoided as a result of this knowledge. Documenting of particular shot making provides the golfer with information to make sound shot making decisions, having greater likelihood of occurring, which positively affects confidence. For as long as you wish to play your best golf, the data gathered to monitor your own abilities and tendencies will provide confidence in your shot making by permitting you to adopt strategies based on the highest percentages for being successful with every shot you take.

Section 2 - Implementation Benefits

Taking the initiative to implement an effective means of monitoring, recording and evaluating skills for on-course play provides many advantages to golfers. Some of the immediate benefits or advantages awarded as the result of On-Course Assessment implementation include:

1. Improved Practice Session Effectiveness

By recording your performance on the golf course, you are in a more advantageous position to address the concerns that are really preventing you from scoring well. The added value of on-course assessment is what is gained through practice time effectiveness. An on-course performance assessment tool is essential for identifying weaknesses or strengths, where practice rewards the golfer with improvements in areas having a real and responsive effect, in areas having the greatest effect on future play. In addition, the On-course Assessment information gathered also permits true weaknesses to be identified to strategically set the appropriate objectives and challenges for attainment during practice sessions. Providing accurate determination of areas of weakness during competitive play provides opportunity to identify actual on-course improvement targets, raising confidence in those areas needing improvement.

2. Negative Influence Elimination

The strategy also serves as a tool helping to eliminate or control negative influences by focusing the golfer's attention on something constructive and positive following every shot. In addition, On-Course Assessment serves as a deterrent to the formation of distractions by preoccupying the golfer with performing a very valuable activity, not letting the mind wander to introduce distractions causing scoring disasters.

The on-course assessment strategy engages the golfer in an activity providing consistent performance feedback, keeping the golfer in the moment and engaged in an activity specifically supporting the elimination of negative influences, rather than dwelling on the outcome of a suspect shot, which can often trigger successive negative thoughts or distractions that must be dealt with.

3. More Effective Game and Course Management

The information and data gathered during on-course assessment provides reliable and pertinent information for more effective course and game management. Effective management of your game or the strategizing of tactics to use when playing a particular course requires a sound knowledge of your capabilities, inclinations, and tendencies as a golfer. The advantages of a golfer knowing their capabilities and quarks are to manage their game where strengths can be utilized and weaknesses minimized, plus risks lowered and rewards maximized. It is only the golfer that has a sound knowledge of their abilities that is provided these advantages.

4. Promotes Mind State Stability and Integrity

This strategy creates an interdependency and integration of an approach helping improve the integrity and resiliency of the golfer's mind state and confidence levels. The stability of mind state comes from an activity providing the elements necessary to support and build confidence levels. With a conscious effort to ensure activities provide ample opportunity for positive reinforcement, the quantifying of performance metrics naturally permits the setting of performance targets arming the golfer with the capability to see measured improvements in skill, resulting in higher confidence levels. This ability alone provides the golfer the reassurance confidence levels can be built for any area of the game, adding to the stability of the mindset. The integrity or stability of the mindset is also reinforced knowing actual on-course playing data is the best information to have upon which to base your shot-making decisions. Taking the time to assemble the best information available upon which to base shot making decisions certainly adds merit to the additional confidence and improvement experienced. This strategy creates a very stabilizing effect to the model by supporting the interdependencies of the strategies and the benefits this integration brings to the establishment of a Positive Competitive Mindset.

Golfers will generally agree with the value in establishing a formalized system of information gathering and will initially be excited about making an effort to improve their games, but interest is soon lost and they eventually terminate their efforts. The process of gathering performance information requires the sacrifice of time and discipline, to keep the information collected current and comprehensive. Golfers have an inclination to drop this type of activity or not even bother to give it consideration. First, many golfers do not see the value of the process. Independently implementing each strategy presented under the PCM Model has the purpose of reducing scores and accelerating improvement, but through the implementation of multiple strategies the benefits are compounded. As more strategies are put in place the golfer fortifies a playing environment fostering a mind state more suited to competitive play.

If there is little value seen being aware of on-course abilities, or if disgruntled by the effort and time required to maintain a current database of your shot execution skills and tendencies, then some golfers will mistakenly avoid or drop this strategy. In addition, golfers may not be aware of the types of information to collect or find it difficult to establish an effective recording methodology for data that takes the drudgery out of gathering information that is extremely useful to them. Whatever the reasons for not evaluating on-course play, a positive aspect to establishing an ongoing evaluation of your shot-making tendencies is that the process will become automatic in a relatively short period of time. Let the process become routine, as described in the Routine strategy. Much like the golf swing itself, at first there are conscious efforts and actions to get the swing right, but over time, the swing becomes automatic with little or no conscious thought. Your data gathering will become routine and automatic, to the point where minimum effort is needed to maintain related data.

Section 3 - The Shot Assessment Tool

Let's introduce a data gathering tool recording a wide range of on-course play information, and designed to eliminate much of the drudgery associated with gathering this type of data. The tool provides for the recording of on-course play in a convenient scorecard type format. The decision to include an on-course assessment card was to cater to the golfer not fond of having to tote and tend to electronic devices. A single card providing a wealth of information, regarding all shots taken does provide some elements of convenience, when the alternative is considered. However, electronic devices do serve the advantage of maintaining the data gathered and reporting on this data in various ways. The method you choose for recording on-course play is a matter of preference and your resourcefulness to manage the data gathered.

Whether it's with pencil and paper using a scorecard type tool, or inputting data directly into devices like a GPS device, cellular smartphone or a device specifically for golf data management is completely your choice. Application of the data and information gathered to guide practice sessions will be presented, permitting the tailoring of practices, based on this valuable information and enabling ability to accurately tailor their growth for the greatest benefits in actual play. You can introduce on-course performance objectives permitting measured growth in any area related to the data gathered. As a result of making the effort to record important aspect of your game allows for the establishment of performance target identification in this area. The golfer is then able to utilize practice time to specifically address any skills supporting the achievement of targets directly affecting play.

Immediately below is a sample of the On-Course Assessment Tool used to record a golfers play on a hole-by-hole basis. The tool permits the fast and easy recording of the shots executed for a hole, as well as important key aspects or characteristics of these shots. The card also provides for the recording of traditional statistics related to play like sand saves, green in regulation, number of putts…etc. A portion of the information recorded on the data-gathering card relates directly to the Proximity Acceptance strategy. Since the golfer is already recording on-course performance data, the maintenance of the Proximity Acceptance Strategy and the recording of this data are already built into this recording card for obvious gains in efficiency.

Hole 10	Par	Ydg	Hdcp			Score		Putts		GIR	
Tee Shot	Length	Club	FIR			D		S	L	R	Penalty
						P		P	L	S	
2nd Shot	Length	Club	Lie			D		S	L	R	S Save
			F	R	B	T	P	P	L	S	
3rd Shot	Length	Club	Lie			D		S	L	R	Save
			F	R	B	T	P	P	L	S	
1st Putt	Length	Read	Actual		Grade			L	R	Above	
		R-L	L-R	R-L	L-R	UP	DN	L	S		Below
2nd Putt	Length	Read	Actual		Grade			L	R	Above	
		R-L	L-R	R-L	L-R	UP	DN	L	S		Below

Below is a listing of the information gathered on this simple to use tool.

Upper and Right Bordered Area

Hole Number, Par of Hole, Yardage of Hole, Handicap of Hole, Score on Hole, Number of Putts on Hole, Green in Regulation on Hole, Number of Penalty Stroke on Hole, Sand Save on Hole, Save on Hole

Tee Shot

Tee Shot Yardage, Tee Shot Club, Fairway/Green Hit in Regulation (y/n), Tee Shot Shape (Slice, Hook, Push, Pull – circles or check placed appropriately on card), Yardage Left of Target - Yardage Right of Target – yardage indicated in space provided, Yardage Past Target-Yardage Short of Target – yardage indicated in space provided.

2nd Shot

2nd Shot Yardage, 2nd Shot Club, Fairway/Green Hit in Regulation (y/n), Lie (Fairway, Rough, Bunker, Trouble– circle or check placed appropriately on card), Tee Shot Shape (Slice, Hook, Push, Pull – circles or check marks placed appropriately on card), Yardage Left of Target - Yardage Right of Target – yardage indicated in space provided, Yardage Past Target-Yardage Short of Target – yardage indicated in space provided.

3rd Shot

3rd Shot Yardage, 3rd Shot Club, Fairway/Green Hit in Regulation (y/n), Lie (Fairway, Rough, Bunker, Trouble– circle or check placed appropriately on card), Tee Shot Shape (Slice, Hook, Push, Pull – circles or check marks placed appropriately on card), Yardage Left of Target - Yardage Right of Target – yardage indicated in space provided, Yardage Past Target-Yardage Short of Target – yardage indicated in space provided.

1st Putt

1st Putt Length – length indicated in space provided, Original Read (Left to Right or Right to Left - circles or check marks placed appropriately on card), Actual Putt Shape (Left to Right or Right to Left - circles or check marks placed appropriately on card), 1st Putt Grade (Uphill Or Downhill - circles or check marks placed appropriately on card), 1st Putt Distance Short or Long – distance (ft) indicated in appropriate space provided, 1st Putt Distance Off Line Left or Right – distance (ft) indicated in appropriate space provided, 1st Putt Result (Above or Below Hole- circles or check marks placed appropriately on card)

2nd Putt

2nd PuttLength – length indicated in space provided, Original Read (Left to Right or Right to Left - circles or check marks placed appropriately on card), Actual Putt Shape (Left to Right or Right to Left - circles or check marks placed appropriately on card), 2nd Putt Grade (Uphill Or Downhill - circles or check marks placed appropriately on card), 2nd Putt Distance Short or Long – distance (ft) indicated in appropriate space provided, 1st Putt Distance Off Line Left or Right – distance (ft) indicated in appropriate space provided, 1st Putt Result (Above or Below Hole- circles or check marks placed appropriately on card)

You can see a simple tool is capable of gathering a great deal of key information regarding all aspects of your game. Use of this tool is a valued strategy of the Knowledge Component of the Positive Competitive Mindset, based on the magnitude and importance of information and knowledge gained, regarding capabilities and shot execution inclinations. The tool designed to be completed quickly, providing key diagnostic capabilities for all aspects of play, and conveniently documenting capabilities and tendencies, providing a sound and detailed record of a round of play. Obviously, the full benefit of the card is dependent on printing it on heavier paper stock. There is a great deal of convenience in a pencil and card data gathering method. Naturally golfers are already well aware of the ease of use and convenience of a card that is always on their person.

The assessment card or electronic device always being in your possession does serve two primary purposes. First, the data recording does take a couple minutes to record, therefore having the card readily accessible at any time, provides convenience for ensuring this valuable information is collected. Second, the process of monitoring your competitive play keeps your mind in the moment, focused on positive productive thoughts, and eliminating the varied destructive thoughts often originating immediately prior to shot execution. The first commitment in adopting a Positive Competitive Mindset alluded to earlier in the book, related to the elimination of any emotional attachment to any shot executed, and is wonderfully supported by this strategy. Golfers may see the recording of this data as a nuisance, but the actual data gathering process serves as an excellent way of eliminating negative influences, and supporting a healthy Positive Competitive Mindset, by keeping the golfer occupied with valuable and productive tasks, at a time when distractions and negative thoughts often emerge.

Having knowledge of your capabilities and inclinations greatly improves the success rate of your shots causing a marked positive influence on your mental mindset and confidence, which further improves play. You want to establish yourself in this win-win situation by getting into the confidence breeds success, success breeds confidence cycle. If you agree that the information and ideas presented concerning this topic are logical and sound, then you see real value in its implementation. If this is the case, then you must make a commitment to establishing your system and sticking to it. The benefits you reap from your efforts will result in progressively marked improvement in your game.

Effective Data Usage

With the availability of GPS devices and Smartphones having applications making it simple to input shot by shot information and customize reporting of the data, these new resources are eliminating the drudgery of keeping records. Whatever the preference for gathering and managing on-course performance data, a means of utilizing this information must be implemented, to maximize the usefulness of the information gathered.

A key element to have included in the information, provided through the management and reporting of data collected are trend comparisons for different aspect of play. For example, knowing the percentage of Fairways Hit in Regulation for the last 5 rounds, as compared to the previous 5 rounds, provides immediate and recent feedback of any changes specific to this statistic. Comparing specific data in this manner, for any aspects of recorded play, provides prompt response for determining positive or negative changes in your game's metrics. The golfer is in the position of not only knowing their capabilities, but can flag any recent negative changes regarding any aspect of their game, for prompt and accurate remediation of issues and concerns.

Do not get caught in the trap of keeping a running average of aspects of play, because this information can greatly skew perceptions, obscuring diagnosis of issues and concerns. In addition, a running average loses its significance over time, because the influence of each entry on the average becomes increasingly insignificant. Moreover, what is being learned from the statistics for greens in regulation for a round played 3 months ago? Comparing trends in a data item is essential to providing prompt and accurate remediation of on-course play. Making the comparison of data for more recent rounds of play to rounds occurring prior, immediately opens the door to accurate and prompt addressing of issues, based on better information management, promoting accelerated improvement. Managing data in this manner will help to ensure currency of skills, prompt remediation, and avoidance of unimportant or misleading information.

www.ingramcontent.com/pod-product-compliance
Lightning Source LLC
Chambersburg PA
CBHW080245170426
43192CB00014BA/2567